D1304518

"Reading opens new doors to the world"

British History

ISBN 0-75258-217-8 (Hardback)

This is a Parragon Book
This edition published in 2002
Parragon
Queen Street House
4 Queen Street
Bath BA1 1HE, UK

Copyright © 1999 Parragon

Printed in Indonesia
Created and produced by
Foundry Design & Production

Cover design by Blackjacks

British History

GENERAL EDITOR:
Professor Eric Evans

Contents

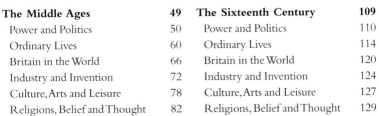

Introduction

NO AREA OF COMPARABLE SIZE has had such a varied and distinguished history as have the British Isles. During the past two thousand years, most of Britain was first occupied as part of the Roman Empire, then became the site of frequent conflict between Celts, Angles, Jutes, Saxons and Danes. The Norman Conquest of 1066 established a new type of leadership on England, and it stuck. Since 1066, no successful invasion on England has taken place, and the political stability, which has been such a pronounced feature of the country's development, owes much to the long thread of continuity that has been woven in a nation whose borders have not been breached.

The themes of integration and diversity are crucial to understanding British history. Out of the frequently warring groups which struggled for supremacy after the retreat of the Roman armies early in the fifth century emerged four significant states: England, Scotland, Wales and Ireland. All had their separate histories, but they have been closely interconnected throughout the last millennium. Whereas historians outside Scotland, Wales and Ireland used to write 'the history of Britain' as if it were basically the history of England, the story of these islands is now more frequently (and more appropriately) understood as a genuinely British one. It reflects conflict at least as much as co-operation. Actual political unification is surprisingly late in coming. England and Scotland, who fought over border territory almost incessantly during the Middle Ages, shared one ruler (usually a member of the

A scene from the Norman invasion, from the Bayeux Tapestry. ▶

Scottish house of Stuart) from the death of Queen Elizabeth I in 1603, but the nation did not become politically united until 1707. Even then, Scotland retained its own legal and educational systems. English power, under the Plantagenet monarch Edward I, had established a position of dominance over Wales from the end of the thirteenth century but administrative unification did not come until the first half of the sixteenth century during the reign of Henry VIII.

Queen Elizabeth I, one of the most famous monarchs in British history. ▲

The area of the British Isles that sustained most conflict over the last millennium has been Ireland, which has endured a succession of religious and political struggles for supremacy. The history of a largely Catholic Ireland cannot be written without understanding the influence, and frequently the social and cultural dominance, of both the Scottish and English Protestant settlers from the sixteenth century. The Catholic Stuart monarch James II tried, and failed, to win back the English and Scottish crowns from Ireland in 1690, when he was defeated by a Dutchman who was the Protestant King of England. Throughout the later seventeenth and eighteenth centuries, English interests and concerns greatly influenced Irish development before fear both of revolution and French invasion forced the British government to offer political union to Ireland in 1800 on terms that its Protestant elite were unlikely to refuse. The troubled history of relations between Britain and Ireland in the so-called 'United Kingdom of Great Britain and Northern Ireland' has been a prominent feature of British history during the last two centuries. It has been characterised by a succession of searches for a mutually acceptable settlement both between Britain and Ireland and between the Protestant and Catholic communities within Ireland. The threat of bloodshed and violence has been almost constant. For a significant period, bloodshed has been a bitter reality.

This book reflects national diversity and integration as one of its key themes. It shows also what a vital role has been played by the immigration and emigration of minority groups. Its construction also reflects another crucial element in the proper understanding of national development. History is not made only by monarchs and by political leaders. The book gives due weight to the role of both ordinary folk and of those who helped forge its rich culture. Knowing how power is exercised, and by which political and social groups, is crucial in understanding the context in which the lives of ordinary people were lived. Those ordinary people also made their own history in the villages, towns and (later on) the great industrial conurbations of Britain. As this book shows, history works 'bottom up' as well as 'top down'.

Inevitably, though, much attention is paid to the three areas in which Britain can claim to be unique. The micropedia charts the development of representative political institutions. It shows how the powers of the monarchs became limited and how, though this was not for the most part the intention of the rulers, Britain emerged as a democracy. It is important to understand how the influence of Britain's middle classes grew, how working people struggled for direct representation and how

The Houses of Parliament at Westminster in London. ▼

women demonstrated that they should not been seen as second-class citizens in terms either of political representation or of their social roles. Britain was also one of the few European nations to manage the transition to democracy in the nineteenth and twentieth centuries without political revolution.

The second British claim to uniqueness lies in its industry. Britain was the first nation in the world to undergo that most thoroughgoing of all transformations, an industrial revolution. How that happened, and with what consequences both for the lives of its citizens and for its role in the world, is one of the central features of the book. It is also closely linked with the third unique element in Britain's history: the development of the British Empire and Britain's world role. By the early twentieth century, Britain ruled over an empire larger than any in recorded history: 'the empire on which the sun never sets'. Though most of the territory that became the 'British Empire' was acquired relatively late, during the eighteenth and nineteenth centuries, Britain was always unusual among European powers in that its main concern over defence was with its coastline rather than with land borders. Britain became the world's leading maritime nation before it became the world's biggest empire and the two factors are closely linked. The success of Britain's industrial revolution depended to a large extent upon the success of its trading overseas. The processes of becoming the world's leading trading nation, the 'workshop of the world', and also the world's most substantial imperial power were closely linked. This book shows how the empire was acquired and how that empire formed Britain's status as the world's leading power in the nineteenth century. It also shows how, and with what consequences, both empire and world status went into retreat as the twentieth century developed.

The organisation of this micropedia allows the reader to follow all of these themes through the centuries. Britain's story is rich and fascinating, complex and important. This book helps to make sense of it all. With luck it should also kindle your enthusiasm to find out more!

PROFESSOR ERIC EVANS

CHAPTER 1
The Ancient World

Power and Politics

7000 BC   THE RETREATING ICE AGE

ALTHOUGH SETTLERS in Britain have been traced back as far as
250,000 BC, the first roots of modern Britain can be dated to about 7000
BC when the retreating Ice Age was the signal for settlers to begin to re-
inhabit the British Isles. Expedition was made easier as land bridges
within the islands and between Britain and the mainland continent still
existed. This was the middle phase of the Stone Age known by historians
as the Mesolithic period. Society was still very basic, but the first signs of
order, based around the practices of hunting, fishing and gathering,
quickly emerged. This period covering the first Celtic settlers lasted for
about 3,000 years before more sophisticated methods of cultivating food
were established.

*As the Ice Age retreated, ancient peoples began to cross land bridges and inhabit the
British Isles.* ▼

4000 BC THE NEOLITHIC REVOLUTION

THE LATE STONE AGE, known as the Neolithic period, marked the introduction of agriculture into the British way of life as people moved away from the traditional hunting and gathering methods. Corn crops were grown, small dairy herds were kept particularly in the Lowlands, the Midlands and south, where the population reached about 3,000. New settlers came from the Mediterranean. The influence of those from the west also continued with evidence that the Irish Sea was used to link different societies from what is now the north-west coast of Wales to the east coast of Ireland. Religious practices also show that people increasingly put great store in the cult of the afterlife, with large stone tombs being built.

2500 BC STONEHENGE

THE NEOLITHIC period saw work begin on one of Europe's most remarkable, mysterious and ancient structures – Stonehenge. To this day its purpose is still not fully known although it is commonly

Stonehenge, one of the most ancient and mysterious legacies of Neolithic Britain. ▲

recognised as a site of worship connected with the summer and winter solstices. Modern Druids still worship the coming of the summer solstice at the site on Salisbury Plain. Work began in about 2500 BC but Stonehenge was rebuilt many times and not completed until about 1100 years later, in 1400 BC. One estimate claims that 30 million man-hours were used up during the prolonged construction of Stonehenge. It reflects the importance of religion in prehistoric Britain and suggests ancient religious leaders played an important part in early society.

Metalwork was one of the earliest Celtic industries, and led to a growth in the economy. ▲

2000 BC ECONOMICS

THE BRONZE AGE, in the period around 2000 BC, saw a growth in trade as Britain's nascent economy began to grow. The Celts' skill in craftwork led to a flourishing metalwork industry both for home use and export. Trade in Irish copper and Cornish tin grew – the metals needed for bronze – as the economy expanded on both sides of the Irish Sea. Although the tin trade was established by the Celts its importance to the British Isles can be gauged by the fact that the last Cornish tin mine, South Crofty, only closed in the late 1990s. Developed later on in the Bronze Age was an axe industry. Later these tools would be exported to the European market, as were Celtic ornaments.

1100 BC MILITARY POWER

THE BEGINNING of the Iron Age – so called because iron succeeded bronze as the basic component of tools and weaponry – saw the pre-

Celtic High Crosses can be found all over Ireland, a testimony to ancient religions and beliefs. ▶

eminence of a military ruling class in parts of prehistoric Britain, especially in the south. As hill forts grew, ever-larger communities appear to have organised themselves into units, which generally gave political precedence to the military. These hill forts had large populations. One in Dorset was thought to have contained 1,000 people. A large urban centre was also found on the site of modern-day Winchester. To the north and west political development took place more slowly. The Romans identified over 20 Celtic tribes, raising the possibility of political differences among the various local communities.

100 BC   THE BELGAE

ONE GROUP of Celtic settlers who had a profound influence on Britain's development were the Belgae tribe who invaded the country in the first century BC. A northern Gallic tribe, they are probably best known for first introducing coinage into the British economy. After the relative decline of the early Iron Age internal markets grew as numeracy and literacy grew. These earliest coins were struck in gold. The Belgae occupied large parts of southern England including Hampshire and Wiltshire, and moved as far north as the Trent River. Once settled their influence extended to those already in the country. The Belgae were among the first tribes to encounter the Romans, and offered strong but ultimately fruitless opposition to the new invaders.

55 BC   CAESAR'S EXPEDITIONS

JULIUS CAESAR, emperor of Rome between 102 BC and 44 BC, left his mark for ever on the British Isles by naming the newly conquered country incorrectly. Caesar called Rome's emerging colony Britannia in the mistaken belief that the Belgae settlers were actually from the Britanni tribe. He led his first expedition in 55 BC following a military sortie into Gaul. This ended in failure as he was beaten back by bad weather. He returned a year later with additional troops and defeated the home army led by the Catuvellauni tribe. Adding Britain to the Roman Empire assured Caesar of great prestige back in Rome as it was considered a fabled island separated from the Continental mainland by a ferocious ocean.

Julius Caesar invaded the British Isles and set up colonies there. ▲

54 BC   THE EXPANSION OF THE ROMAN EMPIRE

AFTER BRITAIN was eventually conquered in 54 BC it became an administrative division – a province – of the Roman Empire. The provinces were divided socially into classes – senatorial and imperial. Britain was at first one imperial province with Roman rule extending as far as the Humber River. Colchester was the provincial capital. In the first and second centuries as Roman rule extended to the Forth, London became the capital. By the third century Britain had been divided into two – a 'Britannia Superior' and 'Britannia Inferior' with York becoming another capital. By the early fourth century two provinces had become four with Cirencester and Lincoln being added as capitals. Towards the end of the fourth century a fifth province was added taking in part of Wales.

AD 43   THE CLAUDIAN INVASIONS

ROMAN RULE in Britain was cemented by one of Julius Caesar's successors – Claudius – emperor between AD 41 and 54. Following internal political disputes in Rome, the newly crowned Claudius turned his attention to Britain almost 100 years after Caesar. In AD 43 he assembled about 40,000 troops for a full-scale invasion of the islands. Despite fierce resistance, British troops could not match the weaponry of the Romans nor did they have sophisticated body armour like the invaders. Roman rule was confirmed when 11 British tribal kings submitted to the emperor. Claudius was present at the capture of Colchester and arrived in town complete with elephants. By AD 47 Roman forces had occupied as far north as the Trent River.

Emperor Claudius continued the Roman invasion of the British Isles. ▶

Roman soldiers massacring the Druids at Anglesey. ▲

AD 61   THE MASSACRE OF THE DRUIDS

THE MAIN religion of Celtic Britain was Druidism. Its principal
philosophy emphasised immortality and the importance of the soul.
Druids were like latter-day priests and occupied a special place in Celtic
society especially when it came to law and education. Entry to the
priesthood took several years to achieve as prospective candidates had to
prove they had understood and memorised the faith's basic principles as
Druids relied on an oral culture. The religion practised animal and some
human sacrifice. Such practices appalled the Romans following their
invasion. In AD 61 Roman soldiers massacred Druids at Anglesey, an
important centre for Druidism, and also destroyed sacred artefacts. After
the Roman invasion Druidism largely disappeared until being revived in
the nineteenth century.

AD 61 BRITONS FIGHT BACK

RESISTANCE TO the Romans among Britons was patchy. Some tribes fiercely resisted, others helped the invaders. Many in the south welcomed the Romans as their arrival ended the political dominance of the local Catuvellauni tribe. The most famous resister – in England at least – was Boudicca. Queen of the Iceni tribe in East Anglia, she led a revolt against the Romans in AD 61. The kingdom of Boudicca's husband Prasutagas was divided between his daughters and the Romans on his death. However, Roman agents seized all the land. When Boudicca protested she was flogged and her daughters raped. Driven by fury, Boudicca's troops inflicted massive defeats on the Romans in Colchester, London and St Albans. After she was eventually defeated Boudicca committed suicide.

AD 78 TROUBLE IN THE NORTH

RESISTANCE TO Roman rule was most marked in Caledonia (Scotland). Despite several attempts, the invaders never fully conquered this part of the British Isles. The border between the Romans and local tribes shifted many times from AD 78 until the end of Roman rule in Britain in AD 440. The Romans got as far as the Forth in the mid-second century, where soldiers constructed a 60-km (37-mile) wall to the Clyde – the Antonine Wall, similar to Hadrian's Wall – to repel attacks from the north. Agricola, governor of Britain for six years until AD 84, was the man who came closest to fully conquering Scotland but his northern incursions were later abandoned. The Romans knew the inhabitants of the unconquered lands as Picts.

Remains of the Antonine Wall, built to protect the Romans from marauding northerners. ▶

AD 300s RELIGION UNDER ROMAN RULE

ROMAN CULTURE also brought with it a new religion – Christianity. Although the extent to which Christianity became entrenched in British society during Roman times is arguable, it is now thought it was more deeply rooted than was previously believed. It appears to have been established during the later period of Roman rule. Although the influence of Christianity was patchy, it seems to have taken root among the wealthier members of ancient British society – such as in parts of Dorset and East Anglia. It was during the same period that a British monk, Pelagius, advocated his heretical views that man could be saved by the exercise of his own will rather than through divine grace – the first but by no means the last time Britain clashed with Rome on religion.

AD 410 THE END OF ROMAN RULE

THE END of Roman rule came about gradually rather than because of one event. The decline began around the beginning of the fifth century. Roman forces were defeated by Picts in the north and Saxons in the south. Internal disputes among the Romans also caused instability. Roman forces in Britain were deliberately weakened to assist in the struggle for power back in Rome. In AD 409 British forces rebelled against the rule of Emperor Constantine III. By AD 410 the Emperor Honorius ended connections with the British part of the Roman Empire. From this time Britain had no central government and local tribes filled the political vacuum. The Romans attempted to regain power in the late 420s AD, when military intervention was once again a possibility.

The Britons rebelled against Roman Emperor Constantine's rule. ▶

Ordinary Lives

4700 BC   ARRIVAL OF THE FIRST NEOLITHIC SETTLERS

ARRIVING IN skin boats, clearing the forests and shrub to make pastures, Neolithic people lived in small farming communities, raising cattle, trading and fighting a continuing battle with encroaching forests. Each time the soil was exhausted from repeated plantings, the forests would creep back and have to be fought all over again. It was a period where nature had to be kept at bay, and this could only be achieved – when it was possible at all – by communal effort, as people worked together to organise irrigation schemes or other enterprises. They probably specialised more than their hunting predecessors, spending time weaving baskets, making necklaces, bracelets and anklets, and probably drinking beer as well, with the forests always in the background.

In prehistory, ape-like peoples came down from the trees and began to forge a hunter-gatherer lifestyle. ▼

600 BC THE CELTIC HIERARCHY

EARLY OBSERVERS of the Celts gained the impression that this doughty and vivacious people were not capable of concerted action for long, if at all. The apparent wildness this suggests did not, however, extend to their social organisation. By the sixth century BC, the Celts had a well-established hierarchy or class system that formed the matrix of their society. At the pinnacle, there was the king or chieftain and below him an aristocracy whose main business was war. Next came the freemen farmers, who were important in their own right since the Celtic

Druid priests and priestesses were revered members of Celtic society. ▲

economy relied heavily on mixed farming. The aristocratic families provided the priests known as Druids, who directed Celtic religious life and performed its often frequently mystical ceremonies.

600 BC THE DRUIDS

AT THE CENTRE of a society that valued music, poetry, boar hunting and horse racing alike, Druids were a revered part of Celtic life. They fulfilled the roles of prophets, bards and priests, and had to train for up to 20 years in an apprenticeship that included learning enormous amounts of poetry. Of great significance were oak trees, mistletoe and wells – which were particularly sacred – and Druids were assisted in their duties by a class of women prophets who were not given the full privileges of Druids, but who could predict the future. The body of a Celt, possibly a sacrificial victim, was found in a peat bog in 1984. His last meal had been wheat, barley and some kind of potion containing Druidic mistletoe.

55 BC   BRITAIN AND THE ROMANS

CAESAR KNEW much about Britain as he prepared to invade in 55 BC.
He had heard of the inhabitants' curious habit of dyeing their bodies blue
with woad and the supernatural aura that, the Romans believed, hung
over the land they called 'Isola Sacra', the Sacred Isle. However, the
warriors who lined the cliffs when Caesar's fleet arrived off the south
coast were no longer only Celts, or the descendants of the Beaker folk or
any of their predecessors. The natural melding of immigrants over time
had made them all proud Britons. And these Britons meant to fight to
keep their homeland and their freedom.

AD 43   CONQUEST

THE ROMAN ARMY, the most powerful military machine of its time,
may have lost battles, but it never lost a war. Even so, the Roman conquest
of Britain was by no means an easy matter, and it was never complete.
There were always Britons prepared to defy the foreign invaders, even after
the conquest was over. Before the Romans prevailed, the Britons'
resistance was ferocious, with its damaging chariot warfare, guerrilla tactics

Julius Caesar, whose vast empire covered large parts of Europe. ▼

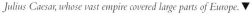

and clever use of forest cover. But the might of Rome could not be thwarted, and ultimately submission was the only option. When the surrender took place at Colchester in the late summer of AD 43, the Roman Emperor Claudius was there in person to preside at the ceremony.

AD 47   THE FOSSE WAY

MOST OF THE FOSSE WAY, one of the main Roman roads, was completed by AD 47, probably as part of the push westwards of the invasion forces. By the end of the Roman occupation, it stretched from Lincoln to Topsham in Devon, via Bath, Cirencester and Leicester, part of a network of roads – nearly 12,000 km (7,500 miles) of which have been identified – that linked major urban centres and helped move troops quickly around the country. The roads were planned as a hub radiating out from London, and many survived into the medieval period. These routes formed the basis of Britain's road system right up to the advent of motorways. The roads also helped bring Roman life and trade to the countryside, and brought Rome to the northernmost limits of its empire.

AD 77   SUBVERTING THE BRITONS

FROM THE FIRST, Britannia proved a difficult province to control, but Gnaius Julius Agricola, Roman governor between AD 77 and 84, is credited with devising a very subtle method of reconciling the Britons to Roman rule. He romanised the province, and so offered Britons

Many relics of Roman rule remain in Britain, including walls, roads, forts and magnificent villas with mosaic floors. ◀

the advantages of Roman life: towns, water supplies, roads, imported luxuries, homes heated by hypocausts (a form of central heating), public baths, theatres and other entertainments such as gladiatorial combat. The contrast between this comparatively pampered existence and the rough, often uncomfortable, life they had led before appealed to many Britons who came to live in the towns, wear Roman togas, eat Roman food and educate their children in Roman schools.

AD 155   FIRE IN VERULAMIUM

A DISASTROUS FIRE in Verulamium (St Albans) in AD 155 destroyed the town for the second time under Roman rule – the first time had been at the hands of the Iceni tribe under Boudicca in AD 61 – but both disasters enhanced its development. Like most Roman towns, it included a forum, bath, amphitheatre and temple, but the new theatre held more people than any hall in modern St Albans, offering free admission to watch bear shows and gladiatorial contests. Clustered around Verulamium and other towns were the villas, no more than half a day's travel away and including accommodation and bath houses for estate workers, which formed the backbone of the new agricultural system. As many as four mosaic schools provided the craftsmen to create their lavish floors.

Gladiatorial contests were a popular sport in Roman Britain. ▶

AD 313 CHRISTIANITY IN BRITAIN

IN AD 313, the Roman Emperor Constantine I was converted to Christianity and with that, this formerly suspect faith took over the Roman Empire. Christianity had been a minority religion – and a persecuted one – among tribes in Scotland as early as AD 205. There had been vicious oppression, together with the torture and martyrdom in AD 208 of a Verulamium (St Albans) man, Albanus, who had sheltered a Christian priest. This time, though, the Christian faith was official. Now, it was the pagans who were hounded.

Emperor Constantine I brought Christianity to the British Isles. ▲

They faced execution if caught performing pagan rites and, though the old beliefs persisted in some areas, all forms of pagan ritual and worship were outlawed in AD 391. Pagan temples were smashed and idols destroyed.

AD 430 BRITAIN FACES DISASTER

THE DEPARTURE of the Romans brought anarchy in its wake. Rome's rule had meant law and order. Now, law and order broke down as the British found themselves helpless before the Anglo-Saxon raiders and marauders from the north. The comparatively healthful Roman way of life now gone, disease asserted itself. Food supplies were threatened and new crop fields were ploughed within the seeming safety of town walls. Richer Britons took to burying their valuables, as always a sure sign of fear and insecurity. The panic was such that in about AD 430, one British leader, Vortigern of Dyfed, made the mistake of recruiting Saxon mercenaries for protection, a move that proved virtually suicidal.

AD 430 ROME'S LEGACY

THE ROMANS left Britain comparatively little of their culture but the marks of their presence are distinct even so. Except for motorways, Britain's road system runs along the routes the Romans selected. Aspects of Roman law remain in the British legal system. There are many Latin words in the English language. Roman villas, public baths and defensive walls provide archaeologists with valuable clues to the Roman way of life. Town names like Manchester or Colchester stand on the sites of Roman

The Romans created a huge network of roads across Britain. ▲

military camps. If this seems little enough to show for 400 years, one reason is that the Romans' successors, the Anglo-Saxons, had their own, well-founded culture and a very different way of life from that of Rome.

AD 480s TOUGH PEOPLE FOR A TOUGH LIFE

THE ANGLO-SAXONS, the Romans' successors, were tough people leading a tough life. Their primitive 'wattle and daub' homes were built from the wood and mud of the forests near or surrounding their villages. They wore simple, roughly made tunics. Shoes were sometimes made of leather, or might consist of thick pieces of woollen material wrapped round the feet and tied round the ankles with leather straps or strips of cloth. The men, who might at any time be called out to fight off unfriendly neighbours or raiders, could easily convert everyday clothing into fighting outfits, by adding leather or chain-mail jerkins over their tunics, and leather belts to hold swords and daggers.

Britain in the World

55 BC JULIUS CAESAR'S INVASION

IN THE 50s BC Julius Caesar carried out the conquest of Gaul, modern France. From the north coast the Roman legionaries could see the white cliffs about 20 Roman miles away. The Romans already knew a good deal about Britain, but after the conquest of Gaul there was an extra incentive to take a closer look. Fugitives had fled there and were soon raiding the new Roman province. In 55 BC Julius Caesar decided to teach the British a lesson. He landed briefly in Kent, but returned the following year with a much larger force of four legions. He led his army in a wide sweep around London smashing the resistance of the British tribes. But having forced them to submit, he left Britain and returned to Gaul.

Although Emperor Claudius was considered mentally retarded as a child, he became a great leader. ▲

AD 43 CLAUDIUS'S INVASION

IN AD 43 the Romans invaded Britain again and this time they came for good. A British chieftain appealed to Rome for help in a war against Caractacus of the Catuvellauni and the Emperor Claudius sent an army of 40,000 men. Claudius had just become emperor after the murder of his nephew Caligula in AD 41 and he was anxious to win a great victory. After being held up at the Medway in Kent, the army crossed the Thames and closed in on Colchester. Once victory was in sight, Claudius hurried

A Roman official and his wife. ▶

from Rome with a band of elephants to lead his army in triumph. He was only in Britain for 15 days before he returned to Rome leaving his generals to carry out the rest of the conquest.

AD 79   AGRICOLA

IN THE 70s and 80s AD the Romans gradually extended their control of Britain. The most important conquests were the work of Agricola (AD 37–93). He advanced into Scotland in AD 79 and built a legionary fortress at Inchtuithil. He planned to cross to Ireland and bring that under Roman control, but after he was recalled to Rome the attempts to occupy Scotland ended and Inchtuithil was abandoned. From then onwards Roman Britain was garrisoned by three legions based at York, Chester and Caerleon in South Wales. For the next 200 years the Romano-British enjoyed an almost unbroken period of peace and increasing wealth. This can be seen in the huge numbers of villas, which were built right across southern England from the second to the fourth centuries.

AD 286   REBELLION

THROUGHOUT THE third century the empire saw an increasing number of civil wars as ambitious generals tried to seize power. Britain was an obvious place to start a rebellion. Not only was it a remote province, but it also had a garrison of three legions, much more than most provinces. In AD 286 Pausanias seized control of Britain and held it for nearly 10 years. In the fourth and early fifth centuries a number of emperors were proclaimed by the British legions and attempted to march on Rome. None was successful. In the meantime the province of Britain continued to be prosperous and remained so long after the last legionaries were recalled to Rome in AD 410 by the Emperor Honorius.

Industry and Invention

PREHISTORY   BECOMING MOBILE

PALEOLITHIC MAN presumably depended entirely on his own feet for transport, and this remained the common mode of transport throughout the Stone Age. Domestication of the ox and the donkey undoubtedly brought some help, although not being able to harness the horse long delayed its effective use. The dugout canoe and the birch-bark canoe had showed man that water transport was a possibility and there is some evidence that by the end of the Neolithic Age the sail had already emerged as a means of harnessing the wind for small boats, beginning a long sequence of developments in marine transport and showing the extent to which humans were already applying their minds to problems.

Relief showing a carpenter using a flint-axe. ◄

PREHISTORY
CHOPPERS AND AXES

DATING BACK to around 2,600,000 years ago, the beginning of the Paleolithic Age, the earliest known tools consisted of variously sized examples of the pebble tool, or chopper. The chopper is thought to be the first tool made and used by human beings. It typically consisted of a water-worn, fist-sized rock, chipped away at one end to create a roughly serrated

Flint was used to create primitive knives, cut with serrated edges. ▲

edge. It was used to cut through the skin and sinews of hunted animals. This was the only tool used by man for almost 2,000,000 years, until the hand axe, a superior version of the chopper was invented. In this tool both the faces of the rock were chipped, making the edge of the hand axe considerably sharper than that of the earlier chopper.

PREHISTORY   MAKING FIRE

THE USE OF FIRE was a technique mastered at some unknown time in the Old Stone Age. The discovery that fire could be tamed and controlled and the further discovery that a fire could be generated by friction between two dry wooden surfaces were momentous. Fire was the most important contribution of prehistory to power technology, although little power was obtained directly from fire except as defence against wild animals. For the most part prehistoric communities remained completely dependent upon manpower but, in making the transition to a more settled pattern of life in the New Stone Age, man began to derive some power from animals that had been domesticated. The bones of a dog, possibly used for hunting in about 8500 BC, have been discovered in the western USA.

8000 BC   EARLY MINING

ARCHEOLOGICAL DISCOVERIES indicate that mining was conducted in prehistoric times. Apparently, the first mineral used was flint, which, owing to its concoidal fracturing pattern, could be broken into

Gradually flint and stone were shaped into different tools and weapons including axes and arrow heads. ▲

sharp-edged pieces that were useful as scrapers, knives and arrowheads. During the Neolithic Period, or New Stone Age (about 8000–2000 BC), shafts up to 100 m (330 ft) deep were sunk in soft chalk deposits in France and Britain in order to extract the flint pebbles found there. Other minerals, such as red ochre and the copper mineral malachite, were used as pigments. Gold was one of the first metals utilised, being mined from stream beds of sand and gravel where it occurred as a pure metal because of its chemical stability.

3500 BC TILLING THE LAND

THE VERY EARLY FARMERS used pointed wooden sticks, sometimes weighted with a stone, to till the soil, but they could only scratch the top soil and this did not produce good crops. These sticks soon developed into a variety of implements including hoes, spades and forks. As early as 3500 BC the greatest basic invention in agriculture had been made, that of the plough. Typically they were made of wood in the shape of a letter A curved at the pointed end so that it made a furrow in the ground when it was dragged along, steered by the ploughman walking behind. It was dragged initially by men then later oxen. By 500 BC an iron blade had been added and by 1000, wheels.

1000 BC   USING IRON

ONE OF THE outstanding technological feats of the Greco-Roman world was the smelting of iron. This technique, derived by unknown metallurgists, probably in Asia Minor, about 1000 BC, spread far beyond the provincial frontiers of the Roman Empire. Iron ore, long a familiar material, could not be reduced into metallic form because of the extreme heat required to perform the chemical transformation, about 1,535°C

Much of what we now understand about the Ancient World comes from Paleolithic art. ▼

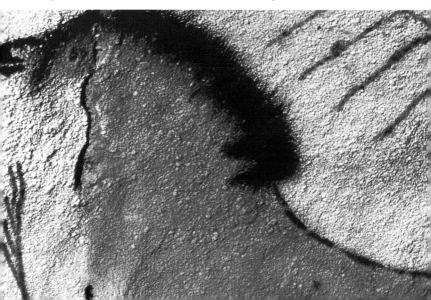

(2,795°F), compared with the 1,083°C (1,981°F) necessary for the reduction of copper ores. To reach this temperature, furnace construction had to be improved and ways devised to maintain the heat. These conditions were achieved only on a small scale, in furnaces burning charcoal and using foot bellows to intensify the heat.

A British kiln dating from Roman times. ▲

100 BC BEGINNINGS OF THE POTTERY TRADE

THE ROMANS made good-quality pottery available throughout their empire from the first century BC to the third century AD through the manufacture and trade of the bright-red, polished ware called *terra sigillata*. The term means literally ware made of clay impressed with designs. *Terra sigillata* was made in Gaul from the first century AD at La Graufesenque (now Millau, France) and later at other Gallic centres, whence it was exported in large quantities to outlying parts of the Roman Empire, including Britain. The body of the ware was generally cast in a mould. Relief designs, patterns and figurative scenes were also cast in moulds (which had been impressed with stamps in the desired pattern) and then applied to the vessels.

55 BC TRANSPORT IN THE ROMAN EMPIRE

THE SAILING SHIPS of this period were equipped with a square or rectangular sail to receive a following wind and one or more banks of oarsmen to propel the ship when the wind was contrary. The carvel-built hull (with planks meeting edge-to-edge rather than overlapping) was developed. The Romans gave much more attention to inland transport than to the sea, and constructed a network of carefully aligned and well-laid roads, often paved over long stretches, throughout the provinces of the empire. Along these highways the legions marched rapidly to the site of any crisis at which their presence was required. The roads also served for the development of trade, but their main function was military, as a vital means of keeping a vast empire in subjection.

55 BC   CEMENT

THE ORIGIN of hydraulic cements goes back to ancient Greece and Rome. The first materials used were lime and a volcanic ash that slowly reacted with it in the presence of water to form a hard mass. This formed the cementing material of the Roman mortars and concretes of 2,000 years ago and of subsequent classic construction work in western Europe. Volcanic ash mined near the city of Pozzuoli was particularly rich in essential aluminosilicate minerals, giving rise to the pozzolana cement of the Roman era, from 55 BC, used by the Romans in many of the fine buildings of their empire. The term cement, meanwhile, derives from the Latin word *caementum*, which meant stone chippings such as were used in Roman mortar, not the binding material itself.

Although built mainly for military purposes, the roads helped improve trade in Roman Britain. ▼

AD 122   A WALL TO STOP BARBARIANS

HADRIAN CAME to Britain in AD 122 and arranged for the building of the famous Hadrian's Wall from AD 122–126. This was a continuous Roman defensive barrier that guarded the north-western frontier of Britain from barbarian invaders. The wall extended from coast to coast across the width of Britain, running for 118 km (73 miles) from Wallsend (Segedunum) on the River Tyne in the east to Bowness on the Solway Firth in the west. At every ⅓ Roman mile there was a tower, and at every mile a fortlet (milecastle) containing a gate through the wall, presumably surmounted by a tower, and one or two barrack-blocks. The fortlets, towers and forts continued for at least 42 km (26 miles) beyond Bowness down the Cumbrian coast.

The remains of a Roman temple on Hadrian's Wall. ▼

Culture, Arts and Leisure

PREHISTORY THE DAWN OF CULTURE

IT IS HARD TO separate the different aspects of culture – music, religion, architecture, poetry – and see exactly how each fitted into the pattern of life, as it changed between Neolithic and Saxon times. But we can be sure that prehistoric culture included a deep sense of connection with the land, through the changing seasons, and – judging by the alignments in sites like Stonehenge – to the stars and planets. Later cultures used to form social bonds, and memorised long tracts of heroic songs and poetry beyond anything that is possible today. Although there were probably no literate kings between Alfred and Henry I two centuries later, writing and learning had become considerably more widespread by the time the Normans arrived.

2600 BC AVEBURY STONE CIRCLE

'AVEBURY DOTH as much exceed Stonehenge in grandeur as a Cathedral doth an ordinary Parish Church', said the antiquary John Aubrey, and more than 4,000 years after it was built it is difficult to understand exactly what role the enormous stone circle played. It is surrounded by a 426-m (1,300-ft) earth bank, and each

The southern inner circle at Avebury, Wiltshire; the purpose of these monoliths remains a mystery. ▲

remaining stone weighs up to 40 tons, but the two avenues of stones, 2.4 km (1.5 miles) long, which once snaked through the site, are now gone. Was it a great sun temple, or a 'moongate' – a place where heaven and earth meet – as some archeologists suggest? We will probably never know for certain, but we can be sure that its purpose was central to people's lives.

450 BC   ARRIVAL OF THE BARDS

HISTORIANS CAN never be sure about the arrival of the Celts across Britain, but they were probably here by 450 BC, and they brought with them a verbal loquacity and fascination with music that has remained to a great or lesser degree ever since. Wandering bards would entertain the gathered Celts with songs and music on the lyre or harp, praising chieftains gone by in epics learned by heart. Bards and poets were a Druidic branch and learned their craft for up to 20 years, often in schools, committing a great deal of poetry to memory. The highest class of poet, or *ollam*, was equal to a minor king and would travel with a retinue of up to 24 companions, defending themselves with the magical power of satire.

AD 84   FOUNDATION OF BATH

LEGEND HAS IT that Bath dates back as far as the legendary British king Bladud around 860 BC. But the construction of the Roman Baths there, known as *Aquae Sulis*, certainly began around AD 84 near the Fosse Way, and they were soon the centre of a major healing centre dedicated to the Celtic god Sulis and the Roman goddess Minerva. The baths themselves fell into disuse in the fifth century, and the town may have stayed ruined

for 300 years after that. The remains of the baths stayed undiscovered until the eighteenth century, but – along with Roman mosaics, altars and temples – they are a monument to the Roman design that strongly influenced the fashionable people who flocked to the same springs a thousand years later.

Characteristic of Roman opulence are the magnificent mosaic floors that can still be seen in many Roman ruins. ◀

Religions, Belief and Thought

2800 BC   STONEHENGE

A CENTRAL FEATURE of Stonehenge is its size; it is a surprisingly small construction. It continues, however, to hold a fascination in the history of British culture. Probably begun in about 2800 BC, it developed in a number of stages and may have been in use until about 1100 BC. Stonehenge was likely to have been the focus for religious and ritual functions but beyond that it is difficult to be sure. What Stonehenge does is draw attention to the sophistication of those who planned and built it. The calculations necessary to order the stones, to understand the movement of the Earth, Sun and Moon would have required careful observation of the skies. This suggests a thinking and sophisticated people, exploring fundamental religious and philosophical questions and reflecting on their place in the universe.

Stonehenge is believed to have been the site of ancient religious rites and festivals. ▼

2750 BC   LONG BARROWS

NEAR TO AVEBURY, and overlooking the earth work and mysterious mound of Silbury Hill (built about 2750 BC), is the Long Barrow at West Kennet. Barrows serve as burial places and West Kennet is one of the most significant memorials to the dead. The small areas inside the barrow are now empty but there is the smell of death about the place, not a chilling fear, but the simplicity of a resting place of lives well spent. To bury the dead with some possessions or some protection and/or food for the future, implies some sort of belief in a journey beyond this life. Is the need to bury the dead, the creation of ritual, and the gifts for an (unknown) future life the bedrock from which religious thinking emerges?

2600 BC   SPREAD OF IDEAS

THE CELTS adapted many of their ideas from their contemporaries in the south of Europe. The archeology of earlier periods shows there was considerable movement of peoples exchanging new ideas and new practices. It is not possible to know much of the religious beliefs of Neolithic, Bronze and Iron Age peoples; we can only draw inferences from their creation of quoits, henges and barrows and how they buried their dead. Movements in the skies, tides and seasons affected them. Human sacrifice was not unknown as a feature of some rituals and that sacrifice would have been for, or to, something. Religion in a preliterate society was a social tool, welding together through story and ritual the diverse needs of society. This finds its most potent expression in the ritual surrounding death.

The wealth of Celtic artifacts found by archeologists reveals much about their religious beliefs and customs. ◀

The Avebury Stone Circle is just one of many mysterious legacies of ancient Britain's religious practices. ▲

1500 BC   BRYN CELLI DHU

THE CHAMBERED cairn of Bryn Celli Dhu in Anglesey is a variation on the model of prehistoric burial monuments. It appears to be constructed as a series of circles. This may be significant for it would create a link with the circles, spirals, images and labyrinths common across Europe that act as a motif of eternal pilgrimage. The chamber is clearly a burial monument but it seems to link the symbol of circles with that of the barrow. If the first signs of human culture are linked with burial rituals (going back around 500,000 years BC) then there is a long history of belief in some form of existence after death. The placing of many bodies in a foetal position suggests a return to the 'birth state'; a preparation for a new birth place, perhaps.

1300 BC   BURIAL RITES

THERE APPEARS to have been a change in burial rites in northern Europe from about the thirteenth century BC. A change from burial (or placing the body in a barrow or tomb) to cremation took place. This may suggest a more sophisticated understanding of what awaited one after life on earth. The body would be burned and the ashes placed in a pot. A Bronze Age etching on a piece of pottery shows a chariot being used in a funeral. It is drawn by two horses and preceded by a horse being led by a handler. The chariot bears the ashes of the dead person in a container. The analogy to some forms of modern state funerals is clear. It is likely the horse would have belonged to the dead person and have been sacrificed.

600 BC   CELTIC SOCIETY AND THE DRUIDS

AROUND THE sixth century BC the Celts became a powerful influence across parts of Europe. A society was created in which people were bound to each other by obligations, duties and responsibilities. There was a priesthood, members of whom, owing to the preliterate nature of the society, were probably story-tellers and organisers of ritual and tradition. The religion, Druidism, was probably the religion of the Celts in Britain but it appears to have been linked with the sun and moon worship of previous ages. Old faiths were adapted to meet new needs and newer religions. 'They (the Gaulish nation) employ the Druids as ministers for such sacrifices (human) because they think that, unless the life of man be repaid

Celtic High Crosses were erected on monastic lands as protective symbols and points of worship. ▶

for the life of man, the will of the immortal gods cannot be appeased,' wrote Caesar in his *De Bello Gallico* (BK VI).

AD 300   EVIDENCE FOR CHRISTIANITY

CHRISTIANS HAVE left little evidence of their presence in Britain during the first centuries AD. The Chi-Rho symbol appears on some mosaics and on some silverware, though it is occasionally found in the midst of pagan or pre-Christian symbols. The Chi-Rho sign was used as a symbol by Christians because the Chi and the Rho are the first two letters of 'Christ' in Greek. The great monuments to Romano-Christian religion are found in the mosaics of Frampton and Hinton St Mary and the wall paintings of Lullingstone; but otherwise the evidence is patchy. One cemetery in Dorset suggests a large wealthy Christian community – but other cemeteries around the country revealed nothing.

The scholar, historian and theologian, The Venerable Bede. ▲

AD 304   ALBAN – THE FIRST CHRISTIAN MARTYR

THE FIRST CHRISTIAN known to have been martyred in Britain is recorded as Alban. The Venerable Bede, writing hundreds of years later, says he was a layman from the city of Verulamium and had given shelter to a Christian priest fleeing from persecution, but the first reference to the 'blessed martyr Alban' occurs in about AD 480. While he hid the priest, they talked and Alban was converted to Christianity. The story tells that when the soldiers came to arrest the priest, Alban wrapped the priest's cloak around himself and was martyred in his place. Legend says his death (probably in AD 304) took place on the hill where St Alban's Abbey now stands. Bede also refers to the martyrdoms of Aaron and Julius at Caerleon in Gwent and of many more.

Constantine's conversion began a new era of Christianity in England.▲

AD 312   THE EDICT OF MILAN

THE EDICT OF MILAN in AD 312 was the obvious consequence of
Constantine's succession to the title of emperor and his conversion to
Christianity. For 300 years Christianity had been an illicit religion and had
suffered severe persecution. Like all 'new religions' it had also suffered
periods of unpopularity. Now, for the first time, Christians could be open
about their commitment and rapid advances could be made. The evidence
for such advance, while rich in other European countries, is thin in
Britain. In AD 359 British bishops attended the Council of Rimini but
could not pay their own expenses. This suggests the Church in Britain was
poor and not well organised with members drawn from the less wealthy
members of the community.

AD 380   PELAGIUS

PELAGIUS WAS only the second Briton of this early period (Alban being
the other) who has a discernible personality. His name is associated with
the heresy of Pelagianism, something that has remained a strong attraction
for the British ever since. Pelagius objected to the emphasis put on the
complete sinfulness of human beings so their only chance of salvation was
through the grace and forgiveness of God. He had a strong faith in the
inherent possibility of each person to reach perfection without the
intervention of God's grace. He left Britain as a young man and never
returned but his message was brought to his homeland by Agricola, a
follower, early in the fifth century. Pelagius was condemned and
excommunicated by the pope. Though an unorthodox Christian he
foreshadowed the rise of ethical humanism, albeit in a Christian context,
and the struggle of the British with the Christian doctrine of original sin.

AD 397   NINIAN

'NYNIA, A MOST venerable and holy man, of the nation of the Britons,
who had been instructed properly in the faith and the mysteries of the truth
at Rome.' So Bede describes the first bishop to live among the Picts in
Cumberland and southern Scotland. He studied in Rome and may have
returned to Britain as early as AD 397. What is known of him is found in
Bede's work more that 300 years later and the twelfth-century writings of

St Aiden founded a monastery on the island of Lindisfarne in northern England to spread the Christian word. ◀

Ailred of Rievaulx, so it is difficult to be certain about the details of his teaching and history. He did found a monastery at Whithorn in Galloway, which came to be known as the 'White House'. This became the base for Ninian and his monks' evangelistic mission up into the east-coastal area of Scotland.

AD 429   AFTER PELAGIUS

SO CONCERNED were the authorities in Gaul about heretics in England that two bishops, Germanus Bishop of Auxerre (AD 418–48) and Lupus, Bishop of Troyes (AD 427–79) were asked to go there to instil some discipline into the Romano-British Church. They arrived in AD 429 and, among other things, visited the shrine of St Alban. They preached against the liberal teachings of Pelagius 'not only in the churches but also at the cross roads and in the fields and lanes'. Germanus had been a fighting man and obviously had great strength of character. He appears to have found the Britons timid and lacking in self-confidence though the implications of Pelagius's teaching suggests a people at peace with itself and able to take a relaxed view of human nature.

AD 430   ST PATRICK

PATRICK'S FAMILY, who lived near the sea in Bannavern, were attacked one day and Patrick was taken to Ireland by pirates. His birthplace is not known, although there are various English and Welsh claimants. He looked after cattle before escaping to Gaul. He received a vision asking him to return to Ireland and in about AD 430 he was made a bishop for the Irish.

He seems to have travelled over most of northern and central Ireland during the next 30 years. He tried to introduce a diocesan form of government but the rural nature of the country defeated him. Although the hymn the 'Breastplate of St Patrick' has long been popular, the earliest known version was three centuries after Patrick's death.

Thirteenth-century manuscript depicting St Patrick, patron saint of Ireland. ▼

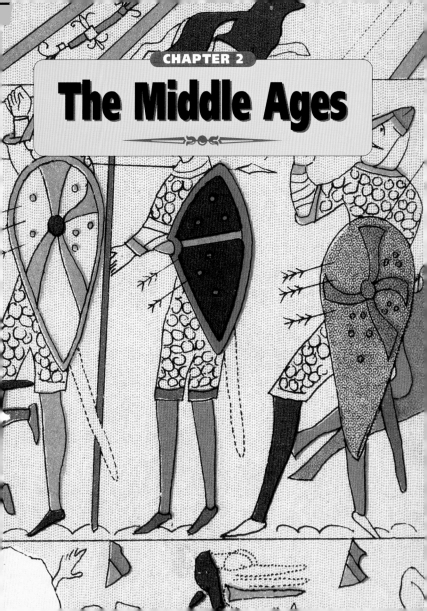

CHAPTER 2
The Middle Ages

Power and Politics

AD 500s   GERMANIC INFLUENCE

THE ANGLO-SAXONS were a German people composed of three main groups – Angles, Saxons and Jutes. Their connection with Britain was established before the sixth century when the Saxon leader Aelle landed in Sussex. Trade routes between the south coast and German ports grew under the Romans. Saxons had previously led a series of pirate attacks on the south coast. When they arrived, Kent was soon conquered by the Jutes and Saxon kingdoms were established in Essex and Middlesex. Wessex and Sussex soon followed. East Anglian and Northumbrian kingdoms were also set up. Although less civilised than the Romans, kinship ties proved strong under the Anglo-Saxons. Their influence on British life can still be noticed by the number of town names ending in –ing, –ington, or –ingham.

AD 600s   KINGS AND QUEENS

THE STRUGGLE for power in Britain during the seventh century remains one of the bloodiest periods in the country's history. By the time the Anglo-Saxons had asserted their dominance, Britain was ruled by a large number of different kings. One estimate claims there were 'dozens' of English kings at this time. The Britons had largely fled to Wales, while the Anglo-Saxons controlled large parts of England. The

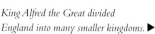

King Alfred the Great divided
England into many smaller kingdoms. ▶

most powerful kingdoms to emerge were Wessex, Mercia, East Anglia and Northumbria. Leaders of the larger kingdoms also ruled over smaller areas outside their own bailiwick. The most powerful leader was known as the *Bretwalda*, which meant Lord of Britain. The Anglo-Saxons also developed a council – the Witan – composed of noblemen and bishops, which was designed to limit royal power.

AD 793   THE VIKING INVASIONS

THE LATE EIGHTH century saw Britain invaded for the first time in two centuries as the Vikings began their colonisation. History used

Vikings attacking the English coast. ▲

to portray them as bloodthirsty barbarians. This may be an exaggeration; though some of the battles were indeed gruesome, the Vikings' reputation as rapists and pillagers may owe as much to propaganda as to fact. Evidence suggests they were also successful merchants. The areas they controlled became much more prosperous – especially those in eastern England – and trade flourished as the economy expanded. The traditional view of Vikings – the term derives from an old Saxon word for pirate – may derive from their initial sorties into England, which saw the sacking of three holy sites, Lindisfarne, Jarrow and Iona between AD 793 and 795.

AD 878 THE RISE OF WESSEX

THE VIKING INVASIONS, though decisive, were not complete. They still met resistance from Saxons, the most famous of whom was King Alfred. One of England's greatest heroes, Alfred ruled the kingdom of Wessex, between AD 871 and 899. Despite appalling odds, his army defeated the Danes at Athelney in AD 878 and followed this with a decisive victory in Wiltshire in the same year. In AD 886 he captured London and his rule was recognised by the Danish. His successes are not confined to only military victories. Alfred extended the use of the English language, encouraged learning, stressed the importance of widespread literacy, courted intellectuals, wrote books, translated Latin, began the *Anglo-Saxon Chronicles* that detailed life between the ninth and twelfth centuries and originated the Royal Navy.

AD 900s THE AGE OF WESSEX

HAVING ESTABLISHED its rule through Alfred the Great, the kingdom of Wessex was able to consolidate its rule throughout the tenth century. Alfred's successors, including Edward the Elder, Aethelstan and Eadred, proved themselves to be largely competent in the face of renewed threats and further invasions from the Danes. Internal political life in

Viking helmet and mask found at Sutton Hoo. ◀

the southern parts controlled by Wessex was more militaristic than that under the control of the Danes. The role of the kings also grew in importance. Instead of being only overlords, the new monarchy now presented themselves as quasi-religious figures. Royal authority was more keenly felt, literally, when representatives of the royal household carried out flogging on law breakers. Monasteries also received increased royal patronage.

1016 THE DECLINE OF THE ANGLO-SAXON ORDER

THE ACCESSION of Cnut (Canute) to the throne in 1016 marked a brief period of renewed Danish dominance and the beginning of the end of Anglo-Saxon rule. Following the rule of Aethelred the Unready, who ordered the massacre of all Danes in his kingdom, the Danish launched a counter-assault on Wessex. Cnut was accepted by the Danish army and began reform of the English rulers dividing the country into four earldoms. Cnut was succeeded by his sons Harold and Harthacnut but they were to be the last Danish rulers. The Anglo-Saxons, in the form of Edward the Confessor, returned to the throne in 1042. His successors included the last Anglo-Saxon king, Harold II, who was defeated by William the Conqueror.

Danish king Cnut, ruler of England from 1016. ▲

1066 STAMFORD BRIDGE AND HASTINGS

ON 25 SEPTEMBER 1066, Harold Godwinson defeated the king of
Norway, Harold Hardraada, and his arch enemy and brother Tostig at the
battle of Stamford Bridge, near York. But within days of his victory news of
the Normans arrival at Pevensey reached Harold. Mustering his forces, he
marched to Sussex to meet the invaders and ultimately secure his place in
history. The battle between the English army and the Normans took place
at Senlac Hill, five miles from Hastings. Although holding the advantage in
numbers, the English were undisciplined and out-fought by their enemy.
The battle lasted a single day during which Harold was killed after an
arrow pierced his eye. The victory was later commemorated by the
building of Battle Abbey near the site.

Scene from the Bayeux Tapestry, depicting the Norman invasion. ▼

1086 DOMESDAY BOOK

THE *Domesday Book*, today housed at the Public Record Office, was the most comprehensive record of property compiled in Europe during the Middle Ages.

William the Conqueror's Domesday Book. ▲

It was part of William the Conqueror's attempt to consolidate Norman rule by maximising as much revenue in taxes as possible. The money-raising tactics were resented, and in many shires this led to rioting. Almost every English county – only London, Winchester and the four most northern shires escaped – was visited by the king's representatives. Every village had to give details of landowners, and the size, use and value of their land. The *Domesday Book* eventually came in two volumes, *Little Domesday*, dealing with East Anglia, and the other with the remaining counties.

1087 WILLIAM THE CONQUEROR'S SUCCESSORS

BY THE TIME OF William the Conqueror's death in 1087, the family tensions that would eventually end the Norman dynasty were already beginning to show. William was succeeded in England not by his eldest son Robert, who controlled Normandy, but by his second son, William II, better known as Rufus because of his red complexion. He was once described as being 'hated by almost all his people' and almost certainly died at the hands of an assassin while hunting in the New Forest. Both William II and his successor – his brother, Henry I – had to establish their rule over England through war with Robert. Henry's successes as king were notable in the areas of finance, where he extended the role of the Exchequer, the forerunner of today's Treasury.

1100s   THE *CURIA REGIS*

THE NORMAN and Angevin kings developed a new Parliament, seen now as one of the earliest forerunners of today's modern body. The *Curia Regis* was a legislative body that created and enacted new laws. It was also a court that adjudicated on matters such as land and property disputes. Its importance declined though, when the machinery of government, especially bureaucracy, grew. One of the departments to take on its work in the twelfth century was the Exchequer, the forerunner of today's Treasury. A further major political reform of the time was the development of the borough. Derived from the Anglo-Saxons' *burh*, the borough remains a political unit in Britain to this day.

1200s   THE CHURCH UNDER THE NORMANS

ONE AREA where Norman rule changed the social landscape of Britain was religion. French religious orders and monks were brought to the

newly invaded country and were granted land to build new monasteries. At the time of the invasion in 1066 there were just 1,000 monks and nuns in England. By the early thirteenth century this figure had swollen to 13,000. Cathedrals, such as Durham and Ely, were built to emphasise the new regime's religious beliefs. Catholic Christianity remained the dominant form of religion throughout this time – the religious tenets of Rome appear to have been taken on board by the population at large. Non-Christian faiths such as Judaism were rarely tolerated and in the thirteenth century all Jews were expelled from Britain.

Ely Cathedral, one of many cathedrals built after the Norman invasion. ◀

1295 MODEL PARLIAMENT

THE CONCEPT of modern Parliament owes much to the late-thirteenth-century Model Parliament and the nineteenth-century historians who gave the body its grand title of the 'Model Parliament'. The name came about because of its political make-up, which was said to be more representative than the Parliaments that followed later. Parliament was summoned by Edward I who occupied the throne between 1272 and 1307. Edward soon found himself clashing with Welsh armies and, later during

Edward I, who summoned one of the earliest Parliaments in 1295. ▲

his rule, with the Scots. He needed to convene a Parliament in order to raise revenues for his wars. The body was duly summoned in November 1295. It comprised of earls and barons and members of the clergy as well as representatives from each city and borough.

1314 SCOTTISH CONQUEST

EDWARD I left an unpleasant legacy for his successors. His shrewdness in administrative matters was not matched in his dealings with the rest of the British Isles, and England found itself at war with both Wales and Scotland. The English army was routed in several battles with the Scots, commanded by William Wallace, most notably at Bannockburn in 1314. But the English court was also preoccupied with its own internal warring factions, that would shape the development of the country over the next two centuries. Specifically, the principle that the crown should pass to the eldest son made it more likely that the country would end up with a king it did not want and certainly did not need.

Manuscript depicting the Hundred Years' War between the French and the English. ▲

1337 THE HUNDRED YEARS' WAR

ENGLAND'S MAIN overseas enemy during this period was France. Between 1337 and 1453 the two countries embarked upon a prolonged period of conflict. At the heart of the struggle was political sovereignty and trade. France was worried by the power of the English territories in its country, and was also fearful of England's growing economic influence, especially in the region of Flanders. The claim of English monarchs to the French crown was another anxiety. England was troubled by France's support of Scotland's struggle for independence. The Hundred Years' War broke out when Gascony was confiscated from the English. By the time the conflict was resolved the English, after a series of defeats led in part by Joan of Arc, retained control of only Calais on the French mainland.

1381 THE PEASANTS' REVOLT

SOCIAL POLITICS during the Middle Ages led to a series of uprisings collectively known as the Peasants' Revolt in 1381. Peasants and artisans rebelled against the imposition of a poll tax and the government's decision to collect arrears. Most serious of all the uprisings was in Kent, where protesters were led by Wat Tyler. Having seized Rochester Castle, Tyler led a march to London in June. Confronted eventually by the king – Richard II – the protesters dispersed but not before the chancellor and archbishop of Canterbury had been murdered by the rebels. Wat Tyler was also killed, by the Mayor of London, William Walworth.

Richard II sailing down the Thames to confront the peasant rebels. ▶

Richard ij allant à la rencontre des serfs anglais révoltés

Ordinary Lives

AD 570   ANGLO-SAXON INVADERS

AS THE ANGLO-SAXONS penetrated deeper and deeper into Britain, the Britons were pushed eastwards, leaving their lands to be settled by the invaders. Vortigern's mercenaries were among them. The Britons fought back as best they could and found a Romano-British leader who was later romanticised into the legendary 'King' Arthur. It is believed that Arthur used Roman cavalry tactics in guerrilla strikes against the inexorable advance of the Anglo-Saxons, but the advance continued nevertheless. By about AD 570, small estates, usually belonging to one man, his family and his followers, had begun to take shape. Eventually, these were consolidated into Anglo-Saxon kingdoms such as Mercia (eastern and southern England), Northumbria (north-east England and south-east Scotland) and Wessex (south and south-west England).

Wells Cathedral, one of the first great Saxon constructions. ▼

AD 700s SAXON SOCIETY

WELLS WAS ONE of the first great cathedrals founded by the Saxons. The people who designed and built it lived nearby in small houses with sunken floors, and wore jewellery fastened with large ornate brooches. Their social lives were orientated around great Saxon mead halls, 24 m (80 ft) or more in length, and hung inside with tapestries, ornamental drinking horns and shields. Here they would listen to the minstrels with harps and repeat popular tales like that of *Beowulf*. It was a formal society, which reserved activities like hunting and hawking for the lords, and cooking and milking for the women. But women were protected by law from marrying men they did not like, and could own land and property and divorce easily.

AD 789 OFFA'S DYKE

THERE WERE vicious rivalries between the Anglo-Saxon kings that led to civil war and anarchy. One of the most ambitious of these monarchs was Offa, who seized power in Mercia in about AD 757 and afterwards made his realm supreme south of the Humber. In about AD 789, Offa built a huge 257-km (160-mile) long earthwork, later known as Offa's Dyke, to protect his territory from attack. The dyke was 2 m (6 ft) deep, with a 7.6-m (25-ft) earth rampart, strengthened by timber palisades and a stone wall. However, only four years after the dyke was completed, new invaders appeared in the east who were far more dangerous and terrifying than any home-grown enemies: the Vikings from Scandinavia.

Offa's Dyke, built to protect the district of Mercia from attack. ▶

1070   TROUBLE FROM SCOTLAND

EDGAR THE ATHELING, was a closer relative to Edward the Confessor than was William the Conqueror and had a better right to the throne. He found a willing supporter for his claim in his brother-in-law, the Scots king Malcolm III who, in 1070, sent an army to ravage northern England. Two years later, Malcolm struck again in an apparent attempt to annexe Northumbria to his own realm. William struck back with full, retributive force and on 15 August 1072, when the two kings met at Abernethy on Tayside, Malcolm was obliged to submit and hand over his son Duncan as a hostage. When Malcolm also agreed to eject Edgar from his court, the boy fled across the English Channel to Flanders.

1073   HEREWARD THE WAKE

THE YEAR AFTER he took part in the looting of Peterborough Abbey, Thegn Hereward, known as Hereward the Wake, staged an uprising of his own in the treacherous, marshy Fenlands near Ely. This time, the Normans came in force to deal with him, and though Hereward and his men held out for months against assaults from both land and sea, their cause was ultimately doomed. Cunningly, the Normans confiscated lands belonging to monks near Ely, precipitating their surrender. With that Hereward's resistance was critically weakened. Inevitably, his own men were obliged to

surrender too, but Hereward himself managed to escape. Nothing is definitely known about him after this, but legends about this great hero-patriot from Lincolnshire proliferated long after he was dead.

Hereward the Wake, leader of a rebellion against the Normans. ◀

1080 MURDER AT DURHAM

THE HATRED of Saxon for Norman did not manifest itself only in uprisings and battles. Savage personal vendettas shadowed these bigger set-piece events. One of the most horrific acts of vengeance occurred on 14 May 1080 when Walcher, the Norman bishop of Durham, and one of his relatives, Gilbert, took refuge in a church to escape a furious mob who were convinced that the bishop had murdered a Saxon thane. Walcher, in fact, had tried his best to calm the arrogant behaviour of Norman knights under his command, but this counted for nothing as the mob set the church on fire, forcing Walcher and Gilbert out into the street. As they and their followers emerged, they were seized and summarily killed.

Canterbury Cathedral, the site of St Thomas Becket's murder. ▲

1171 MIRACLES AT CANTERBURY

FOURTEEN MYSTERIOUS cures were recorded in the first year of the shrine of St Thomas Becket (*c.* 1120–70) at Canterbury, all within a few months of his murder by four knights loyal to Henry II (1133–89). The miracles led to a cult in Becket's name and brought pilgrims flocking from all over England along the Pilgrim's Way and from all over Europe. Medieval travel was so dangerous that the Church included travellers in prayers along with prisoners and the sick. Crosses were erected in lonely roads, lanterns kept burning in churches at night and pilgrims would gather together – along with minstrels, bears, jugglers and herbalists – on their way to the shrines or great fairs, like Stourbridge, St Giles or Bartholomew Fair in London.

1267   GUILD BATTLE

A FIERCE BATTLE between the London guilds of Goldsmiths and Taylors in 1267 involved 500 people and left many of them dead. It took place against the background of the growing influence of the guilds, which were setting standards for craftsmanship, fixing prices and wages, controlling the entry of apprentices and regulating trade. The Exchequer had moved from Winchester in the twelfth century, followed by the development of permanent courts of justice in the thirteenth. By this time, London was thriving under economic expansion, exporting wool and cloth, which was shrunk and scoured by a network of water mills around the countryside. In one 45-m (150-ft) section of London's Cheapside, as many as 15 bustling shopfronts were recorded.

1348   KNIGHTS OF THE GARTER

EDWARD III (1312–77) launched his Order of the Garter with 26 knights – including himself and his 18-year-old son, the Black Prince (1330–76) – on the eve of the outbreak of the plague, known as the Black Death. The first meeting was held in Windsor as the first deaths began outside. Edward wanted to create a new version of the Arthurian ideal of a Round Table dedicated to chivalry and courtly love. He feasted in Windsor dressed in white

Edward III – founder of the Order of the Garter – and his knights. ◀

and silver, wearing a tunic with the words: 'Hay, Hay, the white swan! By Goddes soul, I am thy man'. For the population outside, romance was more difficult than marriage: under a ruling by Pope Alexander III (d. 1181), young people could freely exchange marriage vows anywhere they liked. This remained the law in England until 1753.

1348 THE BLACK DEATH

AT THE TIME the fatal plague known as the Black Death was a mystery, but the combined outbreaks in 1348, 1361, 1369 and

Scenes in London during the plague; in the fourteenth century it caused a drastic drop in the population of England. ▲

1374 left between a third and a half of the population dead – including the new archbishop of Canterbury, just six days after his consecration. No social class escaped, and the final outbreak was particularly fatal to young people. It was known as the 'pestilence of the children'. The Black Death was probably the greatest demographic disaster in European history, and in England the population plunged from close to six million to just three million, then carried on drifting downwards. In the long-term, it discouraged labour-intensive arable farming, raised wages and even led to paid holidays. Scientists did not understand that bubonic plague was spread by rat fleas for another six centuries.

Britain in the World

1066   HAROLD GODWINSON

ON 5 JANUARY 1066, Edward the Confessor died. He was childless. Edward had been a weak king and it was perhaps no surprise when Harold Godwinson, Earl of Wessex was proclaimed king almost immediately. He had been at Edward's side when he died and stated that Edward had named him king at the point of death. Although no one had actually heard Edward say this, no one challenged him. There is little doubt that Harold was a popular king. He was the most powerful man in England and a very successful general. Although there appears to have been no opposition to Harold's succession, Harold soon found that he had two rivals, William of Normandy and Harold Hardraada, King of Norway.

1066   HARALD HARDRAADA

HARALD HARDRAADA was King of Norway and a descendant of the Danish king of England, who had reigned from 1016 to 1042. When he heard news of Edward's death, he decided to try to seize the throne of England. Harald was a famous warrior and he was supported by Sweyn, the king of Denmark and by Tostig, the brother of Harold Godwinson, who had been exiled in 1064. He was obviously a very dangerous opponent and in September he landed in

Edward the Confessor, whose death led to foreign attempts to seize the sovereignty of England. ◀

Yorkshire and defeated an English army at the battle of Fulford Gate, near York. While Harald was celebrating, King Harold marched north and made a surprise attack on the Norwegian army. Harald, Sweyn and Tostig were all killed and the army was destroyed at the Battle of Stamford Bridge on 25 September 1066. It appeared that England was safe.

1066   THE BATTLE OF HASTINGS

WILLIAM OF NORMANDY landed in England only three days after the Battle of Stamford Bridge against the king of Norway. When Harold heard the news he marched south immediately and advanced to meet William at Hastings. For some reason he did not wait to collect reinforcements and so arrived at Senlac, the site of the battle, with only 6,000 men against William's 7,000. Harold may have been over-confident, he was after all the king of a large country and William was only a duke, or Harold may have been trying to prevent damage to his estates in Sussex. Whatever the reason, Harold's decision proved fatal. On 14 October the English army was defeated at Hastings and Harold was killed. On 25 December 1066 William was crowned king of England in Westminster Abbey.

The death of Harold in the Battle of Hastings, from the Bayeux Tapestry. ▼

1100s A PROVINCE OF NORMANDY

THE NORMAN Conquest changed England dramatically. William took possession of all land and only eight per cent was left in English hands. French became the language of government. England also changed from being a powerful independent kingdom, to becoming a province of an increasingly influential empire based in north-west France. William obviously preferred Normandy and spent most of his time there and his eldest son William took the title of duke of Normandy when William I died

Edward I, who attempted, but failed, to regain land in northern France. ▲

in 1087. Henry II, who became king in 1154, spent only about one-third of his reign in England. As far as Henry was concerned, it was his French possessions that were the most important.

1189 RICHARD THE LIONHEART

HENRY II died in 1189 and he was succeeded by his son Richard. Richard had taken a vow to go on a crusade only a few months before his father's death and left England almost immediately. He was away for almost five years. The crusade lasted for two years, but on his way home Richard was taken prisoner by Leopold, Duke of Austria, and was held to ransom for 150,000 gold marks, a sum equal to two years taxes. It was the effort to collect this vast sum that partly gave rise to the legend of Robin Hood and his efforts to help the poor. When Richard finally returned, he left again to fight a series of campaigns in France. He was shot by an archer in 1199.

1272   EDWARD I

WHEN KING JOHN died in 1216 he was succeeded by his nine-year-old son, Henry III. Henry made several attempts to invade France and these were partly responsible for his increasing unpopularity with the English Barons. In 1264–65 there was a civil war between the Barons led by Simon de Montfort and Henry's forces, led by his son Edward. When Henry died in 1272, his son succeeded as Edward I. He attempted to restore English prestige and sent expeditions to Gascony to re-establish English authority. Edward was able to retain control over Gascony, but was unable to regain any of the lands in northern France.

1327   EDWARD III

EDWARD III became king at the age of 15, in 1327. After defeating the Scots at Halidon Hill in 1333, Edward turned his attention to France. The French king, Philip VI, was supporting the Scots and Edward wanted to stop their interference in English affairs. In 1338 he invaded France, in response to attacks on Gascony by Philip VI of France. Edward also claimed the throne of France through his mother Isabelle, who was a French princess. In 1340 the English navy under Edward III won its first great victory at Sluys and gained control of the Channel. Edward then made a truce with the French until 1345.

Edward III laid claim to the French throne and led a series of attacks on France. ▶

The longbow was deployed to great effect by the English during the Hundred Years' War. ▲

1346 CRÈCY

IN 1346, EDWARD III invaded France and met the French army at Crècy. The result was a catastrophic defeat for the French. For the first time on the Continent, Edward used the longbow, which the English had encountered in Wales. Almost 2 m (6 ft) in length and requiring tremendous strength, it had the power to penetrate chain mail and even plate armour on occasions. When the French knights charged, they galloped into a hail of arrows. This sequence of events was to be repeated in several battles during the next 80 years. Edward followed up his victory at Crècy by capturing Calais in 1347, using artillery. The surrender of the burghers of Calais is commemorated in a statue in the town to this day.

1360   THE BLACK PRINCE

AFTER THE TREATY OF BRETIGNY in 1360, Edward, the Black
Prince, governed Aquitaine, the area in south-west France that included
Gascony. He became involved in a series of campaigns against the French,
led by Bertrand du Guesclin. The French avoided battle and concentrated
on wearing the English out by a war of attrition. The people of Aquitaine
became more and more opposed to the English as Edward imposed extra
taxes to pay for the cost of the war. Eventually, in 1371, he left France and
returned to England. Edward, the Black Prince, died in 1376 from plague,
just a year before his father, Edward III. He is buried in Canterbury
Cathedral and there is a chapel dedicated to him in the crypt.

1374   JOHN OF GAUNT

THE BLACK PRINCE
was replaced in France by
his brother, John of
Gaunt. John proved to be
an incompetent soldier
and within three years
most English possessions
in France had been lost.
By 1375 only five towns
remained in English
hands: Calais, Cherbourg,
Brest, Bayonne and
Bordeaux. John of Gaunt
returned to England in

*Effigy of Edward, the Black Prince in
Canterbury Cathedral.* ▲

1374 and tried to take power, but when Edward III died in 1377, he was
succeeded by Richard II, the son of the Black Prince. Richard reigned for
22 years, before being deposed by John of Gaunt's son, Henry, in 1399.
Richard was probably murdered in 1400 and Henry IV established the
House of Lancaster. During the reigns of Richard II and Henry IV there
was little fighting in France, but when Henry IV died in 1413, his son
Henry V invaded once again.

Industry and Invention

AD 500s IRON EVERYWHERE

BEGINNING ABOUT the sixth century, and for the next thousand years, the most meaningful developments in metallurgy centred on iron-making. Britain, where iron ore was plentiful, was an important iron-making region. Iron weapons, agricultural implements, domestic articles and even personal adornments were made. Fine-quality cutlery was made near Sheffield. Monasteries were often the centres of learning for the arts of metalworking. Monks became well known for their iron making and bell founding, the products made either being utilised in the monasteries, disposed of locally or sold to merchants for shipment to more distant markets. In 1408, the Bishop of Durham established the first water-powered bloomery in Britain, with the power apparently operating the bellows.

An iron-age farm. ▼

AD **800s** **THE POWER OF WATER**

MEDIEVAL TECHNOLOGY soon applied itself to harnessing water and wind power. The Romans had pioneered the use of water power in the later empire, and some of their techniques probably survived. The type of water mill that flourished first in northern Europe, however, appears to have been the Norse mill, which used a horizontally mounted waterwheel to drive a pair of grindstones directly, without the intervention of gearing. Examples of this simple type of mill survive in Scandinavia and in the

Shetlands. It is possible that a proportion of the 5,624 mills recorded in the *Domesday Book* in 1086 were still of this type. Most of the Domesday water mills were used for grinding grain, but later they were also used for sawing wood and crushing vegetable seeds for oil.

AD **900s** **EXPANSION OF FARMLAND**

WIDESPREAD EXPANSION of farmed land occurred throughout western Europe between the tenth century and the later years of the thirteenth. In France, new villages were built and new farms carved out of the forest and the waste, while in England, a great deal of land on the

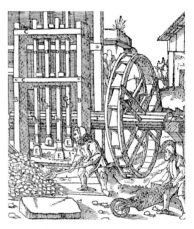

Waterwheels are believed to have been used in the British Isles since the ninth century. ▲

boundaries of the open fields was taken in and cultivated. All this new cultivation was carried out with the same implements and tools; the same crops were cultivated and animals bred as before. In remote and desolate places, monastic organisations created great estates. These estates were formed to feed growing populations rather than to improve technical skills. A new literature of farming arose, although it was directed to the attention of great lords and ecclesiastical magnates rather than to the illiterate majority of husbandmen.

Medieval agriculture: oxen were commonly used to pull ploughs, as horses were expensive to maintain. ▲

AD 900s   HORSE AND PLOUGH

A WHEELED asymmetrical plough in known to have been in use in some parts of western Europe by the late tenth century. Illuminations of manuscripts and calendars a little later in date show a plough with two wheels fitted with a rudimentary mould-board and a coulter. This plough could invert the soil and turn a true furrow, thus making a better seedbed. The horse collar, which replaced the old harness band that pressed upon the animal's windpipe, was one of the most important inventions in the history of agriculture and appeared at this time in Europe. The rigid, padded horse collar enabled the animal to do heavier work; ploughing as well as haulage. Many peasants continued to use oxen because horses were more expensive to buy and to keep.

1000s THE ROMAN INFLUENCE

RELATIVELY FEW structures survive from the Dark Ages, but the later centuries of this period were an age of improvement in building. Romanesque and Gothic architecture embodied significant technological innovations. The architect-engineers studied classical building techniques and solved the problems of constructing very tall masonry buildings while preserving as much natural light as possible. They used the cross-rib vault, the flying buttress and great window panels that provided scope for the new craft of the glazier. The Romanesque style, with stone arches, vaults and domes spanning interior

Romanesque architects drew on classical influences for their inspiration. ▲

spaces, did not really begin until the later part of the eleventh century. Stone was very important and from 1050 to 1350 more stone was quarried in France alone than in the whole history of ancient Egypt.

1100s THE CANNON

THE FIRST EFFECTIVE cannon appeared during the twelfth century made of wrought-iron bars strapped together, but although barrels continued to be made in this way for some purposes, the practice of casting cannons in bronze became widespread. The technique of casting in bronze had been known for several millenniums, but the casting of cannons presented problems of size and reliability. Bronzesmiths drew on the experience of bell founders experienced in medieval church building, as the casting of a large bell posed the similar problems of heating a substantial amount of metal and of pouring it into a suitable mould. Bronze, however, was an expensive metal to manufacture in bulk, so that the widespread use of cannons in war had to wait for improvements in iron-casting techniques.

1180 INLAND TRANSPORT

MEDIEVAL TECHNOLOGY made very little contribution to inland transport, although this period did see some experimentation in bridge building and in the construction of canals. Lock gates were first developed on canals as early as 1180, when they were employed on the canal between Brugge (Bruges, now in Belgium) and the sea. Roads remained indifferent where they existed at all and were not looked after or maintained in any way, and vehicles were clumsy throughout the period. Most wayfarers, like the pilgrims described by Chaucer in his *Canterbury Tales,* travelled on horseback (or on foot), and this was to remain the best mode of inland transport for several centuries to come.

1300s ALCHEMY AS SCIENCE

IN THE TWELFTH century, Christian scholars began to make translations from both Arabic and Greek works including the literature of alchemy. By 1250 alchemy was familiar enough to enable such encyclopedists as Vincent of Beauvais to discuss it fairly intelligibly, and by 1300 the subject was under discussion by the English philosopher and scientist, Roger Bacon and the German philosopher, scientist and theologian, Albertus Magnus. To learn about alchemy was to learn about chemistry, for Europe had no independent word to describe the science of matter. In the works of Bacon and Magnus change was discussed in a truly chemical sense, with Bacon treating the newly translated alchemy as a general science of matter for which he had great hopes.

The science of alchemy increased in popularity throughout the fourteenth century. ◀

1300s CRAFT GUILDS

CRAFT GUILDS, also called 'mysteries' (from Latin *ministerium*, 'occupation'), were European medieval occupational associations, usually comprising all the artisans, and often the suppliers, retailers and wholesale merchants, concerned with a specific branch of industry or commerce. A weavers' guild is recorded at Mainz (now in Germany) as early as 1099 and others are recorded in London and other cities of England during the reign of Henry I (1100–35); but the greatest period of guild expansion occurred during the fourteenth century. The primary economic objective of most craft guilds was the establishment of a complete monopoly over all who were associated together in the pursuit of a common profession, but the ability of the craft guilds actually to exercise their authority was subject to serious practical limitations.

1362 REACHING TO GOD

AS NEW BUILDING designs stretched skywards, the spire at Salisbury Cathedral was built over the crossing of the nave and transept, which had not been designed to accommodate it, and the tall crossing piers began to buckle under the added weight. Strainer arches had to be added between the piers to brace them against buckling. This was the first time that stone columns were slender and heavily loaded enough to be observed to bend or buckle. Salisbury's spire was therefore built as a composite structure of stone cladding laid over a timber frame and tied together at the base with iron bands to resist spreading, it rose to a total height of 123 m (404 ft) when it was finished in 1362.

The spire at Salisbury Cathedral, which needed innovative engineering tecniques to support its height. ▶

Culture, Arts and Leisure

AD 698   THE LINDISFARNE GOSPELS

THE LINDISFARNE GOSPELS, written and illustrated by a monk called Eadfrith, remain one of the most beautiful creations of Saxon England, and they can still be seen in the British Museum. Lindisfarne was a monastery in Northumberland, which flourished under the Bishop of Lindisfarne, St Cuthbert (*c.* AD 635–687), and became the centre for Irish missionary activity in the north of England. His body is now in Durham Cathedral, but in AD 698, the year the gospels were created, the first miracles were reported at his tomb in Lindisfarne, which is perhaps why the gospels are also known as the Gospels of St Cuthbert. Two years later, the Psalms were translated into Anglo-Saxon. The monastery was destroyed by the Vikings in AD 793.

Illumination from the Lindisfarne Gospels. ▲

AD 891   *ANGLO-SAXON CHRONICLE*

THE *Anglo-Saxon Chronicle* is the main literary source for Saxon history, and was started in AD 891, during the reign of the learned king, Alfred the Great (849–99) and continued in various forms until 1154, in the case of the version in Peterborough Abbey. It provides a year-by-year digest of the main events, though there are periods when the information is very sketchy. It is particularly detailed about the triumphs of the reign of Alfred and the disasters of Ethelred the Unready (966–1016). Manuscripts of the first section were widely available in the 890s AD, and now there are seven different versions still in existence. The chronicle was used by medieval historians such as William of Malmesbury (*c.* 1095–1143).

1066　CONSECRATION OF WESTMINSTER ABBEY

THERE IS EVIDENCE for a Roman settlement underneath what is now Westminster Abbey, and probably some kind of Anglo-Saxon settlement as well. But it was Edward the Confessor (1005–66) who made the abbey the important site it is today – though the current abbey is mostly the result of rebuilding under Henry III (1207–72). Edward moved his palace to Westminster from Winchester, and began extensive rebuilding work to the abbey in the 1050s. It was finished on 8 December, eight days before Edward's death, and was therefore ready to witness two coronations in 1066, those of both Harold II (c. 1020–1066) and William

Westmister Abbey, the site of coronations since 1066. ▲

I (1027–87). Contemporary sources suggest that Edward's new abbey was the most sumptuous Saxon building ever built.

1110　THE FIRST MIRACLE PLAY

THE FIRST RECORDED miracle play was performed in Dunstable in Kent in 1110, and the genre flourished in England from the thirteenth to the fifteenth centuries. Miracle plays were performed, using characters from the Bible or mythology, by wandering players – often from guilds – usually on the street on a wheeled stage, or sometimes on platforms next to the road, for processions. The stories were familiar and the words of some plays have been passed down to the present day. They probably developed out of liturgical processions, and were given a boost by a papal edict in 1210 forbidding the clergy to appear on stage. Performances took place on festival days, especially Corpus Christi. Later, stories began to develop on non-biblical subjects in the same format.

1277 IMPRISONMENT OF ROGER BACON

ROGER BACON (*c.* 1220–92) is best known as one of
the pioneers of science teaching, though he never
succeeded in his aim of getting science recognised as
part of the curriculum of Oxford University, where he
lived and worked. As a Franciscan friar and a scholar in
mathematics, optics, astronomy and alchemy, he was also
one of the first science writers. In the end he succumbed
to a cold – it is said – after an experiment to test whether
snow could preserve a chicken. His interest in alchemy
and his attacks on the local theologians were enough to
destroy his academic career, and he was sent to prison
for unorthodox teaching in 1277. Stories of his bizarre
experiments made him a well-known figure in popular literature.

*Early scientist
Roger Bacon.* ▲

1350 *SIR GAWAIN AND THE GREEN KNIGHT*

BY THE TWELFTH century, the legend of King Arthur and his knights
had been appearing in literature as far south as Spain and as far north as
Iceland. The stories fuelled Celtic resistance in Wales and Scotland, with
the idea of Arthur's imminent return – scotched in 1191 by the discovery
of his grave at Glastonbury Abbey
– and were also fuelling the
growing popularity of chivalry
and romance in Britain. Prose
romances about Arthur began
appearing again in England from
the second half of the fourteenth
century, culminating in *Sir
Gawain and the Green Knight*:
2,500 lines of alliterative verse
following the knight Gawain's
moral dilemmas as he clings to his
chivalric values. The anonymous
author probably came from the
West Midlands.

Arthur and the Knights of the Round Table. ▼

1375 'THE BRUCE'

THE STUARTS inherited the Scottish throne in 1371 from the Bruce family, but it was Robert the Bruce's (1274–1329) pact with France – known as the Auld Alliance – that kept the English out of Scotland throughout the Hundred Years' War. Scottish independence was articulated in the only surviving poem of the Aberdeen poet John Barbour (*c.* 1320–95), 'The Bruce'. Barbour had studied in Oxford and Paris, and from 1372 was Clerk of Audit and Auditor of the Exchequer for the first of the Stuart kings, Robert II (1316–90). His poem gives a patriotic account of the liberation of Scotland and Bannockburn (1314). His other poems, including 'The Stewartis Original' – tracing the genealogical descent of the Stuarts from Banquo – have disappeared.

1387 *THE CANTERBURY TALES*

THE CANTERBURY TALES by Geoffrey Chaucer (*c.* 1340–1400) was an immediate success, and proved to be one of the most influential books in the language, helping to set the style of English spoken in south-east England as the main language of literature, instead of French and Latin. Chaucer had an eventful life himself, living above Aldgate as the Peasants' Revolt played out underneath in 1381, and later becoming an MP. He is buried in Westminster Abbey, not as a poet – though his tomb later became the nucleus for Poet's Corner – but as a royal servant who leased a house in the Abbey precincts. The humour of the tales and his other works meant that they were among the first texts to be printed.

The Canterbury Pilgrims, made famous in Chaucer's Canterbury Tales. ▶

Religions, Belief and Thought

AD 597 COLUMBA

COLUMBA (OR COLUM) was a powerful force. It was said of him, 'A typical Irishman, vehement, irresistible, hear him curse the niggardly rich man or bless the heifers of a poor peasant'. His name means 'dove' but there was more of the lion about him. Although of princely birth, he chose to be a monk. Columba left Ireland and sailed to Iona where he was out of sight of Ireland and so less tempted to return home. Life was austere in the monastery he founded in AD 563, but it became a stepping stone for missionary work in Scotland and the Isles. He met the Druids and 'Christ is my Druid' was his weapon against them. He died just after Augustine landed in Kent and the conversion of England to Roman Christianity was to begin.

AD 597 THE CONVERSION OF ENGLAND

POPE GREGORY, apparently moved by the sight of British slaves in Rome, asked Augustine to go to Britain. He led an expedition to evangelise the nation. The mission would have enormous consequences for the history of Britain for the reverberations of Augustine's landing echoes down the centuries. The nature of Christianity in Britain would change and there would be a more organised and coherent Church that would both support and criticise the leadership, be it chieftain or king. The very different organisational style of the Celtic Church would be muted and never fully be absorbed into the dominant power of Roman Christianity. The conversion of Britain, which began in AD 597, was a pebble tossed into a pool from which ripples continued for well over a thousand years.

The ruins of the Norman priory on Lindisfarne. ◄

AD 635   AIDAN AND THE MISSION TO THE NORTH

AIDAN CAME FROM Iona in AD 635 and set up a monastery on the island of Lindisfarne. He travelled widely often with King Oswald who was happy to act as his interpreter. Fervent and enthusiastic, Aiden was rarely in his monastery but this fusion of Church and State ceased when Oswald was killed in battle in AD 642. Aidan died in AD 651 and his monastery continued and perhaps flowered under Cuthbert (AD 634–87). A shepherd boy, Cuthbert became Bishop of Lindisfarne. He loved to fast and lived an austere life, and was a monk rather than a bishop. He knew the Church in England would have to fall into line with the rest of western Christianity but he was a true Celt, worthy of its tradition.

AD 664   HILDA AND THE SYNOD OF WHITBY

THE ISSUE of Celtic versus Roman Christianity was brought to the fore in AD 663 when Oswy, king of Northumbria, became aware he would be celebrating Easter when his wife, who was a Roman Christian, would be keeping her Lent fast. A Synod was called at Whitby under the supervision of its abbess, Hilda. When Oswy came down in favour of the Roman Christians 'with a smile', it was clear Christianity in Britain would be allied to Rome. This would remain so for nearly nine hundred years. Hilda, who ruled over the double monastery (male and female) at Hartlepool and Whitby, until her death in AD 680, showed how devotion to the new religion could capture powerful, outstanding women.

St Hilda of Whitby, receiving Caedmon. ▶

3. Bede

Historian and Theologian, The Venerable Bede. ▲

AD 731   BEDE

'A CANDLE OF THE CHURCH, lit by the Holy Spirit' and 'the father of English historians' are two tributes to the work of the Venerable Bede (AD 673–735). He entered Wearmouth monastery at the age of seven but in a year or two was transferred to Jarrow which, apart from visits to Lindisfarne or York, he never left. He was renowned as a scholar, theologian, historian, scientist and poet. His book *Ecclesiastical History of the English People* (AD 731) is extremely important for knowledge of the history of the Church in England. He believed passionately in unity and while he travelled little he was concerned that although political unity did not exist, there should be Catholic uniformity in the Church.

AD 900s   THE END OF THE FIRST MILLENNIUM

DUNSTAN WAS BORN in AD 909 and became the most able and powerful archbishop for many years. Educated by Irish monks in Glastonbury, Dunstan became Abbot of Glastonbury in *c*. AD 943, which has been called 'a turning point in the history of religion in England'. He set about establishing other monasteries based on the Rule of St Benedict. In about AD 970 a meeting was held to modify the Benedictine Rule to the English situation, for example, prayers for the king were to be said at each service. Dunstan became Archbishop of Canterbury from AD 960–88 and revitalised monasteries. Many monks became bishops and he created a framework of monastic and Church government that remained in place until the Reformation.

1100s BUILDING CATHEDRALS

IN MEDIEVAL England there were 19 cathedrals, which often contained holy relics or the remains of saints. Cathedrals like St Pauls, which were not linked to monasteries, often used the nave for all sorts of secular purposes. The cathedral, however, was where the bishop's throne was and therefore had status over perhaps grander churches in the same diocese. Durham

St Paul's Cathedral, one of 19 cathedrals built in medieval England. ▼

Cathedral, built in the early twelfth century, had Romanesque pillars and arches. What the cathedrals provided was undoubtedly great art and they helped to unify the nation, but these massive beautiful buildings reminded mere mortals of their frailty and of the power and authority of the Church.

1170 BECKET AND HENRY II

'WILL NO ONE RID ME of this turbulent priest?' This is the question dramatically associated with the death of Thomas Becket. A Londoner of Norman stock, he had been Archdeacon of Canterbury when Henry II made him Chancellor of England in 1155. When the position of Archbishop of Canterbury fell vacant, Henry insisted Becket be consecrated. Becket thought it a joke but was ordained a priest on 2 June 1162 and consecrated archbishop on 3 June. From that day he became an opponent of the king and the manner of his life changed. He spent five years in exile because he feared for his life. In 1170 he returned but he had enemies at court and among his fellow bishops. On 29 December 1170 Becket was murdered in his own cathedral. Henry was full of remorse and did penance at Canterbury but his power did not decline.

The murder of Thomas Becket in Canterbury Cathedral. ◀

1221   GROWTH OF MONASTICISM

BY THE EARLY fourteenth Century there were 900 monastic houses and about 17,500 monks and nuns. In the eleventh century, all houses were Benedictine; by the thirteenth century there were a variety of houses to choose from. Now people took monastic vows because they wished to and they could choose which type of life they preferred: teacher, ascetic, contemplative etc. In the twelfth century a new form of religious life came into being. Mendicant friars, not responsible to diocese or bishop, could walk through boundaries of parish, diocese and country. The first to come were the Dominicans in 1221 to be followed in 1224 by the Franciscans, then the Carmelites. The liberty of the friars and religious orders was, in part, forged in the conflict to give the pope supremacy over kings and princes.

1300s   WRITERS AND MYSTICS

RICHARD ROLLE (c. 1300–49) was a hermit, considered mad by his friends and close relatives. His most famous work *The Fire of Love* (1343) encouraged delight in private prayer; in fact his experiences may have been charismatic. *The Cloud of Unknowing* appeared about 1350. An anonymous work, it is absorbed with the transcendence of God living in a 'dark cloud of un-knowing'. If Walter Hilton (d. 1396) and *The Ladder of Perfection* reminded the reader of the performance of everyday duties in honour of God, the *Revelations of Divine Love* by Lady Julian of Norwich (c. 1343–1413) represented all the best elements of English mysticism. The book is based on 'showings' or revelations. Her work expresses her all-enquiring faith in the message of Christ: 'all shall be well, and all shall be well, and all manner of things shall be well.'

1349   THE DEATH OF WILLIAM OF OCKHAM

A BRILLIANT scholar, William of Ockham (c. 1290–1349) was a radical and the phrase 'Ockham's razor' has survived for over 600 years. The phrase 'entities are not to be multiplied without necessity' is not found in his works but captures the spirit of his philosophy; that is 'if everything in some science can be interpreted without assuming this or that hypothetical entity, there is no ground for assuming it'. By insisting on the possibility of studying logic and human knowledge without reference to metaphysics or theology, Ockham's work encouraged scientific research. Aquinas, the Great Teacher, may have been a theologian but Ockham, as far as logic was concerned, was a secular philosopher. He was the last of the scholastics and the forerunner of a theological revolution. He probably died in the plague of 1349.

1377   JOHN WYCLIF CONDEMNED

THE LIFE OF WYCLIF (c. 1328–84) illustrates the diminished authority of the pope; so much so that Wyclif has been called the 'morning star of the Reformation'. He taught in Oxford and until the mid-1370s was quite orthodox, being driven to 'heresy' eventually through his concern for the poor and a horror of worldly ecclesiastics. He was condemned by the papacy (1377) who were deeply wounded by Wyclif's claim that the pope was the 'anti-christ'. Wyclif did not condemn the Great Revolt of 1381, and was perhaps the only university intellectual to inspire a popular movement against the Church – the Lollards. After the Council of Constance (1414–17) his bones were dug up and burned.

Reformer and theologian John Wyclif. ◄

A page from Wyclif's translation of the Bible. ►

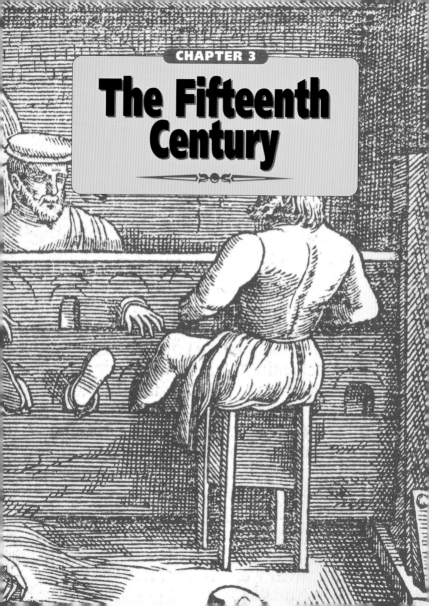

CHAPTER 3

The Fifteenth Century

Power and Politics

1415 THE DEFEAT OF WALES

THE POLITICAL entity of Wales was the kingdom. Although several strong kingdoms existed, the sheer number of these aided English conquest. England was able to call on vastly superior forces in terms of manpower. Between the ninth and thirteenth centuries, Wales's ability to repel English attackers gradually weakened. The most dominant Welsh

kingdoms were those of Gruffudd ap Llywelyn, who was the king of Gwynedd and Powys in the eleventh century. Other notable leaders include Hywel Dda and Llywelyn ap Iorwerth. By the thirteenth century, English supremacy had been established in Wales. In the early fifteenth century, the revolt of Owain Glyndwr over land issues in the north Powys region, against Henry IV, was defeated in 1415.

1455 WARS OF THE ROSES

THE PRIZE of the English crown sparked a battle between two dynastic houses in the fifteenth century – the Lancasters and the Yorks. After Edward III died (1377), both houses claimed a right to the throne. The ensuing war earned its

Claims to the throne by Lancasters and Yorks led to the Wars of the Roses. ◄

name from the use of the red and white roses as symbols for Lancaster and York respectively. After a protracted dispute, originating as a rebellion against weak government and worsening particularly during the reigns of 'weak' kings Richard II and Henry VI, open warfare broke out in 1455. In the 1460s and '70s after many battles including Yorkist victories at Mortimer's Cross and Lancastrian victories at Hexham, the crown swung backward and forth between the two houses. During a period of relative calm under the leadership of Edward IV, war began again after his death in 1483. Peace came two years after the death of Richard III in 1485.

1485 THE DEATH OF RICHARD III

RICHARD III (1452–85) has become known as one of the most notorious kings ever to rule England. This may be partly to do with the history written by the Tudors, whose description of him formed Shakespeare's dramatisation. He came to the throne in 1483 after the death of his brother Edward IV. However, the manner in which he came to be king ensured his name would be remembered for ever in history. As guardian of Edward IV's son, the 12-year-old Edward V, Richard imprisoned him and his younger brother in the Tower of London. The brothers later disappeared, almost certainly killed on Richard's order. Although he had been successful in dealing with other uprisings, Richard was defeated and killed in August 1485 by Henry Tudor (Henry VII).

Henry VII at the Tower of London; Henry succeeded the throne after defeating Richard III at the battle of Bosworth. ▲

Ordinary Lives

1400s CITIZENS PETITION

THE FIRST commission on the filthy air of London was set up by
Edward I as long ago as 1285, but by the fifteenth century, the burning of
sea coal from Tyneside and the herds of animals made the experience of
living in London even worse. Citizens petitioned their complaints about
the 'grate stenche and so evel savour' of the swans, geese, poultry and sheep
kept around the city and its outskirts. Raw sewage tended to be thrown
from upstairs windows into the streets, which stank of a horrific mixture of
offal, slops and kitchen refuse – in spite of the city corporation's attempts
to clean the streets by setting days for putting out rubbish for collection.
Homes, with their new red-tiled roofs, had low boards in each doorway to
stop the foul flood seeping inside.

Early playing cards, which became popular in England in the fifteenth century. ▼

1461   PLAYING CARDS

THE FIRST MENTION of playing cards in England was in a letter written by Margery Paston on Christmas Eve 1461. She belonged to a family of Norfolk gentry whose letters to each other have survived – and she described them as if they were commonplace. Two years later, the import of playing cards was banned to encourage local producers. Most playing cards at the time were made of ivory, parchment or wood, and they were coloured by hand. Standard playing cards today carry representations of Elizabeth of York, the daughter of Edward IV, as the queen. Board games similar to backgammon were also popular, and many children's games – like chess, hide-and-seek and blind man's buff, which was then known as hoodman blind – would be recognisable now.

1474   CAXTON SETS UP HIS PRESS

WILLIAM CAXTON (c. 1420–91) first came across printed books in Bruges, where print technology had spread from the work of Johann Gutenberg (c. 1400–68) in Mainz. Caxton went to Cologne to acquire the skill and the equipment, and produced the first printed book in English in Bruges in 1474, *The Recuyell of the Historyes of Troye*. He opened his own printing shop in Westminster two years later, and printed about 100 titles there, many of them tracts about health, law and religion. His second book, *The Game and Playe of the Chesse*, was his own translation of a book by a Dominican friar from Rheims. It was not until 1509 that another English printer existed in England, though English books were being imported after being printed abroad.

A page from one of the first books printed by Johann Gutenberg. ▶

1480s THE RISE OF HERESY

WITH THE RISE of literacy and the
emergence of the Lollards a century before,
the authorities grew increasingly concerned
about the rise of heresy towards the end of
the fifteenth century. Scapegoats were
needed at a time of enormous religious and
economic upheaval, as the Reformation
gripped society, and inflation – followed by
deflation – gripped the English economy. A
century later, English wages in real terms

*Shakespeare's Globe; the first
theatres began to appear in England
in the late fifteenth century.* ▲

had reached their lowest point for seven centuries, but while some were
trying to hold back the tide of history, the new class of Scottish and
English merchants were benefiting from the relative prosperity, and the
Welsh relaxed under a Welsh dynasty on the English throne. In London,
the first theatres were appearing, and beginning to perform plays that have
survived ever since to spread English culture around the world.

Desiderius Erasmus ▲

1499 ERASMUS VISITS LONDON

THE DUTCH Renaissance scholar Desiderius
Erasmus (*c.* 1469–1536) arrived in England in
1499 for the first time, on his search for wealthy
patrons and intelligent company. He particularly
admired the habits of London girls: 'They kiss you
when you arrive,' he wrote to a contemporary
back home. 'They kiss you when they go away and
they kiss you when they return. Go where you
will, it is all kisses.' Erasmus was a key figure in the
Renaissance. His 1516 translation of the New
Testament into humanist Latin had a great impact,
and by 1539 the whole Bible had been translated
into English. But four years later, Henry VIII
(1491–1547) had changed his mind about the
translation, and forbade women, apprentices and
labourers to read it.

Britain in the World

1415 THE BATTLE OF AGINCOURT

HENRY V invaded France in 1415. He advanced through Normandy, seizing the port of Harfleur and then faced the French army at Agincourt on 25 October 1415. The English were outnumbered three or four times, but Henry chose a muddy field for the battle, where the French knights would be forced to attack between two woods, which would restrict their movement. It was very similar to the battlefield of Waterloo, which Wellington would choose in 1815 for the final struggle with Napoleon. Henry used the same tactics as those that had been used at Crécy and Poitiers. As the French knights charged they were showered with arrows from the English longbows and Henry's army triumphed.

1431 HENRY VI

THE SUCCESS at Agincourt led to the reconquest of Normandy and the Treaty of Troyes in 1420. Henry V was appointed regent of France, and when he died in 1422, his son Henry VI was acclaimed king of France. But Henry VI was only six months old at the time and although he was crowned king of

The marriage of the weak king, Henry VI. ▶

France in Paris in 1431, during his reign English control of France gradually slid away. Paris was lost in 1436 and Gascony in 1442. Normandy was recaptured by the French in 1448 and all English attempts at reconquest failed. By 1453 only the town of Calais remained in English hands. The Hundred Years' War was over. The English kings had failed in their attempt to conquer France, although their claim lives on today in the Royal Standard.

1453   THE END OF THE HUNDRED YEARS' WAR

THE HUNDRED YEARS' WAR began in 1338 and lasted until 1453. It was a series of attempts by the English kings to establish their claim to the throne of France. At first the English were very successful, but towards the end of the fourteenth century many areas were recaptured by the French. Henry V then regained control of much of France and his son, Henry VI, was the only English king to be crowned king of France. After Henry V's death, however, the English possessions were gradually lost during the reign of Henry VI, who suffered from mental illness.

1485   THE BATTLE OF BOSWORTH FIELD

DEFEAT IN THE HUNDRED Years' War turned English attention inwards. For the next 30 years the barons of England fought over the succession to the crown. The struggle was decided when Richard III was defeated and killed by Henry VII at the Battle of Bosworth Field in August 1485. The defeat came after a large section of his forces, under the leadership of Lord Stanley, deserted Richard's cause. Henry VII (1485–1509) avoided all foreign wars, except for an invasion of France in 1492, which he called off when the French offered him £50,000. From being a major power in Europe during the reign of Henry V, England was now of almost no importance. Henry VII concentrated on security and financial strength at home and was prepared to leave foreign adventures to others.

1497   WESTWARD HO

IN THE SECOND HALF of the fifteenth century the nations of Europe began to explore the world. The Portuguese were the first, Prince Henry the Navigator sent sea captains south along the coast of Africa, until Vasco da Gama reached India in 1497. Portuguese and Spanish sailors began to explore the Americas and, in 1497, the first English expedition set sail under John Cabot. For the next 400 years the English explored all corners of the known and unknown world. By the end of the nineteenth century they had created an enormous 'empire on which the sun never set'. In the eighteenth century the most important part of that empire was the American colonies.

1497 JOHN CABOT

JOHN CABOT was a Genoese merchant who settled in England in 1495. He had travelled extensively in the eastern Mediterranean and, when he heard about Christopher Columbus's discoveries, decided to sail west to try to find a short cut to Asia. He set sail on 2 May 1497 and reached land on 24 June. Almost certainly this was the coast of Newfoundland. He returned to England and then led a second expedition the following year with five ships. One turned back, but the other four were all lost. Cabot's second expedition had come to nothing, but he had begun a tradition in English seafaring and had started the English occupation and conquest of North America.

Merchant and explorer John Cabot. ▶

Industry and Invention

1400s LITTLE BOMBS

A GRENADE is a small explosive, chemical or gas
bomb that is used at short range. The word grenade
probably derived from the French word for
pomegranate, because the bulbous shapes of early
grenades resembled that fruit. Grenades came into
use around the fifteenth century and were found to
be particularly effective when exploded among
enemy troops in the ditch of a fortress during an
assault. They eventually became so important that
specially selected soldiers in seventeenth-century
European armies were trained as grenade throwers, or
grenadiers. After about 1750, grenades were virtually
abandoned because the range and accuracy of
firearms had increased, lessening the opportunities
for close combat. Grenades did not come back into
use on an important scale until the Russo-Japanese
War (1904–05).

*The invention of
grenades was to change
the nature of warfare.* ▲

1400s MELTING IRON

IRON HAS LONG been considered one of the most important metals. It
was originally made by heating an ore such as haematite, which contains
iron oxide, in a charcoal fire. When the fire died down a spongy mass of
iron remained that could be hammered into shape. Bellows were invented
in the European Middle Ages and were commonly used to speed
combustion, as in a blacksmith's or ironworker's forge, or to operate reed or
pipe organs. In the fifteenth century, cylindrical furnaces were built and
cold air was pumped in at the base. These were the forerunners of the
modern blast furnaces. The temperature was high enough to melt the iron
so that it could be run off at the bottom as pig or cast iron.

1450   A SENSE OF TIME

MEDIEVAL INTEREST in mechanical instruments flourished throughout the fourteenth and fifteenth centuries, as shown by the development of the mechanical clock. The oldest example, driven by weights and controlled by a verge, an oscillating arm engaging with a gear wheel, survives in Salisbury Cathedral, England. Clocks driven by springs soon appeared, making it possible to construct more compact mechanisms, thus preparing the way for the portable clock. The problem of overcoming the diminishing power of the spring as it unwound was solved by the invention of a simple compensating mechanism, the fusee, a conical drum on the shaft that permitted the spring to exert an increasing movement, or tendency to increase motion, as its power declined.

1455   A NEW WAY OF PRINTING

IT WAS IN THE fifteenth century that printing with movable metal type was made possible. The first large-scale printing workshop was the one established at Mainz by Johannes Gutenberg, which was producing a sufficient quantity of accurate type to print a Vulgate Bible in about 1455. The printing press itself, vital for

Early pendulum clock; mechanical timepieces first appeared in the fifteenth century. ▲

securing a firm and even print over the whole page, was an adaptation of the screw press already familiar in other applications, including the winepress. The printers found an enormous demand for their product, so that the technique spread rapidly and by 1500 almost 40,000 recorded editions of books had been printed in 14 European countries, with Germany and Italy accounting for two-thirds of this number.

Culture, Arts and Leisure

1451 WELSH BARDIC TRADITION

BY THE TIME of the mysterious disappearance of the Welsh
independence leader Owen Glendower (*c.* 1359–1416), the Welsh bardic
tradition had been almost eradicated. But by the mid-fifteenth century,
there was a revitalisation of Welsh poetry under the influence of Dafydd ap
Gwilym (*c.* 1320–80), writing about nature with passion and humour and
using a flexible verse form known as the *cywydd*. Eisteddfods – meaning
'sitting of the learned' – had formerly been held regularly in the capitals of
the Welsh princes, and were revived as well. One was held in Carmarthen
in 1451, voting
Dafydd ap Edmwnd
(1425–1500) as its
most distinguished
poet. By the following
century, the Bible was
also being translated
into Welsh.

1484 THE COLLEGE OF ARMS

THE HIGH Middle
Ages was a period of
spectacular aristo-
cratic display, at the
heart of which was
the colourful science

*Coats of Arms were adopted by
royalty and the aristocracy.* ◀

of heraldry – the method of identifying families using a symbolic language of pictures. Family insignia had been embroidered on the surcoat of knights since the previous century, until the practice was restrained by Henry V (1387–1422). Heralds, meanwhile, had changed their traditional role as announcers, diplomats and tournament organizers to define heraldry, and Edward IV (1442–83) gave their profession a formal existence by setting up the College of Arms in 1484. The importance of heraldry was demonstrated later by the execution of Henry Howard, Earl of Surrey (c. 1516–1547), for quartering his own coat with the royal coat of arms.

1485   *LE MORTE D'ARTHUR*

HISTORIANS ARE UNSURE about the true identity of Sir Thomas Malory (c. 1416–71), but he may have completed his distillation of the English and French versions of the Arthurian legends while in Newgate Prison on charges of rape and theft. But if, as some sources suggest, Malory helped the pioneer

King Arthur's Round Table, at Winchester Castle. ▶

printer William Caxton (*c.* 1420–91) with the text of his book before printing in 1485, it must have been somebody other than the prisoner. *Le Morte D'Arthur* was enormously influential, at a time when a Welsh king had taken the throne, naming his son and Prince of Wales Arthur (1486–1502). A century later, Arthurian enthusiast Edmund Spenser (1552–99) was able to tell his queen that her name, realm and race all derived from 'this renowned prince'.

1490s   THE GROWTH OF LITERACY

'I BOUGHT THIS BOOK when the Testament was abrogated, that shepherds might not read it,' wrote a Gloucestershire shepherd in his illegal bible. 'I pray God amend that blindness.' (a writ by Robert Williams keeping sheep upon Seynbury Hill). The growth of literacy towards the end of the fifteenth century affected all classes, and together with the Italian Renaissance was enormously influential on art and architecture, but it also laid the foundations for a flowering of English literature that formed the basis of its astonishing creativity through the centuries. A period that began with the spectacular Duke Humphrey Library in Oxford, at the very beginning of printed books, ended with the poetry of Edmund Spenser and Sir Philip Sidney, and the plays of Marlowe and Shakespeare.

1499   THE RENAISSANCE REACHES ENGLAND

THE FIRST WHIFF of the Renaissance reached the British Isles at the very end of the fifteenth century with the arrival of Desiderius Erasmus (*c.* 1469–1536) for the first time in 1499, and with his translation of the Bible into Latin in 1516. The same influence is apparent in the tomb of Henry VII (1457–1509) in Westminster Abbey – carried out by Italian craftsmen – and the broad expanses, courtyards and terracotta busts of Roman emperors at Hampton Court Palace. The palace was built by Cardinal Thomas Wolsey (*c.* 1472–1530), appointed Chancellor for life by Henry VIII (1491–1547), but forced to hand over Hampton Court to the king for his own use when it was completed in 1526. The palace was later extended by Sir Christopher Wren (1632–1723).

Hampton Court Palace, built for Cardinal Wolsey and home to Henry VIII. ▶

Religions, Belief and Thought

1400s   PERSECUTION OF THE LOLLARDS

WHEN JOHN WYCLIF died he left behind a group of followers who were ready to face martyrdom in order to spread their faith. The Lollards, the name is probably taken from *lollaer*, which means 'to mumble (prayers)', consisted of educated laymen and some disgruntled clergy who were very critical of the Church and the unworthiness of many of its clergy. Henry IV ascended the throne and supported those pursuing heretics; almost immediately William Sawtre, a leading Lollard, was burned to death. The movement was strongest in the Welsh borders and the industrial towns of the Midlands. Lollards insisted on the Bible being available to the laity, and believed in biblical preaching as well as objecting to ecclesiastical authority. In that sense they prefigured Reformation and English Protestantism.

Prisoners in the Lollards Tower. ▼

1499 COLET AND ERASMUS

JOHN COLET'S (1466–1519) lectures on the 'Epistle to the Romans' marked a step forward in biblical research. He tended to be critical of the state of morality in the country but still managed to be popular and well liked. He founded St Paul's School for 153 poor boys in 1509. His emphasis on the unity of divine truth, concern for historical context and his literal approach to texts excited Erasmus and, no doubt, influenced Thomas More. Erasmus (*c.* 1466–1536) was born in Rotterdam, became a monk in his childhood but soon came to regret it. He became friends with More and Colet on his arrival in England in 1499. His best known work, *In Praise of Folly* (1514), was written in More's house and is a witty satire on lay and ecclesiastical society. His studies on the text of the Bible influenced scholars for many generations but, surprisingly, he did not welcome the Reformation.

Humanist theologian
Desiderius Erasmus. ◄

Vreelmg   Calis

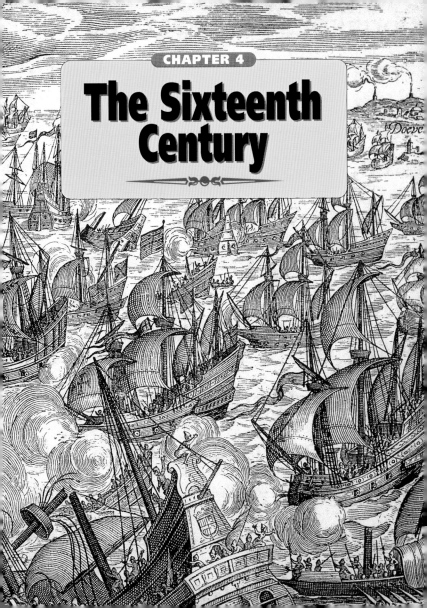

CHAPTER 4

The Sixteenth Century

Power and Politics

1509   HENRY VIII BECOMES KING

JUST 18, HENRY VIII came to the throne in 1509. But the seeds of his infamous dispute with the Catholic Church had already been sowed. Guided by councillors, Henry VIII was instructed to marry Catherine of Aragon, which he duly did, marking the beginning of his infamous marital life. He became heir to the throne when his elder brother Arthur died in 1502. During his first years of rule he concerned himself largely with foreign policy, defeating both the French and the Scottish in battle, in 1512 and 1513. However, erratic fighting, prompted by Henry's belief that war was the 'sport of kings', left England near bankruptcy in the 1520s.

1530s   DIVORCE CRISIS

HENRY VIII fell in love with Anne Boleyn while married to Catherine of Aragon. Exasperated by Catherine's failure to produce a male heir, Henry sought a divorce. Henry insisted his marriage be annulled by the English

Henry VIII, founder of the Protestant Church of England. ◄

Church. This was not feasible, however, as it had been sanctioned by Rome. He appealed to Pope Clement VII but his request was denied as the pope's political master was Catherine's nephew. To prove he could divorce Catherine, the king had to prove Rome had no dispensation over his case. This he was eventually able to do during the 1530s, installing himself as head of the English Church. Anne was pregnant when she married Henry but bore him a daughter, Elizabeth I, not a son. Anne Boleyn was later executed on a trumped-up charge of adultery.

1530s WAR ON THE MONASTERIES

IN THE 1530s, with Henry's rule over the Church of England established, the king set about on his dissolution of the monasteries. His motivation for this appears to have been a desire to win back political support in the country as well as to restore his financial position. By this time Henry VIII was bankrupt and by annexing the monasteries, he was able to redistribute wealth in England overwhelmingly in favour of the monarchy and landed gentry, and away from the Church. The dissolution of the monasteries was overseen by Thomas Cromwell. A notable thinker and writer of the age, Sir Thomas More, was executed in 1535 for his opposition to Henry's religious policies. Sir Thomas, who wrote *Utopia*, refused to deny papal supremacy.

Anne Boleyn, second wife of Henry VIII. ▲

Mary I, who re-established Catholicism in England. ◀

1553 MARY'S CHALLENGE TO PROTESTANTISM

MARY BECAME queen of England and Ireland in 1553, following the death of her brother Edward VI, despite his attempts to ensure the throne passed to the Protestant Lady Jane Grey. Mary was the daughter of Catherine of Aragon, and like her mother, she was a devout Catholic. Upon her succession she set about halting the anti-Catholicism practised by her half-brother and his advisers. Her policies, especially her decision to marry her Spanish cousin Philip, proved unpopular. Still she continued with her policies and officially reconciled England to Rome. Like her father, though, she was defeated by nature. She died childless in 1558, failing to produce a Catholic heir. Her religious fervour earned her the nickname of 'Bloody Mary'. More than 300 Protestants were executed as heretics during her reign.

1556 THE KING'S COUNCIL

THE ARCHITECT of what was later to become known as the 'Tudor Revolution' was Thomas Cromwell. Through Cromwell's promptings, the Privy Council, which still exists today, was established. The Council represented a streamlining of the king's decision-making process and a

Elizabeth I never married and became known as the 'Virgin Queen'. ▶

reform of his financial institutions, known as the King's Council. Its 19 member officers were drawn from the royal household as well as members of state. It developed its own seal in 1556. Cromwell's fate, though, was execution for treason. He fell from Henry VIII's favour after persuading him to marry Anne of Cleves. Legend has it that Henry 'found her so different from her picture … that … he swore they had brought him a Flanders mare'.

1558 ELIZABETH I

POLITICALLY AND economically Elizabeth I has marked herself out as one of the most cautious rulers ever to sit on the throne. She was also a very shrewd leader. She became queen in 1558 when the country was still marked by deep religious divisions. She refused to be used as a focus point for the Protestant factions but reversed laws promoting Catholicism established by her sister Mary. Abroad, she attempted to resist being drawn into wars with the great Catholic powers of Spain and France, yet her fame was assured through her defeat of the Spanish Armada in 1588. At home she practised economic prudence. She financed Parliament from her own money and called in coinage from previous reigns.

Ordinary Lives

1526 DEBASEMENT OF THE COINAGE

HENRY VIII first broke the tradition of standard metal coins in 1526, reducing the quality of the silver. He did so again in 1544, just as he was having to support the biggest English army ever sent to France. The debasements worsened the serious inflation that beset the first 60 years of the sixteenth century. Food prices almost tripled in that time, which suited merchants with fixed rents but impoverished many others. A similar inflation in Scotland led to a major change in diet, from one based on meat to one based on barley and oats. Elizabeth I (1533–1603) restored the coinage, but faced a serious currency shortage as a result. She and Mary of Guise (1515–60) experimented with machine-milled coins in Scotland – to the fury of the mints.

1547 THE VAGRANT ACT

THE VAGRANT ACT of 1547 laid down that an able-bodied tramp could be defined as a slave by two magistrates, if anybody wanted him to work for them. That meant being branded with a V on the forehead and being kept in slavery for two years. The Act proved impossible to enforce. Throughout the early Tudor years, people had lived in fear of the beggars

Metal coins had been standard for many centuries before Henry VIII began to reduce their quality. ▼

'coming to town', and city gates were watched around the clock to prevent the bands of a hundred or so vagrants, ploughmen thrown off their land, or former soldiers from the Wars of the Roses who wandered around the countryside from entering the cities. By the end of the century, parishes were allowed to levy local rates to pay for work for the poor, a system that became known as the Old Poor Law and one that stayed in force until 1834.

1550s CHANGES IN THE SOCIAL ORDER

THE INTRODUCTION of tobacco has been credited to Sir Walter Raleigh (1554–1618) and sweet potatoes to Sir John Hawkins (1532–95). Both spread rapidly among the growing middle classes, the existence of which blurred the previously distant gap between the rich and the poor. In 1553 a law was passed that tried to regulate people's richness of clothing, reserving gold, silver, furs and crimson, scarlet and blue velvet to earls, but it was hard to enforce, and the Tudors were already encouraging the new gentry. More members of the middle classes were being appointed as local justices, charged with controlling 'disorderly alehouses' and 'unlawful games'. Talented public servants from the middle ranks were being promoted, like Thomas Wolsey (c. 1472–1530), a butcher's son from Ipswich, and Thomas Cromwell (c. 1485–1540), a trader's son from Surrey.

1563 THE OFFENCE OF WITCHCRAFT

THE END of the fifteenth century marked the beginning of the 'witch craze' across Europe, as people increasingly regarded 'witches' as a scapegoat for the disorientation of the times, and by 1563 to be a witch

Witchcraft became a capital offence in 1563. ▶

Shakespeare and his contemporary playwrights. ◀

was a capital offence in England. Before the end of the century, as many as 174 people would be indicted for 'black witchcraft' in Essex alone and half of those were executed. In the next 150 years across Europe, as many as 40,000 people – most of them women – would be put to death. The purge was particularly brutal in Scotland, where torture was legal, and by 1649 witches could be tried on the basis of unsupported anonymous allegations. As late as 1878, Essex villagers were charged with assaulting an old woman they claimed was a witch.

1571 SHAKESPEARE'S FIRST DAY AT SCHOOL

THE GREAT PLAYWRIGHT William Shakespeare (1564–1616) was the son of a Stratford-upon-Avon glove-maker who never learned to read, but who sent his son to a free grammar school in 1571. The grammar school day, from 7 a.m. to 5 p.m., included Latin, grammar, religion, geography, music and arithmetic, and pupils had to provide their own books, candles, quill pens, knives to sharpen the nib, inkhorns and boxes of sand for ink-drying. At the same time, poorer children were learning to read, sometimes in classes held in the church porch. As many as 300 new schools opened in England during the century, and by the end of it, there had been an explosion of literacy: almost half of London's criminal classes could read.

1572 MASSACRE IN PARIS

AS A PROTESTANT minority in a strongly Catholic France, the
Huguenots had long been vulnerable. Nothing, however, compared to the
horrors that overtook them in Paris on 24 August 1572. On the orders of
King Charles IX, Huguenot homes were attacked and pillaged and their
inhabitants brutally murdered. Huguenot shops were looted and
destroyed. On 25 August, the government ordered a halt, but the killing
went on and turned towns like Rouen or Toulouse into scenes of carnage.
The mobs stormed into prisons where Huguenots had been confined for
their own safety, hauled them out and slaughtered them. By the time the
massacre finally died down in October, it is estimated that 40,000
Huguenots had been slaughtered.

The massacre of the Protestant Huguenots in France led to their flight to England. ▼

1572   THE HUGUENOTS IN BRITAIN

MANY IN ENGLAND were shocked and appalled when news of the massacre arrived, together with the first Huguenot refugees who landed at Rye in Sussex, on 27 August 1572. Human sympathy soon gave way to curiosity and then to a certain amount of wariness as the Huguenots turned out to be different Protestants from the majority in Britain, whose faith the newcomers regarded as papist. The Huguenots were much more ascetic, dressed far more plainly, as their strict Calvinism required and seemed, at first, to want little to do with the general population. In fact, one of the first things the Huguenots did was accept invitations to already established French Protestant churches in London, Canterbury and Norwich, and keep themselves apart.

1572   FLEEING PERSECUTION

IT IS NO SMALL MATTER to leave home and an established way of life for another, different country. Especially hard when, as happened to the Huguenots, the land they once called home has turned against them and become a hostile place. At first, all such migrants seem to have gained is physical safety. For the rest, they must start again and strive to survive. Earlier migrants such as the Celts or Anglo-Saxons arrived when Britain was still forming as a country and there was space for added variety. The Huguenots, on the other hand, were the first to arrive as foreigners in a country with a long-established identity and way of life. Their job was to fit in and gain acceptance.

Henri IV of France ended Huguenot persecution with the Edict of Nantes. ▲

1572   EXILES LONGING TO GO HOME

THE HUGUENOTS' initial diffidence came partly from their belief that Britain was a temporary stopping place and that one day, they would be able to return to France. However, another 26 years passed before any hope emerged of an end to their exile, when King Henri IV of France published the Edict of Nantes in 1598, giving Huguenots freedom of worship. Those Huguenots who did not take this as evidence of a new start for their faith in France proved wise. By 1685, opinion had once more swung against them as King Louis XIV revoked the Edict and turned what had for some years been a steady trickle of Hugenot migrants into a mass exodus, bringing an estimated 50,000 Huguenots to Britain.

1590   THE GREAT BED OF WARE

TUDOR TIMES WERE a bawdy period of raucous innuendo, but also a period of increasing luxury and romance. The Great Bed of Ware – the 3.6 m (12 ft) square bed made around 1590 as a tourist attraction in a series of Hertfordshire inns – combined both, and was famous enough to be mentioned by Shakespeare in *Twelfth Night* in 1601. Homes were warmer, and beds tended to have soft feather mattresses and pillows rather than logs. Mutual love was also now an acceptable reason for marriage, though early marriages arranged by tyrannical parents remained the norm – Bishop William Chaderton (*c.* 1540–1608) disastrously married his nine-year-old daughter to a boy of 11 in 1592. The definition of husband in 1590 was one who 'hath authority over the wife'.

The Great Bed of Ware. ▲

Britain in the World

1553 'BLOODY' MARY TUDOR

MARY TUDOR became queen in 1553 on the death of her younger half-brother Edward VI. She was the daughter of Catherine of Aragon and had been brought up as a Catholic. During her reign, Catholicism was revived in England and about 300 Protestants, including the Archbishop of Canterbury and two other bishops, were burnt at the stake. More unpopular, however, was Mary's marriage to Philip of Spain, later to be Philip II, King of Spain. The marriage drew England into a war with France in 1557, which was at first successful, but in January 1558 the French captured Calais the last English possession across the Channel. Mary died soon afterwards; she said that Calais was engraved on her heart.

1558 ELIZABETH I

ELIZABETH succeeded her sister in 1558. She signed the treaty of Cateau-Cambresis with France in 1559, which promised the return of Calais to England in eight years time. However, in 1564 Elizabeth gave up all claims to Calais in exchange for 220,000 crowns. Elizabeth wanted to restore the depleted English treasury and

Elizabeth I attempted to restore good relations with Spain and France. ◄

avoid any foreign entanglements. She followed the same policy with Spain, carrying on extended negotiations with the king, Philip II, and trying to prevent English sea captains attacking Spanish ships and colonies on their voyages. But as the scale and wealth of Spain's American empire grew, Elizabeth found the task more and more difficult. Philip II was also a devoted Catholic and wanted to return England to what he believed was the true faith. In the 1570s and early '80s there were many sources of friction.

1577 DRAKE'S CIRCUMNAVIGATION

FRANCIS DRAKE was a nephew of John Hawkins, the main founder of the slave trade. Like other sea captains Drake began to attack Spanish ships in the 1570s and in 1577 sailed west in an attempt to circumnavigate the world. Drake crossed the Atlantic to the Spanish Main, then sailed down the coast of South America, through the

Sir Francis Drake, who indulged in piracy during his explorations. ▲

Magellan Straits and up the west coast of South America. On his way he attacked Spanish ships and colonies. He sailed as far north as Drake's bay in California, naming the region New Albion and claiming it for England. He then crossed the Pacific, sailed through the East Indies and across the Indian Ocean, round the Cape of Good Hope and north to England, completing his voyage in 1581.

1584 SIR WALTER RALEIGH

ENGLISH·INTEREST in the Americas was revived in the 1560s, when John Hawkins began transporting slaves from Africa to Spanish America. But the real breakthrough in the colonisation of America came in 1584, when Walter Raleigh sent out an expedition to found a colony in what he called 'Virginia', in honour of Queen Elizabeth I, the Virgin Queen. Raleigh also believed the legend of 'El Dorado', the Golden Man, which stated that American Indians threw a golden figure into a lake as

Sir Walter Raleigh, leader of several expeditions to the Americas. ▲

sacrifice. In 1616 he led an expedition up the Orinoco River in South America in attempt to discover it, but failed and returned in disgrace.

1588 THE SPANISH ARMADA

THE SPANISH ARMADA, all 132 ships, sailed in May 1588 and reached the Lizard on 19 July. The English fleet avoided a major battle and instead shadowed the Spanish ships up the Channel. The smaller, lighter English ships sniped at the large slow-moving galleons, but did little real damage to them. Spanish morale seems to have been badly affected, however, not only by the English attacks, but also by the poor quality of their cannons and roundshot. Nevertheless, when the Armada anchored off Calais on 27 July, it was still more or less intact. The following night, Drake attacked the Spanish fleet with fireships; many Spanish ships cut their anchor cables in order to escape. On 29 July the only full-scale battle was fought between the demoralised Spanish and the triumphant English.

1590   THE FLOTA

THE DEFEAT of the Armada in July 1588 ended any prospect of an invasion of England, but it did not end the war with Spain. English ships continued to raid Spanish ships and in 1589, 91 ships were brought into English ports. The greatest prize of all, however, was the *Flota*, the Spanish treasure fleet that sailed each year from the Spanish Main. In 1590 Philip II took the extraordinary step of ordering it not to sail, and in 1591 it was only allowed to sail with a heavy escort. Even so, it was attacked off the Azores by Sir Richard Grenville. Although the attack failed, the Spanish ships were so badly damaged that most sank in the severe storms that followed the battle.

The defeat of the Spanish Armada by the English. ▼

Industry and Invention

1500s RENAISSANCE

AN ASPECT OF the Renaissance often overlooked is the scientific revolution that accompanied it. For centuries the authority of Aristotle in dynamics, of Ptolemy in astronomy and of Galen in medicine had been taken for granted. Beginning in the sixteenth century, their authority was challenged and overthrown, and scientists set out by observation and experiment to establish new explanatory models of the natural world. There was a fundamental shift of emphasis to a progressive, forward-looking attitude and increasingly to seek practical applications for scientific research. Meanwhile, the traditional crafts flourished within the expanding towns, where there was a growing market for the products of the rope makers, barrel makers (coopers), leatherworkers (curriers) and metalworkers (goldsmiths and silversmiths), to mention only a few of the more important crafts.

The scientific revolution in the sixteenth century led to new discoveries in many fields of science. ▲

1500s ALCHEMY AND MEDICINE

MEDICAL CHEMISTRY was founded in Europe by its great publicist, Paracelsus (1493–1541), who was the sworn enemy of the malpractices of sixteenth-century medicine and a vigorous advocate of 'folk' and 'chemical' remedies. By the end of the sixteenth century, medicine was divided into warring camps of Paracelsians and anti-Paracelsians, and the alchemists began to move *en masse* into pharmacy. Paracelsian pharmacy was to lead, by a devious path, to modern chemistry, but the alchemist's pursuit of gold making still persisted, though methods sometimes differed. The impression given is that many believed they had the secret of gold making but that most of them had acquired it from someone else and not from personal experimentation.

1550   THE HUMBLE POTATO

THE POTATO was used by Andean Indians for 200 years but was introduced to Europe in the mid-sixteenth century, reputedly to England by the explorer Sir Walter Raleigh. Potatoes began being imported properly in 1550 and they became the staple diet for many people. The crop was for many years stored by piling the potatoes up into clamps that were tightly covered with straw and earth. The Irish Potato Famine of 1845–49 was the worst famine to occur in Europe in the nineteenth century. The crop failed in successive years caused by late blight fungus which destroys the tubers of the potato plant. Potato crisps were invented in France but manufactured from 1920 in England by Frank Smith.

1565   GROWTH OF A WORLDWIDE HABIT

WHEN CHRISTOPHER COLUMBUS discovered the Americas, he found the natives using tobacco in much the same manner as it is used today. The American Indians believed it to possess medicinal properties, which was the main reason for its introduction into Europe. Tobacco was important in Indian ceremonies, such as the smoking of the pipe of peace. Evidently the natives of North and South America had developed crude methods of tobacco culture. The extension of tobacco growing to practically all parts of the world began with its introduction into Europe: France, 1556; Portugal, 1558; Spain, 1559; and England, 1565. Portuguese and Spanish sailors then took tobacco from Europe to all parts of the world.

Modern tobacco plantation; tobacco was brought back to Europe by Columbus. ▶

1570 THE THEODOLITE

THE EARLIEST MAPS were drawn from observations made by travellers and could be very inaccurate over large areas. Considerable evidence was gathered using the information brought back by explorers in the fifteenth and sixteenth centuries, but more precise mapping began with the development of the theodolite by a self-educated English mathematician, Leonard Digges, in 1570, and triangulation in 1617. The theodolite was based on an instrument designed by Hero around AD 100 and measures horizontal and vertical angles. It consists of a telescope mounted between two side supports in a trunnion so that it can be moved up and down in a vertical plane, while the trunnion can also be rotated horizontally. The angles through which the telescope moves are measured from circular, graduated scales.

Sixteenth-century map of South America. ▼

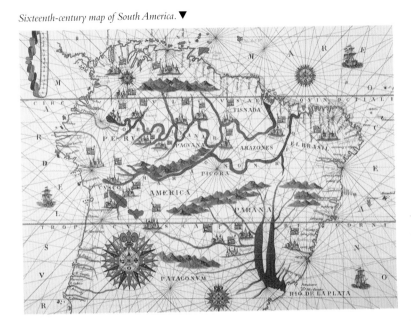

Culture, Arts and Leisure

1526 HANS HOLBEIN AT HENRY'S COURT

HANS HOLBEIN the Younger (*c.* 1497–1543) was another of the European humanists, one of Erasmus's wide circle of friends, who made their home in England. He arrived in 1526, and after 1532 he rarely left, building up a unique memory of Henry VIII's court with his superb portraits of the most eminent people in the land, many of which are housed in the National Portrait Gallery in London. His portraits included some of the candidates for Henry's various marriages, and it was on one of these rare visits abroad, that Henry asked him to paint Anne of Cleves (1515–57). Enchanted, Holbein 'expressed her imaige verye lyvelye' and Henry married her – although he dismissed her shortly afterwards as a 'Flanders mare'. Holbein died of the plague in 1543.

1549 BOOK OF COMMON PRAYER

THOMAS CRANMER, the Archbishop of Canterbury (1489–1556) was a key figure in the English Reformation, bold enough to marry the niece of a Lutheran theologian while clerical marriage was still illegal, and eventually burned at the stake under Mary I (1516–58). He was also the main architect of the religious changes under Edward VI

A portrait by Hans Holbein, who became renowned for his paintings of nobles at Henry VIII's court. ▲

(1537–53), constructing the Prayer Books of 1549 and 1552, the Ordinal of 1550 and the Thirty-Nine Articles of the Anglican faith. But it was as author of the Prayer Book, the only legal liturgy in the Church of England between 1549–54 and 1559–1645, and the basis of the 1662 Book of Common Prayer, that Cranmer is best remembered. His genius for prose and his soaring phrases have spread throughout English literature.

1575 TALLIS AND BYRD

THE SO-CALLED 'Father of English Cathedral Music', Thomas Tallis (*c.* 1505–85), was a Gentleman of the Chapel Royal and was able to write church music for Catholic Mary I and her Protestant sister Elizabeth I alike. In fact in 1575, Elizabeth granted Tallis and collaborator William Byrd (1543–1623) a monopoly of music printing and publishing in England. Byrd became organist of Lincoln Cathedral at the age of just 20, and stayed a Roman Catholic, but together their music formed the basis of church music for the new Anglican Church, bridging the gap with the old Catholic liturgy.

1576 THE FIRST THEATRE

THE FIRST purpose-built theatre in England opened in Shoreditch, London in 1576, built by the actor and carpenter James Burbage, the father of Richard Burbage (*c.* 1569–1619). It became the home of the Lord Chamberlain's Men, one of whom was the young playwright, William Shakespeare (1564–1616). When the lease on the land ran out in 1597, they dismantled the theatre, carried it to the south bank of the Thames and used it as building material for the famous Globe

The Globe Theatre in London, one of the earliest theatres in England. ▲

Theatre. Richard Burbage was also a shareholder of the Blackfriars Theatre, in the abandoned Blackfriars monastery on the other side of the river, and went on to play the leading roles in Shakespeare's *Hamlet*, *Othello*, *King Lear* and *Richard III*.

1593 THE DEATH OF MARLOWE

THE PLAYWRIGHT Christopher Marlowe (1564–93) was only 29 when he met his mysterious and violent death in a Deptford tavern, probably as a secret agent. Marlowe was a free-thinker, a homosexual and wildly indiscreet, and his writings led to accusations of atheism, blasphemy and subversion. They reached a climax with his play *Edward II*, the tragedy of a homosexual king undermined by his barons – paving the way towards Shakespeare's sophisticated historical tragedies – and *Doctor Faustus*, Marlowe's story of a man's pact with the devil.

Religions, Belief and Thought

1515 HENRY VIII AND THOMAS WOLSEY

HENRY VIII (1491–1547) studied theology and Canon law for his defence of the Catholic Church. He appointed Thomas Wolsey (1475–1530) as Lord Chancellor and Chief Councillor in 1515 and the pope made Wolsey legate for life. There were, however, signs of dissent in England: frustration with excesses of the clergy; the rise of Christian humanism; anti-clericalism and the ban on the availability of the Bible in English. To this was added the king's divorce. Henry therefore passed laws so that all temporal and ecclesiastical authority lay with him, the 'Supreme Head of the Church of England', for purely political reasons. Wolsey co-operated with all the king's wishes but when he was not able to secure the king's divorce from Queen Katharine, he was deprived of his Chancellorship and arrested on a charge of high treason. He died on his way to the trial.

Wolsey fell from the king's favour when he was unable to procure his divorce. ▶

1535 THOMAS CROMWELL AND THE DISSOLUTION OF THE MONASTERIES

CROMWELL (1485–1540) had been an aide to Wolsey and became Henry's vice-regent in 1532, although he was wholly subordinate to the king. He put into effect the dissolution of the monasteries after 1535. Nothing could save them because they owed allegiance to powers outside England and Wales; the king was bankrupt; and the king had to use the monastic estates to buy support against Rome. By 1539, 560 monastic institutions had been closed. One consequence of their closure was the destruction of great buildings, libraries and works of art. Henry remained a Catholic all his life – albeit a Catholic without a pope. Cromwell did promote an enlightened Puritanism following the example of Erasmus but his reward was execution.

Mary I's reign was characterised by persecution of the Protestants in England. ▲

1536 EXECUTION OF WILLIAM TYNDALE

TYNDALE (d. 1536) had left Britain in 1524. Hebrew, the language of the Old Testament, was taught nowhere at that time. Printing had revolutionised the spread of knowledge across Europe. Books deemed to be heretical poured into England and after Tyndale's departure copies of his translations were smuggled into England in bales of wool. He had a naive belief that a translation from the original tongue would clarify interpretation, it would be purged 'of false glosses' – but his glosses were too Protestant and he was executed. Henry VIII did have an ear for such things, however, and Miles Coverdale produced a Bible translation in 1536. In 1538, the Great Bible based on Tyndale and Coverdale was produced and placed in every parish. So from 1538 onwards it was possible to study the Bible in English without punishment.

1554   PROTESTANT PERSECUTIONS

MARY'S REAL GOAL as queen was reunion with Rome. In 1554 Cardinal Pole landed in the country and absolved it from sin and established reunion. In practice, the persecutions and martyrdoms of Catholics and opponents of the monarchy witnessed under Henry and Edward now reverted to Protestants. The number of Mary's persecutions (est. 274) has probably been exaggerated. Her willingness to allow about 800 Protestants to leave meant she was subject to anti-Catholic propaganda from other European countries and those Protestants flocked back on her death in 1558. The savagery of persecutions affected public opinion. Mary and her archbishop died within hours of each other – they were not mourned.

1558   THE ELIZABETHAN YEARS

IT WAS IN THE reign of Elizabeth I that the Anglican Church became the rock upon which Tudor stability was built. Elizabeth was to be known as 'Supreme Governor' not 'Supreme Head'. In 1563, Thirty-Nine Articles were approved as defining the Anglican Church's doctrine and in 1571 clergy were to subscribe to these or resign their livings. The Church was clearly Protestant, and though it retained altars and vestments, toleration was not granted to Catholics. The main threat to Elizabeth, particularly after her excommunication by the pope, was a league of Catholic nations. This was

Elizabeth I sought to restore the Protestant faith that her sister Mary had driven from the country. ▲

eased when in the early 1560s John Knox returned from exile to Scotland and preached the Calvinist way of reform. However, the Puritans and the Catholics did not lie down – both sides were persecuted and in 1584–85 it became treason to be a Catholic priest in England.

CHAPTER 5

The Seventeenth Century

Power and Politics

1603 THE STUARTS

THE STUART dynasty was one of the least successful in British history despite lasting almost 400 years, first as rulers of Scotland and then of England as well. The family, which was originally from the French region of Breton, ruled Scotland from 1371 to 1714 and England from 1603 to 1714. The Stuart connection to the English throne came through the marriage of James IV to Margaret Tudor. Their granddaughter was Mary, Queen of Scots. Although Elizabeth did not recognise Mary's son, James I, as heir, he still succeeded her to the throne in 1603. In 1625 he was succeeded by Charles I. The accepted spelling 'Stuart' is the French form of the name 'Stewart'; and this eventually became the accepted form in England.

The execution of Charles I. ▲

1625 THE ASCENSION OF CHARLES I

IN WHITEHALL on 30 January 1649, Charles I became the first monarch to be tried for treason and beheaded. The road to his execution was long and complex. He came to the throne in 1625, when disputes immediately arose with Parliament over his attempts to raise revenues through taxation. His reign was also punctuated by protracted disputes over the long-standing issue of religion. Charles dissolved three parliaments between 1625 and 1628. From 1629 he tried to rule without the aid of Parliament. Following a further attempt to work with Parliament, which failed, civil war broke out. Captured by the Scots and handed over to the English, he escaped, but was later captured and executed after his supporters were defeated.

1640   THE SHORT AND LONG PARLIAMENTS

AFTER AN 11-YEAR GAP Charles recalled Parliament. On 13 April 1640 he convened the Short Parliament, but after further disputes the Parliament was dissolved less than a month later. The king was attempting to get funds for the Bishops' War, which had promoted further religious hostilities between Scotland and England, but many in Parliament were reluctant to grant him any revenues before their grievances were redressed for the dissolution of Parliament 11 years before. The Long Parliament was more successful. Further disputes led to the outbreak of civil war in 1642. In 1648 it established the Commonwealth. In 1660 it dissolved itself in favour of the restoration of the monarchy.

1650s   OLIVER CROMWELL

FOLLOWING THE civil war and the execution of Charles I, Oliver Cromwell found himself the most powerful living Englishman. A former student of Cambridge and MP for the city, Cromwell had

Republican leader Oliver Cromwell. ▶

The arrival of William of Orange and Queen Mary to the throne of England became known as the 'Glorious Revolution'. ▲

distinguished himself during the war, although he was not without critics, especially the Levellers who wanted to rid society of social distinctions but were ultimately opposed by Cromwell. His military record was sullied by a campaign in Ireland where he controversially ordered the massacre of citizens in Drogheda and Wexford. The key player during the 11 years that England was a Republic, Cromwell assembled what was known as the Barebones Parliament in 1653. This Parliament consisted of 140 men, most of whom were chosen by Cromwell himself.

1653　THE REPUBLIC

BETWEEN DECEMBER 1653 and May 1659 England entered the period known historically as the Protectorate. This came into place after the failure of the 'Barebones' Parliament and at its head was Cromwell. He was made Lord Protector and had vast powers. But as with the monarchy, there were disputes between the country's leader – Cromwell – and Parliament. Cromwell dissolved his first parliament in 1655. The situation was reaching crisis point with the second parliament when he died in September 1658. Despite this the Protectorate did achieve some success. Most notable among these was the decision to allow Jews to return to England in 1655 albeit without political equality. Education reforms were also introduced by Cromwell.

1688　THE GLORIOUS REVOLUTION

FOLLOWING THE RESTORATION of the monarchy in 1660, James II claimed the throne in 1685. A devout Catholic he refused to take an anti-Catholic oath but nevertheless succeeded Charles unopposed. In 1688 a Catholic heir – also Charles – was born into a period where Catholicism was reasserting itself within the British Establishment. Alarmed, seven prominent statesmen invited the Protestant William of Orange to come to England, with an idea of him taking the throne. William then mustered an army which landed at Torbay, Devon, in November 1688. He marched to London virtually unopposed. James fled and was eventually defeated at the Battle of the Boyne. The succession of William and the constitutional arrangements that followed have become known as the Glorious Revolution.

Ordinary Lives

1602 THE GROWTH OF LONDON

THE EXPANDING population of London was a constant source of concern for the Tudors, and proclamations were issued in 1580 and 1602 forbidding multi-occupation and any new building within three miles of the city gates. Officials held regular inspections of houses to root out 'lodgers'. The next biggest town – Norwich – covered only 2.5 sq km (1 sq mile), but London's population had mushroomed from 70,000 in 1520 to 200,000 in 1600. With its close-knit muddle of warehouses, homes, markets, churches, shops and brothels, the city was described by one foreign ambassador as 'the filthiest in the world'. Katherine Wheel Alley in Thames Street had nine respectable tenements in 1584. Shortly afterwards, they had been converted to 43.

A London merchant at his books. ▲

1615 MERCHANT ADVENTURERS

THE MERCHANT ADVENTURERS of London had gradually consolidated themselves as England's main overseas trading body. They were granted royal charters in 1486 and 1505, and concentrated on the export of cloth to Germany and the Netherlands. They regained their monopoly in 1615 after the Cockayne scheme had failed to rival their power, when the government tried to break their dominance by banning unfinished cloth exports – an attempt to kick-start the English finishing industry. The cloth industry had by then concentrated in towns and areas of high rural population, causing economic disruption in other regions. In 1614 English traders recorded their highest-ever cloth export figures, but these halved again with the bad harvests in the following eight years.

1640   END OF CENSORSHIP

MARY I (1516–58) had first imposed a registration system on the Stationers' Company in 1556–57, and from 1586 new publications had to get licences from the Archbishop of Canterbury or the Bishop of London. When the system collapsed in 1640 in the run-up to the civil war, it led to an upsurge in publishing and – in a period of great political idealism – the great age of the pamphlet. In 1640 there were just 22 pamphlets published; by 1642 there were nearly 2,000. The free-for-all was followed by more controls under Oliver Cromwell (1599–1658) and a statutory licensing of the press after the Restoration. The pamphlets added to the hothouse atmosphere of radicalism during and after the civil war, where people felt able to talk of 'the world turned upside down'.

1649   THE COMMONWEALTH

AS LORD PROTECTOR, Cromwell found himself increasingly at odds with his parliaments, and decided eventually on direct rule. To oversee local government in all its various forms, he briefly appointed major generals to run each of the 11 districts of England, with powers to interfere in a range of country

Cromwell was established as Lord Protector in England when the monarch was overthrown. ▶

The expulsion of the Jews from Spain; the Jews requested that they be allowed to settle in England. ▲

pleasures, like horse racing, bear-baiting and cockfighting, to force the 'idle' to work, make people responsible for their servants' behaviour and to make sure laws against blasphemy, drunkenness and sabbath breaking were enforced. No news item could now be published without permission, and secretary to the Council of State, John Thurloe (1616–68), oversaw the only two surviving newspapers. To symbolise the end of Cromwellian rule, a maypole was erected in the Strand in 1661.

1655 CROMWELL'S INVITATION

LATE IN 1655, Manasseh ben Israel, a rabbi from Amsterdam, presented a 'Humble Address' to the Lord Protector of England, Oliver Cromwell, asking him to permit Jews to live in Britain. Memories of previous Jewish settlement, in medieval times, were painful, but fortunately, Cromwell, a religious man, was willing to listen as ben Israel told him that if the Jews were re-admitted, this would serve as a signal for the coming of the Messiah. Cromwell's council was more hard-headed. They believed the

Jews could bring economic benefits with them. They were shrewd financiers and diplomats, accustomed to dealing with European monarchs and their ministers. The new English Republic, regarded with contempt in Europe, had a great deal of use for such people.

1666 PLAGUE AND FIRE IN LONDON

THE PLAGUE and fire were together the cause of London's biggest-ever exodus. The plague itself killed 15 per cent of London's 450,000 population, but other badly affected cities included Newcastle, Norwich, Portsmouth, Southampton and Sunderland. Infected houses were isolated and sealed, and mass graves established on the outskirts of

The Great Fire of London, although causing a wave of destruction, finally ousted the plague from the city. ▲

the cities. London's Great Fire in September 1666 finally destroyed the infection there, together with 13,200 houses. A coal duty was imposed to pay for repairs, and strict building regulations drafted to cut the risk of fire. The grandiose rebuilding schemes of Sir Christopher Wren (1632–1723) never came to fruition, but his churches remain a testament to the new brick city that emerged. His St Paul's Cathedral makes Westminster Abbey 'look like crinkle-crankle', said the diarist John Evelyn (1620–1706).

Hunting game was an established practice of the gentry until the Game Laws were introduced in 1671. ▲

1671 THE GAME LAWS

BY THE END of the seventeenth century, the country gentry were on the rise at the expense of the yeoman farmers. Nothing divided them further than the laws passed in 1671 by the Cavalier Parliament that ruled that freeholders worth less than £100 – the vast majority – could no longer kill game, even on their own land. Farming families had long since made a good meal out of a pheasant that had strayed on to their farms, but an artificial definition now divided them from their richer neighbours. Shooting was taking over from hawking as the respectable way for the gentry to kill game birds, which meant that even more of them were killed – and the pickings for the rest, now defined as 'poachers' were all the more meagre.

1686 LAST WITCH-HANGING

ALICE MOLLAND from Exeter became, in 1686, the last witch to be hanged in England, although the witch trials in Salem, Massachusetts, would not begin for another four years. It was a sign that the old paranoid superstitions were beginning to fade, but the witch-hunts had caused enormous suffering – mainly to country women. The last witch trials took place in England in 1711 and in Scotland in 1722. In 1736, the laws against witchcraft were repealed in both countries. Life was changing in the countryside at the same time: by 1683, the wild

Persecution of women accused of being witches began to wane in the seventeenth century. ▲

boar – which had once roved the medieval forests – was finally extinct in Britain. In 1663 the first turnpike tolls had been levied, sending new roads deep into the countryside.

1693   OPENING OF WHITE'S

THE FAMOUS White's chocolate house opened in St James's Street, London in 1693, and by 1697 proprietors were already having to move it to larger premises on the other side of the street. It was soon notorious as a gaming house, influential in the development of the Tory party and White's Club, and attracting such clamorous interest that the fashionable clientele moved upstairs to avoid the crowds. Coffee houses were now increasingly widespread, after the first one opened in Oxford in 1650, and there were 2,000 in London by the end of the century. Wine consumption was down because of taxation, but spirits and beer were shooting up. One tavern in London's Ludgate Hill, Belle Sauvage, was offering drink and a look at a rhinoceros for a shilling.

1694   THE BANK OF ENGLAND

THE GOVERNMENT passed a bill in 1694 for a lottery funnelling £1 million into government coffers, but it was clear that William III (1650-1702) still needed another £1.2 million to fund his French wars. The idea of a reserve bank was launched a month later and the money was raised within 10 days, with the king and queen subscribing first. The bank invested heavily in government stock and used this as security to issue bank-notes – though as £10 was the smallest denomination, they were pretty rare. Even so, the paper money began to fuel inflation, and the price of bread doubled between 1693 and 1699. A Window Tax followed in 1696, as an

The founding of the Bank of England in 1694. ▲

innovative way of taxing property according to size, and stayed in force until 1851. The Bank of Scotland was founded in 1695.

Britain in the World

1600 THE EAST INDIA COMPANY

THE EAST India Company was set up in 1600. It was one of a number of trading companies established at the time. It sent its first mission, headed by John Mildenhall, to India in 1603 and gained the right to trade from the Mogul emperor in 1608. Over the next 50 years the company set up trading stations around India: Surat in the north-west, Madras in the south-east and Bombay on the west coast. Later Calcutta in the north-east was also occupied. In 1664, a similar rival French company was set up and established its first trading station at Pondicherry in 1674. For almost 100 years the two companies competed for control of the trade of India.

1604 PEACE WITH EUROPE

THE WAR with Spain dragged on until 1604, but after the death of Philip II in 1598, it lost much of its focus. Philip III, who succeeded his father, had no interest in attacking England. He lived as a virtual recluse and devoted himself to religion. James I, who had succeeded Elizabeth I in 1603, brought the war to an end in 1604. English rivalry with Spain soon disappeared. Spain became involved in a series of wars with France and was also dragged into the Thirty Years' War. From 1640

The colony originally called New Amsterdam, now New York. ◀

onwards there was also a serious revolt in Catalonia. Following peace with Spain, the English kings became heavily involved in internal politics, which led to the civil war in 1642 and the execution of Charles I in 1649.

1664   NEW YORK

THE ENGLISH were not the only people to establish colonies in America. In 1612 the Dutch set up a trading station on Manhattan Island, and in 1626 they bought the island from the Indians for $24. The colony became known as New Amsterdam. In 1664 the colony was handed over to the English and was renamed New York after the brother of Charles II, James, Duke of York. The new colony led to the establishment of two more. To the west the Quaker, William Penn, set up Pennsylvania and New Jersey was created to the south. Charles II's reign also saw the settlement of the Carolinas and finally in 1733 the state of Georgia was set up.

1688   WILLIAM III

IN 1688, WILLIAM of Orange, the Stadtholder of the Netherlands, became king of England, when James II fled. French support for the Stuarts, and William's desire to protect the Netherlands led to England being drawn into war with France in 1689. William joined the League of Augsburg and landed in the Netherlands with an army. He was defeated in a series of battles from 1692 to 1694, but managed to avoid total disaster. At sea the English navy won an important battle over the French at Cap la Hogue in 1692. This marked the beginning of English dominance at sea, which was to continue until the twentieth century.

William and Mary, the monarchs of the Glorious Revolution. ▲

Industry and Invention

1600s A CHANGE OF FACE

THE PRACTICE of building in stone and brick became common, although timber remained an important building material for roofs and floors and, in areas in which stone was in short supply, the half-timber type of construction retained its popularity into the seventeenth century. After that, brick and tile manu-facturing spread and provided a cheap substitute, although its use declined in the eighteenth century, when classical styles enjoyed a vogue and brick came to be regarded as inappropriate for facing such buildings. Cast iron was coming into use in buildings for decorative purposes. Glass was also beginning to be used on many buildings, developing the industry that still relied on ancient skills of fusing sand to make glass.

1600s NEW HEATING

THE EFFICIENCY of interior heating was improved in the seventeenth century by the introduction of cast-iron and

The half-timber style of building became fashionable in the seventeenth century. ◀

New methods of heating were developed which made use of new materials available. ▶

clay-tile stoves, which were placed in a free-standing position in the room. The radiant heat they produced was then distributed uniformly throughout the space. In addition these stoves lent themselves to the burning of coal, a new fuel that was rapidly replacing wood in western Europe. When European builders had rediscovered the technology of the classical world in brick, stone and timber, a stable plateau was reached in the development of the building arts, with little further advancement. The available materials and techniques were well suited to the churches, palaces and fortifications that their patrons required.

1600s NEW MINES

THE PERIOD from 1500 to 1750 witnessed a steady expansion in the mining of minerals other than coal and iron. Queen Elizabeth I introduced German miners to England in order to develop the mineral resources of the country, and one result of this was the establishment of brass manufacturing. This metal, an alloy of copper and zinc, had been known in the ancient world and in Eastern civilisations but was not developed commercially in western Europe until the seventeenth century. Metallic zinc had still not been isolated, but brass was made by heating copper with charcoal and calamine, an oxide of zinc mined in England in the Mendip Hills. Other non-ferrous metals such as tin and lead were sought out and exploited with increasing enterprise in this period.

1608 LOOKING FOR STARS

THE FIRST OPTICAL telescope was invented in the Netherlands by spectacle-maker Hans Lippershey in 1608. A year later the Italian Galileo Galilei improved the design. These telescopes consisted of two lenses mounted in a tube whose length was the difference between the focal lengths of the two lenses. Galileo was the first to observe mountains on the Moon and the four satellites of Jupiter. His astronomical work led him to believe that Copernicus's world view, that the Earth circled the Sun, was correct, which brought him into conflict with the Catholic Church in 1632. The telescope had a great effect on navigation and travel as well as on the whole science of astronomy.

1620 THE FIRST CALCULATOR

IN 1620, EDMUND GUNTER, Professor of Astronomy at Oxford University, replaced printed logarithmic tables by etching a line of logarithms

Hans Lippershay, inventor of the first optical telescope. ▲

along a 60-cm (2-ft) wooden ruler. This could be used for adding or subtracting lengths measured from the line by dividers. The idea was improved upon by the Reverend William Oughtred in 1621, when he did away with the dividers by sliding one scale over the other. In 1630 this was developed still further into an early type of slide rule by Robert Bissaker. This ruler had fixed and sliding log scales and later a sliding cursor was added. Many more scales were added to slide rules allowing them to be used for many different computations.

1659 NATURAL GAS IN EUROPE

THE FIRST discoveries of natural gas seeps were made in Iran between 6000 and 2000 BC. Many early writers described the natural petroleum seeps in the Middle East, especially in the Baku region of what is now Azerbaijan. The gas seeps, probably first ignited by lightning, provided the fuel for the 'eternal fires' of the fire-worshipping religion of the ancient Persians. The use of natural gas was mentioned in China in about 900 BC. Natural gas was unknown in Europe, however, until its discovery in England in 1659, and even then it did not come into wide use for some time. Instead, gas obtained from carbonised coal (known as town gas) became the primary fuel for illuminating streets and houses throughout much of Europe from 1790 on.

1698 THE LATE STUART PERIOD

PROBABLY THE most important innovations of this period were in power. The researches of a number of scientists, especially those of Robert Boyle of England with atmospheric pressure, of Otto von Guericke of Germany with a vacuum, and of the French Huguenot Denis Papin with pressure vessels, helped to equip technologists with the theoretical basis for the generation of steam power. Thomas Savery took out a patent for a 'new Invention for Raiseing of Water and occasioning Motion to all Sorts of Mill Work by the Impellent Force of Fire' in 1698. Although water-power and wind power remained the basic sources of power for industry, a new prime mover had appeared with the steam engine, with tremendous potential for further development as and when new applications could be found for it.

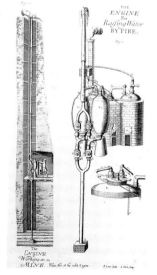

Thomas Savery's mine-pump. ▶

Culture, Arts and Leisure

1601   *HAMLET*

SHAKESPEARE'S MOST famous play was probably first seen in 1601, one of the first plays performed at the Globe Theatre, just before the playwright moved his lodgings from Bishopsgate to Southwark. There Shakespeare continued to write about two plays a year – struggling through a period of unpopularity for the new theatres – while he kept his financial interests at his real home in Stratford-upon-Avon. *Hamlet*, the story of an anguished Danish prince, has fascinated critics and audiences ever since, but it also marked the turning point in Shakespeare's career, between the comedies and histories like *Midsummer Night's Dream* (1596) and *Henry V* (1599) and the great tragedies like *King Lear* (1605) and *Macbeth* (1606). It remains probably his most challenging play.

The revolutionary Globe Theatre, on the South Bank. ▼

1614   *BARTHOLOMEW FAIR*

THE ANNUAL Bartholomew Fair, held in Smithfield every 24 August, was used as the basis of the greatest play by Ben Jonson (1572–1637), the son of a master bricklayer and probably imprisoned after acting in the notorious play *The Isle of Dogs* in 1597. *Bartholomew Fair* was first performed in 1614 and depicted a range of outrageous characters, notably the hypocritical Puritan Zeal-of-the-Land Busy and the Justice Adam Overdo, who are eventually engulfed in the iniquities of the fair. A partnership between Jonson and the architect Inigo Jones (1573–1652) created the spectacular masques of the Stuart court, which combined drama, music, art and dance. They were brought to an end when the civil war dispersed the court in 1642.

Bartholomew Fair in Smithfield, used by Ben Jonson as the setting for his play of the same name. ▲

1625 THE DEATH OF ORLANDO GIBBONS

BY THE DEATH of Elizabeth I in 1603, English music had become the envy of Europe. Orlando Gibbons (1583–1625) upheld the tradition into the reign of James VI and I (1566–1625). By 1619, Gibbons had become one of the 'musicians for the virginals to attend his highness' private chamber', and in 1625 he conducted the music for James's funeral. The new king, Charles I (1600–49), invited Gibbons and the Chapel Royal to Canterbury to welcome his queen two months later, but just before she arrived, Gibbons died from an apoplectic fit. Apart from his sacred anthems, he is best remembered for his songs, notably *Fair is the Rose*, *The Silver Swan* and *Dainty Fine Bird that Art Encaged*.

1631 COVENT GARDEN MARKET

IN AN ATTEMPT to relieve London's over-crowding, the restrictions on new building were loosened under Charles I, and it was with his support that Inigo Jones, who had studied in Italy and Denmark, was able to lay out Covent Garden market in 1631, marking the introduction of mature

Covent Garden Market, the brainchild of Inigo Jones. ▼

Italian Renaissance architecture to England. Jones was also responsible for the Banqueting House in Whitehall, through the windows of which Charles would walk to his execution in 1649. Originally 'Convent Garden', the development was built on land belonging to the Dukes of Bedford. It was later rebuilt, but it marked a change in the way cities looked and was followed after the Restoration by new London suburbs in Bloomsbury and elsewhere.

1644 *AREOPAGITICA*

ARGUABLY THE CENTURY'S greatest poet, John Milton (1608–74) – later to write *Paradise Lost* (1667) – came to political prominence as the propagandist for Parliament against the Royalist cause, defending the decision to execute Charles I, even drafting letters for Oliver Cromwell (1599–1658) to send to foreign rulers. His pamphlets about education and the controversy over his view that a mismatch of minds was a better reason for separation than sexual incompatibility or adultery, were overshadowed by his great defence of freedom of speech. *Areopagitica* (1644) was a protest against the reimposition of censorship by parliamentarians. Almost blind, his life, endangered by his Royalist loyalties, was saved after the Restoration by the payment of an enormous fine and the intervention of fellow poet, Andrew Marvell (1621–78).

1651 *LEVIATHAN*

THE LIFE OF MAN without law, said the philosopher and writer Thomas Hobbes (1588–1679) in *Leviathan* is 'solitary, poor, nasty, brutish and short'. Appalled by the violence of the civil war around him, Hobbes was searching for a more logical basis for ordering human society, following on from the humanism of his friend Sir Francis Bacon (1561–1626). In his long and well-travelled life, he also met other enlightened contemporaries, including Galileo

Thomas Hobbes. ▲

The lifting of the Commonwealth restrictions heralded a new dawn for London's theatres. ▲

Galilei (1565–1642) and Rene Descartes (1596–1650). The publication of the immensely influential and materialistic *Leviathan* in 1651 caused outrage among politicians and theologians, and although he was given a pension by Charles II (1630–85), he was forbidden to write by Parliament and his books were publicly burned.

1662 THEATRE ROYAL, DRURY LANE

WITH THE END of the restrictions of the Commonwealth, Charles II distributed the sole legal rights to arrange performances in Westminster to Thomas Killigrew (1612–83) and Sir William D'Avenant (1606–68). While D'Avenant opened the first indoor theatre in London's Dorset Gardens, Killigrew opened the Patent Theatre, later renamed the Theatre Royal, Drury Lane, in 1662. Just 12 years later it was rebuilt after the first of many fires, to boost its capacity from 700 to 2,000, and it was soon prospering showing the new Restoration dramas by William Congreve (1670–1729) and Sir John Vanbrugh (1664–1726). The Theatre Royal was rebuilt again in 1791, burned down again in 1809 and was rebuilt in its present form in 1812.

1668   POET LAUREATE

THE POET AND playwright John Dryden (1631–1700) was born into a Puritan family, and spent his career adapting to the prevailing political climate, ending up as a Catholic in 1686. This adaptation was all the more important, because Dryden was appointed as Poet Laureate on the death of D'Avenant in 1668, the first poet to hold the title officially. Dryden achieved the position with his poem *Annus Mirabilis* in 1667, describing the Great Fire and naval war with the Dutch the year before. Towards the end of his life, dismissed as Laureate during the Protestant Revolution of 1688, he turned to the theatre and then to translating Latin classics, developing the heroic couplet, which would be adopted by poets in the next century.

1672   THE FIRST CONCERTS

UNTIL 1672, PEOPLE heard music by going to church or organising their own private performances. But that was the year when a violinist called John Bannister, sacked from the King's Musik for misappropriating money, began a series of paid concerts, 'over against the George Tavern in White

Composer George Frideric Handel. ▶

Friars, near the back of the Temple'. His example was soon followed by the musical coal merchant Thomas Britton (1654–1714), above whose shop George Frideric Handel (1685–1759) later played. Other concert societies followed, taking the names from the taverns where they played. For example, the Angel and Crown in Whitechapel, which specialised in the music of Henry Purcell (1659–95). The first purpose-built concert hall was opened in Oxford in 1748.

1675   ST PAUL'S CATHEDRAL

THE RELIGIOUS DISPUTES of the past century meant that very few churches had been built before the centre of London burned down in 1666. The ruins of Old St Paul's Cathedral stayed where they were for eight years before the site was cleared, and Sir Christopher Wren began work on his new classical design. Wren forced through his design against great opposition from the Church authorities in 1675, and the building was finished 35 years later, under one architect, one master mason and one bishop. The use of Portland stone, and Wren's classical style, changed English architecture for ever. Wren was paid £200 a year. 'And for this,' said the Duchess of Marlborough, 'he was content to be dragged up in a basket three or four times a week'.

1689   THE FIRST BRITISH OPERA

WHILE CROMWELL had forbidden plays, he had never forbidden music. Even so, opera did not develop in Britain until 1689, when Henry Purcell was asked to write an entertainment for a young gentlewoman's boarding school in Chelsea. The result was *Dido and Aeneas*, which marked the introduction of this new art form to England. Purcell was also involved in a series of masques, writing melodies around popular historical themes. He had been organist of Westminster Abbey, where he was later buried, and composed music for the coronations of James VII and II (1633–1701) and William III (1650–1702). He also composed much chamber music, and many dance tunes and harpsichord suites. 'We have at length found an Englishman equal with the best abroad,' wrote his collaborator, Dryden.

Under Cromwellian rule, England saw a decline in arts such as music and drama. ◀

Religions, Belief and Thought

1603 THE MONARCHY AND PURITAN EXPECTATION

'I WILL HURRY THEM out of the land' James I is reputed to have said when met with Puritan opposition. James, who ascended the throne in 1603, believed kings received their authority from God and were answerable to him alone. Some Puritans expressed their concern by sailing away on board the *Mayflower* in 1620 to Massachusetts, where they set up a strict religious community. In 1611 the *Authorized Version* of the Bible was published after the Hampton Court Conference of bishops and Puritans under James I's chairmanship. In general, up to the Civil War, the monarchs remained in a tense stand-off with the Puritans. Catholics were regarded as the main target. The Puritans had to deal with Archbishop Laud and many, perhaps thousands, left England for the New World.

1615 NEW VISIONS

JOHN DONNE (1572–1631) Dean of St Pauls, had been brought up as a Catholic. In 1612 he resolved to become a priest and was ordained in 1615. His poetry lives on for us today, but it was as preacher that he came alive to the people of his day. Another poet of the same era, George Herbert (1593–1633), was unlike Donne, a natural believer; Donne was a natural sceptic. Herbert looked for the 'mean' between the 'painted

King James I of England, VI of Scotland. ◀

shrines' of Rome and extreme Protestantism. Mary Ward (d. 1645) was a devoted Catholic and, taking the Jesuits as a model, founded the Institute of the Blessed Virgin Mary in 1609. On going to Rome for approval in 1629 the experiment was suppressed and she was excommunicated for her pains. She founded communities in London and Yorkshire but, although she died in 1645, they did not receive papal approval until 1703.

1642   EFFECTS OF THE CIVIL WAR

IT IS NOT EASY to say how much the civil war (1642–49) was a religious war. Certainly, the Anglicans sided with the king while on the Parliamentary side were Puritans. During the war there was much destruction, churches were burned, works of art broken and destroyed, books torn up and vestments cut to pieces. Parliament abolished the episcopacy. Puritan leaders drew up the Solemn League and Covenant (it became law in 1644) many clergy signed it and continued as Presbyterian ministers. Bishops fled and became a rare species; with the bishops went the Book of Common Prayer, replaced by the Directory of Public Worship; but all was not harmonious in the Puritan camp.

During the reign of James I, a group of gentlemen plotted to kill the king by blowing up the House of Lords – the 'Gunpowder Plot'. ▼

1650s
SCHISMS AND
INDEPENDENTS

THE LIKELIHOOD of replacing an Anglican Church with a model church such as the one that existed in Geneva was always slim. There were strong theological differences between the Puritans. The Baptists, strong in the country before 1640, were a powerful

A Quaker meeting. ▲

influence in the army. The Congregationalists were despised by the Presbyterians, but perhaps the largest group of all was the Quakers. George Fox (1624–91) gathered together a number of smaller visionary independent churches and acquired thousands of followers in the 1650s. The Quaker creed of the Holy Spirit coming directly without mediation of Church or Scripture, together with their passive disobedience, made the

Quakers greatly unpopular with other churches. The term 'Quaker' which started as a term of abuse, has now lost its pejorative meaning and remains a common name for the Religious Society of Friends.

The founder of the Quaker movement George Fox. ◄

1662   THE CHURCH AFTER THE RESTORATION

A NEW PRAYER BOOK was published in 1662 and inaugurated on St Bartholomew's Day the same year. Bishops resumed their seats in the House of Lords and many Presbyterian clergy were ordained and became Anglicans. The Church introduced largely unsuccessful measures that sought to destroy the Baptists, Quakers, etc. The Toleration Act of 1689 was the first formal recognition of religious pluralism. Such tolerance did not extend to Catholics and Unitarians but it was a step forward. The century ended with Christianity being picked over by scientists and humanists. There was a growing humanitarian concern – the poor are always present even if the eternal verities had been demolished.

1696   THE DEISTS

DEISM STATED that while there was a creator who established the world and its process, there was no response to human prayer or need; this was a 'religion of nature', unencumbered by creeds and formularies. This fitted easily into the thinking of many intellectuals. John Toland's book *Christianity not Mysterious* (1696) really began the controversy and Tindal's work *Christianity as old as Creation* (1730) intensified the debate. It was the ultimate argument for natural reason – there was no need for the incarnation. William Law (1686–1760), who abandoned a Cambridge career because he would not swear allegiance to George I, responded by a series of quiet, mystical publications outlining the importance of living a practical Christian life based on an imitation of Jesus.

Quakers were frequently persecuted by other churches. ▶

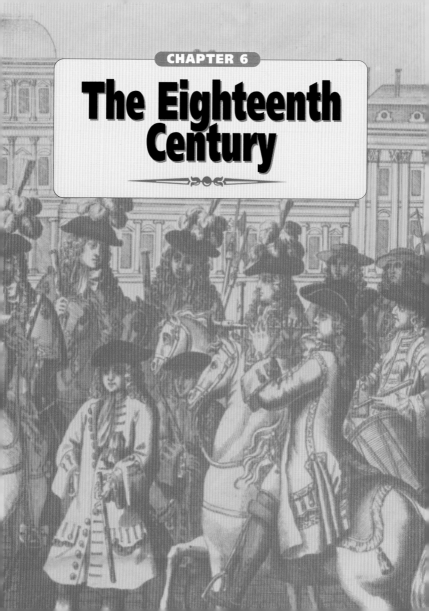

CHAPTER 6

The Eighteenth Century

Power and Politics

1707 THE ACT OF UNION

IN 1707 THE POLITICAL independence of Scotland ended. The road to this arrangement began early in the seventeenth century. In 1603, James VI of Scotland succeeded to the English throne, becoming James I. During the Republic, the countries were temporarily united under the Protectorate. By the beginning of the eighteenth century the Act of Union had been signed. The two parliaments established during this time became one – with the Scottish body disappearing.

Scottish MPs were now to be represented in the Parliament covering England, Scotland and Wales. Despite losing political dominance Scotland was able to retain a separate religious and legal identity, which it maintains to this day.

1715 THE JACOBITE REBELLION

DESPITE THE NEW political arrangements brought about by the Glorious Revolution and the Act of Union, some refused to recognise the new order. Those who refused, commonly known as the Jacobites, were supporters of the House of Stuart who campaigned for almost 60 years for the restoration of the Stuart monarchy. The Hanoverian succession in the early eighteenth century, though, stopped any claims of the Scottish line to the throne by peaceful means. In 1715,

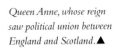

Queen Anne, whose reign saw political union between England and Scotland. ▲

uprisings in both Scotland and England – at Preston – were put down. Further rebellions were attempted in 1719, 1722 and 1745 by the 'younger pretender' Charles Edward Stuart. In Parliament, the Whigs (Scottish Presbyterians) used the long-running dispute to their advantage, claiming the Tories were Jacobite supporters.

1783 PITT THE YOUNGER

WILLIAM PITT became the youngest prime minister of the country in 1783 aged just 24. He had entered politics as an MP just three years previously. Despite his young age, his reputation as a shrewd leader became assured over the period he was in power. Son of William Pitt the Elder, also a politician, his thrust of his leadership lay in attempting to introduce financial reforms (although he was not always successful in these attempts) and, at first, a commitment to parliamentary reform. Pitt was also the leader who introduced income tax into the British political and economic system. In 1800 he steered the bill promoting the union of Great Britain and Ireland through Parliament. He died aged just 46.

William Pitt the Younger, who became prime minister at the age of 24. ▲

Ordinary Lives

1700s   THE HUGUENOT INFLUENCE

THE HUGUENOTS, French Protestants who had settled in Britain, sought to earn their place in British life by making a distinct contribution to it. Their contribution was considerable, and it did not take a long time to become apparent. They excelled in law, banking, insurance, education, the arts and sciences, and glassware and cabinet manufacture. Huguenots introduced white paper into Britain. David Garrick (1717–79), one of Britain's most famous and admired actors, was of Huguenot descent.

In Ireland, Huguenots established silk and poplin industries, and introduced glove- and lace-making and silk weaving. Their horticultural skills influenced the layout of what is now regarded as the typical English garden.

The interior of a weaving factory; the Huguenots introduced a number of such industries, particularly in Ireland. ◄

Jethro Tull's seed drill, which was to revolutionise farming. ▲

1701 ADVANCES IN AGRICULTURE

THE GREAT AGRICULTURAL improver Jethro Tull (1674–1741) invented his famous seed drill around 1701. In 1714 he used his observations of agriculture on the Continent to develop a horse-drawn hoe to pulverise the soil, and described them in his book *Horse Hoeing Husbandry*. Tull may not have had quite the impact with which contemporaries attributed him, but he was still a key figure in the agricultural revolution, which – between 1660 and 1850 – allowed farmers to feed a population that had quadrupled in size, at the same time as improving the quality of the food produced. By 1700, about half of England's agricultural land had been enclosed as a way of using more modern growing methods.

1720   THE SOUTH SEA BUBBLE

THE SOUTH SEA Company was set up in 1711 to trade with South America, but also as an alternative source of government funds to the Whig-dominated Bank of England and East India Company. Eight years later, its scheme to take over part of the government debt led to wild speculation in the company's stock, until the bubble burst in September 1720. Many prominent people, including George I (1660–1727), lost heavily. This was a period when the financial term 'bubble' passed into the language, following financial crashes in Amsterdam and – encouraged by the Scottish financier and notorious gambler John Law (1671–1729) – in Paris. The South Sea debacle led to wide restrictions on forming companies, except by the difficult and expensive route of royal charters.

1739   EXECUTION OF DICK TURPIN

JOHN GAY'S *Beggar's Opera* in 1723 revealed the existence of a nether world of tramps, cheats, thieves, prostitutes and highwaymen – a world of which travellers were only too aware. But there was no official police force

The highwayman Dick Turpin has become one of the best-loved villains in English history. ▼

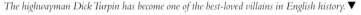

to protect travellers, except for a small patrol of 50 mounted men who guarded the approaches to London. The most celebrated highwayman, Dick Turpin (1705–39), was finally hanged in York. He bowed to the ladies in the watching crowd, and flung himself off the scaffold. The crowd was so delighted that they stole his body and buried it in quicklime to stop it being sold to the notorious anatomists.

1746   THE SUBJUGATION OF THE HIGHLANDS

A BRUTAL PROCESS of pacification began in Scotland after the defeat of Bonnie Prince Charlie (1720–88) at Culloden in 1746. Highland dress was outlawed, and so was the hereditary jurisdiction over clans by their chiefs. Scottish politics all but vanished, as MPs preferred not to risk their careers by raising Scottish issues at Westminster. The collapse of kelp prices after 1815 destroyed the remaining economic power in the highlands, and the clearances that followed replaced much of the population with sheep. Paradoxically, the intellectual and business ferment known as the Scottish Enlightenment was under way in Edinburgh at the same time, led by thinkers like David Hume (1711–76) and Adam Smith (1723–90). By the end of the eighteenth century, Scotland was generating 50 times more money than it had at the beginning.

1751   THE GIN ACT

GIN WAS INTRODUCED into Britain from the Netherlands in the 1690s and became extremely popular as a cheap route to oblivion. The 'gin era' was immortalised by the *Gin Lane* engravings by William Hogarth (1697–1764) and, at its peak, there

One of William Hogarth's famous engravings of 'Gin Lane'. ▲

were 8,659 'dram shops' in London alone – not to mention another 6,000 alehouses. It was widely believed that gin-drinking encouraged vice and idleness, and the government tried to control it by increasing the duties in 1729, and introducing stiff penalties for anyone infringing the regulations in 1736. Both actions proved unpopular and ineffective, so that the duties were reduced again seven years later. The era was finally ended in a moral panic about crime by the Gin Act in 1751, which massively raised the tax on gin once more.

1753   ANTI-TURNPIKE RIOTS

THE FIRST Turnpike Act had been passed in 1663, and allowed the operators to charge tolls to pay for and repair roads. As much as 18,500 km (11,500 miles) of turnpike road were built between 1750 and 1770, speeding up journey times, but sometimes attracting the rage of the locals – notably in the rioting that occurred near Leeds and Bradford in 1753. By then there were six different companies operating wagons between London and Manchester. 'However incredible it may appear,' said one advertisement, 'this coach will actually arrive in London four days after leaving Manchester'. Within 30 years, it was two days. In 1700 it took 10 days to get from London to Edinburgh by coach; by 1750 it was six days and by 1800, only three. By 1763 there were as many as 30 coaches a day between London and Birmingham.

1760s   THE NABOBS

ALTHOUGH LATER Britons in colonial service in India disdained such displays, wealthy eighteenth-century factors (merchants) of the British East India Company returned to Britain to commission portraits of themselves dressed as the phenomenally rich Indian princes, the nawabs, from whom their own nickname 'nabobs' was derived. The merchants wore splendid brocades, jewelled turbans and gem-encrusted footwear, and were attended by small boys, also richly dressed, whom they had brought from India as servants. For many British at home, glimpsing these boys on top of the nabobs' coaches as they drove through the streets was a first chance to see an Indian in the flesh. Planters in the West Indies also brought home black servants and sometimes black nannies for their children.

James Watt's steam engine, one of the greatest inventions of the Industrial Revolution. ▲

1775 WORK CONDITIONS IN THE INDUSTRIAL REVOLUTION

STEAM PIONEER James Watt (1736–1819) and his partner Matthew Boulton (1728–1809) set up their the factory in Soho outside Birmingham in 1775, and the following year they produced the first commercial steam engine. This marked an important development in the Industrial Revolution. Birmingham had already become an important centre in the Industrial Revolution. Some industrialists were responsible employers; some were not, literally chaining men, women and children –

Radical writer Thomas Paine. ▲

sometimes straight from the workhouses – to the tireless new machines. The 1802 Health and Morals of Apprentices Act tried to outlaw children working before 6 a.m. or after 9 p.m., but the act was hard to enforce. The nature of industry was becoming a central social issue.

1792   THE RIGHTS OF WOMEN

INSPIRED BY the French Revolution and Thomas Paine's *The Rights of Man*, the 1790s were a time of radical turmoil, centred around political societies like the Sheffield Society for Constitutional Information, (1791) which advocated pensions, free education and votes for all men.

The societies were banned after social disorder, which began with the bread riots in 1795, when a mob broke the windows of 10 Downing Street, shouting 'No war, no famine, no Pitt, no king!' Paine's ideas were applied to the position of women by the pioneer feminist Mary Wollstonecraft (1759–97) in *A Vindication of the Rights of Women* (1792) and other tracts, which demonstrated the double standards of the day. 'In marriage, husband and wife are one person,' said the great lawyer Sir William Blackstone (1723–80), 'and that person is the husband'.

Mary Wollstonecraft, one of the earliest writers to advocate women's rights. ▼

The Bridgewater Canal was built to provide a route from Lancashire coal mines to Manchester. ▲

1792 CANAL MANIA

THE ENGLISH enthusiasm for canals dated back to the 1761 opening of a canal linking the coal mines in Worsley, Lancashire with the outskirts of Manchester, built by the Duke of Bridgwater (1756–1803) and the self-educated engineer James Brindley (1716–72). The canal was described as 'perhaps the greatest artificial curiosity in the world'. By 1792, the year of 'canal mania', 42 new canals were projected, and canal shares were being bought enthusiastically by local merchants, landowners and manufacturers. At its height, there were 6,400 km (4,000 miles) of inland waterways in Britain, built mainly on local initiative, and dramatically cutting the cost of transporting goods. When the first boatload of coal arrived in Oxford from Coventry in 1790, the church bells were rung in celebration.

1795 SPEENHAMLAND SYSTEM

A MEETING OF Berkshire magistrates at Speen in 1795 responded to the poor harvest and high prices, by drawing up a system of poor relief that could apply to agricultural labourers both out of work and in. The system took account of the size of families and the price of bread, and made up earnings to a basic minimum. The system, known as the Speenhamland System, was widely adopted across southern England. Parliament criticised the idea, and so did the Royal Commission on the Poor Laws in 1832–34, because they believed it depressed wages and was a disincentive to work and save money and an incentive to delay marriage. Most labouring families were then reduced to meals of bread and cheese six days a week, and Speenhamland showed how far real wages had fallen.

The signing of the Treaty of Utrecht in 1713. ▼

Britain in the World

1700   THE WAR OF THE SPANISH SUCCESSION

IN 1700, CHARLES II of Spain died without an heir. There were two
claimants, one French and one Austrian. In his will, Charles named Louis
XIV's grandson, Philip of Anjou, as his successor. England and Austria
formed an alliance to prevent this happening. The English feared that it
would lead to a union of France and Spain. The war led to important
changes to Britain's position in Europe. In 1704 Gibraltar was captured
from Spain and it was ceded at the
Treaty of Utrecht in 1713. At the same
time the French gave up all claims to
Hudson's Bay and Newfoundland in
Canada. England also signed the
Methuen Treaty with Portugal, which
became England's oldest ally. By 1713,
when the war ended, Britain was a
major European power for the first
time for almost 100 years.

1704   THE DUKE OF
MARLBOROUGH

THE GREATEST British successes
during the War of the Spanish
Succession came, unusually, on the
Continent. English and British armies
had a poor record in Europe for much

*John Churchill, 1st Duke of
Marlborough.* ▲

of the eighteenth century. They usually landed in the Low Countries, as
William II had done in 1692 and achieved little (the Grand Old Duke of
York was to do something very similar in 1793), but in 1704 the opposite
happened. The Duke of Marlborough led his army 480 km (300 miles)
across Europe and smashed the French at the Battle of Blenheim. In the

next five years the duke won three more victories at Ramilies, Oudenarde and Malplaquet. The secret of his success was the discipline of the British infantry, steady under fire and also under attack from the French cavalry.

1733   THE 13 COLONIES

WHEN GEORGIA was set up as a penal colony in 1733, there were 13 colonies in America. Each one was different and there were frequent disputes between them over territory. To the north were the more industrial, heavily populated states. Here the most important political factors were merchants and trade. To the south were the more agricultural and rural states, where landowners were predominant. North and south were divided by the line finally drawn by two surveyors, Mason and Dixon, in 1767. What held the colonies together was the constant fear of Indian attacks and, from the 1660s, attacks by French forces from their colonies along the St Lawrence River.

1739   JENKINS' EAR

IN 1738, ROBERT JENKINS, a sea captain, arrived in London with one of his ears preserved in a bottle. He claimed that it had been cut off by the Spanish. Anti-Spanish feelings had been growing in Britain during the 1730s. The settlement of the colony of Georgia in 1733 led to clashes with Spanish Florida. There were also many tales of British sailors being thrown into Spanish prisons and being badly treated. Jenkins' Ear was one of the triggers that led to war being declared on Spain in 1739. There followed a series of attacks on the Spanish colonies in Central America and Porto Bello was taken in November 1739. Within a year, the war with Spain had become subsumed in the far more serious War of the Austrian Succession.

1740   THE AUSTRIAN SUCCESSION

IN 1740, CHARLES VI, the Holy Roman Emperor died. His only heir was his daughter Maria Theresa, who could not succeed. Three claimants tried to take the throne and a major European war ensued. Britain, as in the Spanish War of Succession, was once more involved on the side of Austria, but the British position was more complicated than before: since the Hanoverian succession in 1714 the British kings were also Electors of

Tomb of William Pitt in Westminster Abbey; Pitt was a great leader during the Seven Years' War. ◄

Hanover in northern Germany. George II was anxious to defend his electorate and even led the British army to victory at the Battle of Dettingen in 1743. After that the British suffered a series of defeats and by 1747 the French were about to occupy the Low Countries. However, two naval victories in 1747 turned the tide for Britain. At the treaty of Aix-la-Chapelle, in 1748, all conquests were returned. France handed Madras in India back to Britain and Britain returned Cape Breton in Canada to France.

1756   THE SEVEN YEARS' WAR

IN 1756 WAR broke out again between France and Britain, the main cause this time was clashes between French and British forces in America and Canada. The war resulted in total victory for Britain over France, thanks to the leadership of William Pitt the Elder. After some initial military defeats in Europe and the disastrous loss of Minorca, British forces won a series of global victories; most spectacular of all was 1759, the 'Annus Mirabilis'. In this year the British army defeated the French at Minden and the Royal Navy won victories at Lagos and Quiberon Bay, occupying the island of Belle-Ile off the coast of Brittany as a result. In America the Battle of the Heights of Abraham ended French power in Canada. In the West Indies almost all of the French islands were occupied as well as the Spanish colony of Cuba. Senegal and Goree were captured from France in Africa. In the Far East, Manila was captured from Spain.

1763   THE TREATY OF PARIS

AT THE TREATY OF PARIS in 1763 France agreed to withdraw from
Canada and to reduce her interests in India to a purely commercial basis.
Cuba was returned to Spain in exchange for Florida. In the West Indies
Grenada, St Vincent, Dominica and Tobago were retained by Britain, but
Martinique and Guadeloupe were returned. Britain regained Minorca in
exchange for the return of Belle-Ile. On balance it was a great triumph for
Britain, although the government was criticised for not driving a hard
enough bargain. In fact France was humiliated and looked for the earliest
opportunity for revenge during the American Rebellion. Spain also
resented its losses and backed the American colonists from 1779 onwards.

1768   CAPTAIN COOK

CAPTAIN JAMES COOK made
three voyages to the Pacific. In 1768
to 1771 he sailed around New
Zealand, proving that it was an island
and then returned to Britain around
the Cape of Good Hope. In 1772 to
1775 he became the first man to
cross the Antarctic Circle and sailed
around Antarctica and claimed
South Georgia for Britain. His final
voyage was from 1776 to 1779. He
sailed north through the Bering
Strait looking for passages to the
north-west and the north-east to the
Atlantic. He discovered Christmas
Island and Hawaii, but was killed
before he could return home.
Cook's great achievement was that
he mapped huge areas of the Pacific
and began to disprove the long-held
theory of a great southern continent,
the *Terra Australis*.

*The explorer Captain James Cook, the first
man to cross the Antarctic Circle.* ▲

1775 THE MARATHAS

THE MARATHAS were Hindu princes from southern India, who attacked the Mogul Empire at the end of the seventeenth century. The Marathas were organised into a loose confederacy and for a century they fought both amongst themselves and against the Mogul Empire for control of India. By the late eighteenth century, most of central India

India today; in the seventeenth century Indian Maratha Princes fought the Moguls for control of the country. ▲

was under the control of Maratha princes and this led them into conflict with the British in 1775, when the First Anglo–Maratha War broke out. The Second Maratha War broke out in 1802 and led to the defeat of the Marathas at the battles of Laswaree and Assaye. Most Indian states were then brought under British control.

1783 THE TREATY OF VERSAILLES

BY 1780 BRITAIN found herself at war not only with the American colonies, but also with France, Spain and Holland. In addition a League of Armed Neutrality was formed between Russia, Denmark and Sweden to protect shipping at sea from attacks by the British navy. Many of the territories gained during the Seven Years' War were lost. However, Gibraltar survived a siege lasting almost three years and in the final year of the war the balance was once again shifted by the. In 1782, Admiral Rodney won the Battle of The Saints in the West Indies. The Treaty of Versailles in 1783 confirmed American independence as well as most of the conquests of the war.

1788   BOTANY BAY

THE FIRST Europeans to reach Australia were Dutch explorers in the early seventeenth century. Captain James Cook explored the east coast during his first voyage, naming it New South Wales. It was his reports that led the British government to set up a penal colony at Botany Bay (now Sydney) in 1788. Convicts had been sent to Georgia in the American colonies, but that was impossible after 1783. On 26 January 1788, 11 ships with 717 convicts on board, landed at Port Jackson, later to be known as Sydney. After serving their sentences the convicts were set free and given between 30 and 50 acres of land. Soldiers were given about 100 acres. They were the first European inhabitants of Australia.

Captain Cook arriving at Botany Bay in 1788. ▲

1793   COLLECTING FRENCH TERRITORIES

WILLIAM PITT the Younger had been prime minister for almost nine years when he declared war on France in 1793. His greatest skill was in public finance; he was much less suited to being a war leader. After the failure of the Walcheren and Toulon expeditions, he adopted the same policies as his father had used during the Seven Years' War. He began to mop up French possessions around the world and particularly in the West Indies, where the sugar islands had always been regarded as great prizes. In previous wars these had been used as bargaining counters in the final peace treaty. But the French Revolutionary government simply paid no attention. It was not interested in West Indian islands when it was fighting for its life in Europe.

1793 TOULON

IN APRIL 1793, a British force under Admiral Hood seized the French port of Toulon, hoping that royalists would rally to its support. This did not happen. Although there were revolts against the Revolutionary government in some areas of France, such as the Vendee in the west, the big cities and the south in particular were strongly Republican. Hood held Toulon until December 1793, but was then forced to evacuate it. An important factor in his decision was the use of artillery by a young officer, Napoleon Bonaparte, who dragged his cannons on to high ground from where he was able to bombard the city. The British forces learnt another lesson. This war was not going to be fought in the rather gentlemanly manner of some past European wars.

Napoleon, who began his rise to leadership under Admiral Hood in the 1790s. ▲

1794 PITT'S GOLD

BY 1794 IT WAS obvious that Britain would not be able to interfere in any significant way in the war on the Continent. Nevertheless, the British government wanted to see France defeated. Pitt adopted a policy that had been used during the War of the Austrian Succession; he began to pay subsidies to the Continental powers to persuade them to carry on the fight against France. 'Pitt's Gold' as it became known was little more than a bribe to Austria and Prussia to keep them at war with France. Over the next 10 years or so more than £3,000,000 was sent abroad to provide support for the Austrian and Prussian armies. But it made little difference. In 1797 and 1801 the Austrians and Prussians were forced to accept French terms for peace after crushing defeats.

Industry and Invention

1700s   THE BIRTH OF THE CHEMICAL INDUSTRY

THE GROWTH of the textile industry brought a sudden increase of interest in the chemical industry, because of the problem of how long natural-bleaching techniques took, relying as they did on sunlight, rain, sour milk and urine. The modern chemical industry was virtually called into being in order to develop more rapid bleaching techniques for the British cotton industry. Its first success came in the middle of the eighteenth century, when John Roebuck invented the method of mass-producing sulphuric acid in lead chambers. The acid was used directly in bleaching, but it was also used in the production of more effective chlorine bleaches, and in the manufacture of bleaching powder, a process that was perfected by Charles Tennant at his St Rollox factory in Glasgow in 1799.

Richard Arkwright's Spinning Machine. ▲

1712   NEWCOMEN'S STEAM ENGINE

THE EARLIEST steam engines were the scientific novelties of Hero of Alexandria in the first century AD, but not until the seventeenth century were attempts made to harness steam for practical purposes. In 1698 Thomas Savery patented a pump with hand-operated valves to raise water from mines by suction, produced by condensing steam. In about 1712 another Englishman, Thomas Newcomen, developed a more efficient steam engine with a piston separating the condensing steam from the water. In 1765 James Watt greatly improved the engine by adding a separate condenser to avoid heating and cooling the cylinder with each stroke. Watt then developed a new engine that rotated a shaft instead of providing the simple up-and-down motion of the pump, along with other improvements that produced a practical power plant.

James Watt's pioneering steam engine, based on an earlier model by Thomas Newcomen. ▲

1718　THE FIRST MACHINE GUN

FROM THE VERY first introduction of firearms in the late European Middle Ages, attempts were made to design a weapon that would fire more than one shot without needing to be reloaded. In 1718, in London, James Puckle patented a machine-gun that was actually produced; a model of it is in the Tower of London. Its chief feature, a revolving cylinder that fed rounds into the gun's chamber, was the first basic step toward the automatic weapon; what prevented its success was the clumsy and undependable flintlock ignition. The introduction of the percussion cap in the nineteenth century led to the invention of numerous machine guns in the United States, several of which were employed in the American Civil War.

1742 MAKING STEEL

MAKING STEEL involves lowering the carbon content of pig-iron to below 1.5 per cent and controlling the presence of other impurities. This was first achieved successfully by Benjamin Huntsman, an English clockmaker, in 1742. He melted wrought iron in a clay crucible and added the required amount of carbon, but his method proved very expensive and could only be carried out on a small scale. It was replaced by a process invented independently in the 1850s by American William Kelly and Englishman Sir Henry Bessemer. It came to be known as the Bessemer process. In 1864 Frenchman Pierre Martin and naturalised Briton Sir William Siemens invented the open-hearth process.

1754 ENGLISH PORCELAIN

DURING THE eighteenth century European porcelain had reached a stage where it rivalled that from China. It remained a luxury, however, until it was brought into general use by two Englishmen – Josiah Wedgwood and Josiah Spode. Wedgwood came from a family of Staffordshire potters and in 1754 he established his own pottery trying to

Josiah Wedgwood, the pottery pioneer, whose mass-produced crockery is still popular today. ◀

make cheap earthenware that could compete with porcelain. In 1763 he patented cream-coloured queen's-ware, and followed it with blue jasper-ware. In 1769 he built a new factory near Hanley, where he practised mass-production methods to make crockery for everyday use. His work was supplemented by Spode's invention of bone china in 1800. This looked like porcelain, but was cheaper and stronger. It became widely used and popularised by Spode's willow-pattern.

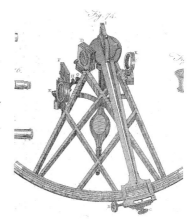

1757 THE SEXTANT

EARLY MARINERS used the Sun by day and the north pole star by night in order to estimate their position. As time went on, better methods of navigation were found with the astrolabe, popularised by Portuguese explorers around 1500, then in 1731 the octant was demonstrated in-dependently by John Hadley of England and Thomas Godfrey of Philadelphia. The more accurate sextant was first made to resemble its present form by a Scot,

▲Top: *an early sextant;* bottom: *the astrolabe, one of the earliest navigational instruments.* ◀

Captain John Cambell, in 1757. In use, the horizon is viewed through a telescope and a fixed half-silvered mirror, while a second mirror is rotated to bring the Sun or a particular star into view alongside the horizon. The angle of rotation gives the altitude of the Sun from which the latitude position can be calculated.

1764   A NEW WAY TO SPIN

JAMES HARGREAVES was the English inventor of the spinning-jenny, the first practical application of multiple spinning by a machine. In about 1764 Hargreaves conceived the idea for his hand-powered multiple spinning machine when he observed a spinning-wheel that had been

James Hargreaves's Spinning Jenny, the first multiple-thread spinning machine. ▼

Engraved by T.E.Nicholson.

accidentally overturned by his young daughter Jenny. As the spindle continued to revolve in an upright rather than a horizontal position, Hargreaves reasoned that many spindles could be turned so. He constructed a machine with which one individual could spin several threads at one time. When he began to sell the machines to help support his large family, local hand spinners, fearing unemployment, broke into his house and destroyed a number of jennies, causing Hargreaves to move to Nottingham in 1768.

1775   DRIVING THE WHEELS OF INDUSTRY

BETWEEN 1775 and 1800, the period over which Watt's patents for his engines were extended, the Boulton and Watt partnership produced some 500 engines, which despite their high cost in relation to a Newcomen engine, were eagerly acquired by the tin-mining industrialists of Cornwall and other power-users who badly needed a more economic and reliable source of energy. Basically, they converted the engine from a single-acting (i.e., applying power only on the downward stroke of the piston) atmospheric pumping machine into a versatile double-acting engine that could be applied to rotary motion, thus literally driving the wheels of industry. The rotary-action engine was quickly adopted by British textile manufacturer Sir Richard Arkwright for use in a cotton mill, which demonstrated the feasibility of applying steam power to large-scale grain milling.

1784   SHRAPNEL

THE SHRAPNEL shell was invented in 1784 by the British Lieutenant (later General) Henry Shrapnel. Shrapnel projectiles contained small shot or spherical bullets, along with an explosive charge to scatter the shot as well as fragments of the shell casing. A time-fuse set off the explosive charge in the latter part of the shell's flight, when it was near opposing troops. The resulting hail of high-velocity debris was often lethal; shrapnel caused the majority of artillery-inflicted wounds in the First World War. During the Second World War it was found that a high-explosive bursting charge fragmented the shell's iron casing so effectively that the use of shrapnel balls was unnecessary, and it thus was discontinued.

Culture, Arts and Leisure

1709   THE TATLER

RICHARD STEELE (1672–1729) first met his collaborator Joseph Addison (1672–1719) at Oxford, and launched *The Tatler* in 1709, publishing three times a week for nearly two years – reporting from various new coffee and chocolate houses in London. When it unexpectedly ceased publication, he and Addison brought their high moral tone to bear through *The Spectator*, inventing a country gentleman called Sir Roger de Coverley, and giving editorial space to some of the leading writers and poets of the age. Having been prosecuted for seditious libel over a pamphlet about the Hanoverian succession, Steele devoted himself to running the Theatre Royal, Drury Lane, developing the dramatic tradition known as 'sentimental comedy' where emotion became the main object of interest.

The first edition of The Tatler *magazine, dated 1709.* ▼

1713   THE SCRIBLERUS CLUB

IN THE WINTER of 1713, in the last days of Queen Anne (1665–1714), a group of Tory intellectuals formed the Scriblerus Club devoted to witty repartee and the ridicule of 'all the false tastes in learning'. The satirical literature that followed was for a time given the title 'scriblerian', and among the distinguished club members were the playwright John Gay (1685–1732), the poet Alexander Pope (1688–1744) and the writer Jonathan Swift (1667–1745).

They devoted themselves to writing the satirical memoirs of an imaginary Whig, called *The Memoirs of Martinus Scriblerus*, eventually published in 1741 – by which time the club had influenced the creation of Gay's *The Beggar's Opera*, Pope's *The Dunciad* and Swift's *Gulliver's Travels*.

1725   CHISWICK HOUSE

PALLADIAN ARCHITECTURE – called after the Italian architect Andrea Palladio (1508–80) had first been introduced to Britain by Inigo Jones, but it lost favour under the influence of Christopher Wren and others. But in the 1720s, neo-Palladianism made a comeback, increasingly associated with Whig politics against the more baroque Tories, and popularised by the architect peer Richard Boyle, Earl of Burlington (1695–1753). His Chiswick House was modelled on Palladio's Villa Rotunda and became a model for a new wave of country-house building. Each room was designed as a perfect cube, and it was intended primarily for entertainment. 'Too little to live in,' said Lord Hervey (1696–1743) about these rooms, 'too big to hang on a watch chain.'

Chiswick House, Richard Boyle's best-known commission. ▼

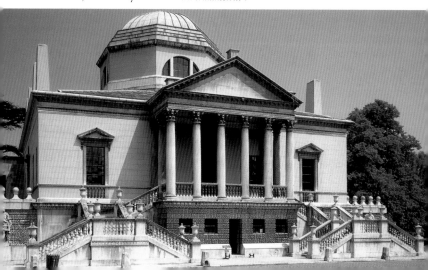

1741   *THE MESSIAH*

GEORGE FRIDERIC HANDEL (1685–1759) was the son of a barber-surgeon from Lower Saxony who became the *kapellmeister* to the Elector of Hanover, later George I (1660–1727). Handel arrived in London in 1711 and went on to dominate the London opera circuit. An invitation to Dublin led to a burst of 25 days' feverish activity to write *The Messiah* in his home near Oxford Street in London in 1741. So busy was he, his meals were left uneaten outside the door. It was admired in Dublin in its first performance, and George II (1683–1760) rose in his seat during the London performance –

George Frideric Handel, whose most famous work The Messiah *was written in London.* ▲

overwhelmed by the 'Alleluia Chorus'. Handel later went blind, his eyes ruined by the same surgeon who had tried to save the eyesight of Johann Sebastian Bach (1685–1750).

1744   **RULE BRITANNIA**

THE MID-EIGHTEENTH century was a period of wealth and growing national consciousness, where the growth of trade and Britain's American empire led to an increasing understanding of nationhood. So it was not surprising that the period also saw the growth of patriotic songs. 'God Save the King' appeared in almost its present form around 1744, and the music for 'Rule Britannia' by Thomas Arne (1710–78) appeared in his masque *Alfred*, performed before Frederick, Prince of Wales (1727–51) at Cliveden House. The words included the phrase 'Britons never will be slaves', and were by the writer and author of *The Seasons*, James Thomson (1700–48). They were adapted five years later by the Jacobites as the anthem for their 1745 rising.

1755 JOHNSON'S DICTIONARY

THE GREAT DICTIONARY of Dr Samuel Johnson, published in 1755, remains one of the milestones in the development of the English language, and it marked the turning point in his own career. For eight years he struggled with the project, working with a team of editors at his London home, and justifying his dictionary definition of lexicographer as 'a harmless drudge'. By 1762, he had been given an annual pension by George III (1738–1820) and had met the Scots lawyer James Boswell (1740–95) who would write his biography (1791), make his name and popularise his eccentric development of the art of conversation. Moralist, journalist, critic, novelist and poet, Johnson knew all the most famous men of his age.

1770 BLENHEIM PARK

A GRATEFUL NATION had bestowed Blenheim Palace on the Duke of Marlborough (1650–1722). The palace was designed by the playwright and architect Sir John Vanbrugh, but the grounds were laid out in the new style – with 1,094 ha (2,700 ac) of natural parks and lakes instead of formal gardens – associated with Lancelot 'Capability' Brown (1716–83). The trees are said to have been planted, not in formal lines, but in accordance with

Blenheim Park, which was planned in the new style pioneered by Lancelot 'Capability' Brown. ▼

Thomas Gainsborough's work has become known as the epitome of eighteenth-century art. ▲

the troop dispositions at one of Marlborough's victories. Brown won his nickname by telling clients their gardens had 'capabilities for improvement', and by the end of a successful career, starting with experience under the great landscape architect William Kent (1686–1748), he had designed more than 140 estates.

1774 THE ARRIVAL OF GAINSBOROUGH

THE GREAT LANDSCAPE and portrait artist, Thomas Gainsborough (1727–88), had moved his practice to fashionable Bath in 1759, developing a distinctive style of painting in the grand tradition of Van Dyck. But it was not until his arrival in London in 1774, where he set up in Pall Mall, that he became the most successful portrait painter of the century, with his fluid and impressionistic style portraying country gentlemen posing in front of their land. He was the only rival to Sir Joshua Reynolds (1723–92), the first president of the Royal Academy and the embodiment of the artistic establishment. Gainsborough caught a chill listening to the trial of Warren Hastings (1732–1818) in Westminster Hall in 1788 and died shortly afterwards.

1787 MARYLEBONE CRICKET CLUB

THE WORD 'CRICKET' was recorded as long ago as 1300, and the game had clearly existed in various forms for centuries, but it was not until 1774 that a committee of the well-to-do met in the Star and Garter pub in London's Pall Mall to draw up the rules formally. In those days there were only two stumps, and no limit to the size of the curved bat, which gave an enormous advantage to the batsman. Games used to take place on White Conduit Fields, and when the club there was dissolved in 1787, the Marylebone Cricket Club (MCC) took its place. The new club, destined to control the game, started in Dorset Square and moved to its present site at Lords in St John's Wood Road in 1814.

1798 *LYRICAL BALLADS*

WHEN TWO POLITICAL radicals, William Wordsworth (1770–1850) and Samuel Taylor Coleridge (1772–1834), met in the Quantock Hills in 1797 their conversation changed the direction of literature. They agreed with each other's sense that eighteenth-century poetry was emotionally artificial, and their *Lyrical Ballads* the following year pointed in another direction. Only four of the anonymous poems in the original edition were by Coleridge. Although one was 'The Rime of the Ancient Mariner', it was described by one contemporary critic as 'the strangest story of cock and bull that we ever saw on paper'. Nevertheless *Lyrical Ballads* founded the Romantic movement in poetry, which became so important in the early years of the next century.

Although the game had been played for centuries, the official rules for cricket were not laid down until 1774. ▼

Religions, Belief and Thought

1738 THE CONVERSION OF THE WESLEYS

JOHN AND CHARLES Wesley were two of 19 children, born into a High Church family. It was not considered surprising that John (1703–91) was ordained with two of his brothers Charles (1707–88) and Samuel (who never became a Methodist). They became friendly with a fervent preacher, George Whitefield (1714–70), and accompanied him on one of his many trips to America. But the Wesley's trip was a disaster and in 1738 they were back in Britain exhausted and near collapse. Within three days of each other in May 1738 they both received separate revelations of the power of their faith. It was this experience that was to change their lives and lead to the rise of Methodism.

1739 DAVID HUME

DAVID HUME'S (1711–76) best-known work *A Treatise of Human Nature* (1739) disappointed him on publication. It fell 'dead-born from the press', he writes. He was a sceptic and a free-thinker. His emphasis lies on the values of custom and instinct as guides to life. If reason is taken as fundamental this will lead to confusion, so custom, which is a summary of knowledge, is a better guide. It is knowledge established by experience. To early readers Hume appeared to argue against the existence of God and the truth of religion, and in his *Dialogues Concerning Natural Religion* (existing in 1751 but published after his death) he demolishes the principal arguments for the existence of God. His purpose was to halt the pretensions of reason and put instinct in its place. His belief about an after-life was that to think of it was absurd. Why should he be concerned? It was irrelevant.

1740s THE RISE AND INFLUENCE OF METHODISM

JOHN WESLEY undertook a travelling ministry, which he sustained for 52 years travelling well over 322,000 km (200,000 miles) and preaching

Scottish historian and philosopher David Hume. ◀

40,000 sermons. By his death in 1791 over 72,000 people in Britain were 'in association' with him and two centuries later there were 18 million Methodists in the world. He lived an austere and demanding life with a clear message: 'Holiness must be perfect love'. The term 'Methodist' referred to the methodical order of life e.g. fasting two days a week, and two services on Sundays (before and after the services in the parish church). The formation of the Methodist Preachers' Conference and their acceptance of Wesley's rights and res- ponsibilities (1784) made separation from the Church of England.

1776   THOMAS PAINE
WRITER AND PHILOSOPHER
Thomas Paine (1737–1809) wrote a
pamphlet in support of the American
Colonialists in 1776. It was called
Common Sense and, at the outbreak of
the French Revolution, he produced in
its defence his most influential work, *The
Rights of Man* (1791–92). So supportive
was it of the Revolution that Paine had
to flee to France. In the second part of
his book he argues that governments
should recognise the natural rights of all
citizens to receive education, old-age
pensions and other benefits of social

*Thomas Paine, author of the pro-
Revolution* The Rights of Man. ▲

welfare. Burke, Paine's opponent may have unintentionally triggered what
he wished to stop. While Burke's pamphlet sold 19,000 copies in six
months, *The Rights of Man* sold 200,000. Paine died in New York having
alarmed governments and offended the Church by promoting an
argument for Deism in *The
Age of Reason* (1794–97).

1785   WILLIAM CAREY
IN 1785, CAREY
(1762–1834) was given
permission to preach as a
Baptist though he had no
formal training. Soon he was
challenging his fellow
ministers with the Great
Commission – 'Go forth and
teach all nations'. He formed

*A missionary conference in India; Baptist missionary William Carey translated the
Bible into six Indian languages.* ▲

the Baptist Missionary Society in 1792 and a year later he decided to go to India. He had been in India for seven years before he baptised an Indian, but he did translate the Bible into six Indian languages and he is a model of the fortitude of the early British missionaries. He founded schools and colleges in India at a time when Britain was doing precious little at home. Carey inspired others but none really possessed the depth of his obsessive drive and evangelical zeal.

1797   WILLIAM WILBERFORCE

THE BOOK *A Practical View of the Prevailing Religious Systems of Professed Christians in the Higher and Middle Classes in this Country contrasted with Real Christianity* (1797) by Wilberforce (1759–1833) was surprisingly popular among evangelicals because of its call for order and acknowledgement of authority. It, and Wilberforce himself, emerged from an evangelical Christian group formed in Clapham in London. Wilberforce was an MP and was able to use that position as a platform to lead the anti-slavery movement. He campaigned for schools for the poor, civil rights for Catholics, prison reform and many other reforms. What is most remarkable about the campaign against the slave trade (finally successful in 1833) was the way in which various interested groups, religious (Quakers and Methodists) and non–religious, put aside their differences and joined forces.

William Wilberforce, one of the leaders of the abolitionist movement. ▶

CHAPTER 7

The Nineteenth Century

Power and Politics

1832 REFORM ACT

AS THE IMPORTANCE of party politics grew and a more literate nation took an ever-greater interest in national matters, voting reform was desperately needed. This was first addressed in the Reform Act of 1832. Most urgently required was reform to the rotten boroughs. These were boroughs where the electorate had shrunk to almost nothing. Borough owners could therefore nominate their own MPs and they were used as a source of influence by the wealthy and powerful. The 1832 Act was brought in by the Whigs after much political debate. Rotten boroughs were largely disenfranchised and the vote extended by some 50 per cent in England and Wales largely among the lower-middle classes. The effect was more limited in Scotland and Ireland.

1834 TRADE UNIONS AND POLITICAL REFORM

IN 1834 SIX trade unionists from the Dorset village of Tolpuddle were transported to Australia amid Establishment fears at the growth of the power of organised labour. Although trade unions had been legal since 1824, the powers that be were increasingly concerned about the threat

The Tolpuddle Martyrs, who were transported to Australia. ▼

Queen Victoria's reign saw Britain at the height of its empirical powers. ◀

they posed. The trade-union movement developed nevertheless and in 1868 the Trades Union Congress was formed. Their development coincided with the growth of further reforms best encapsulated in the Chartist movement around the same time. This asked for reform in six main areas: universal male suffrage, annual parliaments, payment of MPs, equal electoral districts, voting by ballot and an end to property qualification for MPs. Despite widespread support, its influence had died out by the late 1850s.

1837 QUEEN VICTORIA SUCCEEDS THE THRONE

IN 1837 QUEEN Victoria came to the throne where she remained for 64 years. During her reign Britain was transformed into the world's greatest industrial and military power; its urban landscape changed for ever; Parliament was strengthened and the franchise extended. The empire reached its high point, particularly with British rule in India. Queen Victoria eventually became a popular monarch, well loved by the population at large. Paradoxically, despite the many achievements carried out in her name, the monarchy was transformed during her reign. As the constitution evolved it limited the powers of the monarch, leaving it, in the words of Bagehot, to have the 'right to be consulted, the right to encourage, and the right to warn'.

The Great Exhibition at Crystal Palace in 1851. ▲

1851 GREAT EXHIBITION

THE GREAT EXHIBITION of 1851 at Crystal Palace was more than just a day out for the more than six million people estimated to have visited it. It was a demonstration to the world of the zenith of British industrialised power. The event was loved by the public – even the act of travelling to the exhibition by train was an example of British economic strength – and it was all organised by the aristocracy. Prince Albert, Queen Victoria's husband, was the brains behind the event, which revealed over 100,000 exhibits, although not all were British. The event was an unqualified success and marked a transformation in the middle Victorian period. It came to represent the onset of a calmer era in Victorian politics after the constitutional and economic crises of the 1830s and '40s.

1861 DEATH OF ALBERT

THE DEATH of Prince Albert from typhoid in 1861, aged 42, provoked a period of crisis in British political life. A distraught Queen Victoria took to mourning and seclusion for a period of 10 years. Despite her grief the amount of time Victoria spent mourning proved unpopular among the people and was more than a discomfort for senior politicians. Albert, a German cousin of Victoria's, had been a big influence on British political life at this time. At first he was resented among the political Establishment but proved to exert a profound political influence on Victoria. He rid the queen of her anti-Tory feelings and was also influential in the formulation of British foreign policy. For the last 30 years of her life, Victoria only appeared publicly in mourning clothes.

Prince Albert became a much-respected member of the royal family after his marriage to Victoria. ▲

1867 AND 1884 THE REFORM ACTS

THE REFORM ACTS of the mid- and late-nineteenth centuries proved to be watersheds in British political history. Building on the first Reform Act of 1832, the two pieces of legislation extended the franchise to ever-larger numbers of the English people in 1867 (1868 in Scotland). This Act gave the vote to an extra 938,000 people, almost doubling the number of people allowed to vote in elections. The 1884 Act was largely in response to political pressures. By extending the franchise to the counties it increased the number of people able to vote from three million to five million. Constituencies were re-aligned to take account of the increased number of voters and led to increased party discipline within the Commons. 'Party is organised opinion,' said Gladstone, who was Prime Minister at the time of the 1884 Act.

1867 BAGEHOT'S *CONSTITUTION*

THE LATER Victorian era was notable for the works of great thinkers within Britain whose writings would have repercussions all around the world. As well as the concept of Darwinism, the Victorian era also gave birth to the writings of John Stuart Mill, and the novels of Charles Dickens. Karl Marx, working in London, would publish his communist theories. Walter Bagehot wrote his defining work *The English Constitution* in 1867. Darwin's great work – *The Origin of Species* – was published in 1859 and its theories of evolution and survival of the fittest proved a great worry to the Church, among others. J. S. Mill's theory of utilitarianism and his defence of individual freedoms promoted social reforms in the era. Dickens, brought up in poverty, used his novels to rail against the cruelties of industrialisation.

Charles Darwin, whose Origin of the Species, *was to shock the Victorian Establishment.* ▲

1868 BENJAMIN DISRAELI

DOMINATING THE political scene of the late Victorian era were two politicians – Benjamin Disraeli, who was Queen Victoria's favourite, and William Gladstone, a man she came to dislike intensely. Disraeli, the son of a Spanish Jew, was a Conservative prime minister first in 1868 and later between 1874 and 1880. Notably he was responsible for several pieces of social legislation to pass through Parliament. These included the second Reform Act of 1867 and the Public Health Act in 1875. In the field of foreign politics he made Queen Victoria Empress of India in 1876 as well as beginning Britain's ownership of the Suez Canal in 1875. A renowned novelist in his earlier years, he once said 'when I want to read a novel – I write one'.

1868　WILLIAM GLADSTONE

'HE SPEAKS TO ME as if I were a public meeting,' Queen Victoria once said of Gladstone. Although he was not a favourite of the queen's, Gladstone proved himself to be the enduring politician of the Victorian era. He entered Parliament as a Tory but eventually became a Liberal prime minister in 1868. After spending six years in opposition he was prime minister again between 1880 and 1885. One of the main pieces of legislation to pass through Parliament during his leadership was the Reform Act of 1884, which gave the vote to farm labourers. He was prime minister

Prime minister William Gladstone. ▲

again between 1892 and 1894 and unsuccessfully tried to push through bills for Home Rule in Ireland in 1886 and again in 1893.

1874　CHANGING PARLIAMENT

BRITISH POLITICS underwent a major transformation due to the consequences of the Reform Acts of 1867 and 1884. The net result of the Acts was to extend the vote to 60 per cent of adult men in towns – previously it had been 20 per cent – and to 70 per cent in the country. The effect was dramatically felt by the House of Commons fairly soon after the 1867 Act. The Liberal coalition government had disintegrated in 1874, which was not entirely unexpected. However, their defeat at the polls to the Conservatives, their first major electoral defeat for more than 30 years, was unexpected. The extension of the vote increased the focus on the House of Commons and thus its importance in British political life, something that continues today.

Ordinary Lives

1801 GENERAL ENCLOSURE ACT

BY THE END of the eighteenth century, up to three million open fields had been enclosed in the Midlands alone, and the 1801 Act meant that the process became even simpler. Woods and wasteland disappeared, making way for a new pattern of hedges, walls and fences. Some of those who had depended on using common land were thrown off unceremoniously to become labourers or paupers. 'When farmers became gentlemen, their labourers became slaves,' complained the radical William Cobbett (1763–1835). Under the influence of agricultural reformers like Arthur Young (1741–1820), land was becoming more productive and many new breeds of cattle were appearing. Even George III (1738–1820) was writing a regular agricultural column under the pseudonym 'Mr Robinson'.

New breeds of cattle began to appear at the beginning of the nineteenth century. ▼

1816 DEMOBILISATION AND INSTABILITY

THE BATTLE OF WATERLOO and the end of the war was an unexpected economic disaster for Britain, as the demoralised markets on the Continent were unable to absorb stockpiles of British goods, and up to 400,000 members of the armed forces were suddenly thrown on to the labour market. The result was serious unemployment. The 10 per cent income tax was abolished, but replaced with taxes on other products. The poor existed on a diet of potatoes, condensed milk, tea from used tea leaves, white bread mixed with chalk and water from the sewers. The result was serious political upheaval, fuelled by the urban discontent that led to events such as the Peterloo massacre in 1819, mass demonstrations after the transportation of the Tolpuddle Martyrs in 1834 and the Chartist disturbances later.

1829 THE METROPOLITAN POLICE

THE PRISON reformer Elizabeth Fry (1780–1845) made her first horrifying visit to Newgate in 1813, and her campaign to improve conditions coincided with an increase in the number of prisoners. Home secretary Sir Robert Peel (1788–1850) ended the brutal death sentence for theft and began replacing transportation to Australia with penal servitude in Britain, knowing that juries were refusing to convict. The influx of convicts were housed in prison hulks on the rivers. Peel's new police force (est. 1829) in London was deliberately created to be more civilian than military

Prison reformer Elizabeth Fry. ▲

– armed only with a truncheon and top hat – because of political distaste for the system of spies and soldiers on the Continent. It took another 10 years before counties were allowed to have their own police forces.

1837 FIRST TELEGRAPHIC MESSAGE

DURING THE Napoleonic wars, urgent
messages were sent from the Admiralty to
the dockyards by a system of
semaphore stations relayed from high
spots like church towers. Messages
from London took just 12 minutes
to reach Portsmouth. But that all
changed in 1837 when the first
telegraphic message was sent,
sending electromagnetic signals
that made a needle point to
letters of the alphabet from
Camden Town Station to Euston.
Morse code was invented the
following year, and the first railway
telegraph system was working between
Paddington and Slough by 1842. Racing

An early telegraph machine,
designed by J. Brett. ▲

news from Newmarket was sent telegraphically in 1854, the news agency
Reuters was founded five years later. Once the Atlantic cable had been laid
in 1866, telegraphic messages could be sent to the USA as well.

1845 RAILWAY MANIA

THE FIRST SENSE of a railway boom came in 1836, but 'railway
mania' arrived in full force between 1845–47 when 576 companies were
set up and over 14,000 km (8,700 miles) of new track were agreed.
Armies of navvies were cutting tracks or building the new railway towns
like Swindon or Crewe – Crewe did not even appear as a place-name in
the 1841 census. Former draper George Hudson (1800–71), known as
the 'Railway King', was making a fortune speculating in railway shares,
but was on his way to prison and ruin. Under an Act passed in 1844,
companies had to run at least one train every weekday at no more than
a penny a mile. Their trains had already forced towns to synchronise
their times: Bristol, for example, used to run its clocks according to
latitude, 10 minutes behind London.

1855   SUNDAY OPENING RIOTS

BEER HAD LONG been the staple drink of the masses – it was safer than drinking water – but temperance campaigners and preachers increasingly included it along with spirits as the cause of drunkenness. There were no games on Sundays, and morning prayers were read by the heads of middle-class households, but the pubs were open. In 1854, the campaigners forced them to close at midnight on Saturday and – except for brief periods for Sunday lunch and evening – not reopen until 4 p.m. on Monday. Complete Sunday closing was enforced in Scotland from 1853 and Wales from 1881. Furious pub-goers rioted throughout the summer of 1855 in Hyde Park, breaking the windows of carriages in protest. But in 1864, pubs were nevertheless forced to close every night from 1 a.m. to 4 a.m.

1858   JEWISH EMANCIPATION

DESPITE THEIR respectable family life and their willingness to advance by hard work and dedication, Jews still lacked rights of citizenship well into the nineteenth century. In 1753, a proposal to offer

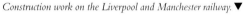

Construction work on the Liverpool and Manchester railway. ▼

Jews citizenship created such a furore in Parliament that it had to be dropped. In the event, Jews had to wait until 1858, almost 30 years longer than the originally equally disadvantaged Catholics, to see their disabilities removed. Lack of citizenship, however, did not affect their ambitions or their resolve, especially strong in Jews, to see their children advance themselves. They certainly advanced. There was a Jewish sheriff of London in 1835, a Jewish baronet in 1841 and in 1855, a Jew, David Salomans, became Lord Mayor of London.

1862   THE NEW COMMUTERS

THE WORD 'commuter' was first used in the 1850s, by which time there were 800 horse-drawn buses in London, and traffic jams were so common that new streets like Corporation Street in Manchester or Shaftesbury Avenue in London were being built to relieve the congestion. The underground Metropolitan Railway opened between Paddington and Farringdon Street in London in 1862, backed by the City of London and Great Western Railway, to speed people into work. By then London's new Victoria Station had opened up opportunities for new suburbs in south London for the new middle classes, where they could live in relative health and still commute to work every morning. The first tram appeared in Liverpool in 1863.

Nineteenth century horse-drawn bus. ▼

1888   JACK THE RIPPER

THE NOTORIOUS series of horrific murders of prostitutes in Whitechapel in 1888 has never been solved. At the time, the mystery gripped the public and brought widespread condemnation of the police, but it also heightened tensions over the latest influx of immigrants to east London, and at least one attempt was made to implicate local Jews. From 1870–1914 as many as 120,000 Jewish refugees from the pogroms in Russia and eastern Europe made their homes in London's East End, Manchester and Leeds. As many as 29 per cent of this new wave became tailors, leading to a revival of the rag trade in east London. Other Jewish immigrants played a prominent role in the tobacco trade: both Player's factory (1882) and Imperial Tobacco in Glasgow (1888) were Jewish enterprises.

1894   THE FIRST MOTOR CAR

THE FIRST motor car seen in Britain was a Benz, imported in 1894, and stopped by police as it crossed London for the first time. Two years later, the law that laid down a speed limit of 4 mph and insisted on a man walking in front carrying a red flag – designed for older, heavier steam vehicles – was repealed, and the Earl of Winchelsea burned the flag ceremonially at the first London–Brighton rally that same year. A new speed limit of 20 mph was imposed in 1904 and by 1914 there were 140,000 cars in the country – and motor-accident deaths were running at almost 1,500 a year. 'What pair of horses could carry a load, as my Daimler has done, of 250 pounds of baggage, myself and my man?' said one car advertisement.

Gottlieb Daimler. ▲
An 1894 rear-engined Velo Benz automobile. ▼

Britain in the World

1805 THE BATTLE OF TRAFALGAR

WHEN THE French fleet escaped from Toulon in May 1805, Napoleon's plan to invade Britain seemed to be working even better than he had expected. Nelson, who had been blockading Toulon for two years, at first thought that the French might be heading for Egypt as they had done in 1798. Only when he had sailed as far as the Straits of Messina did he head west and follow Villeneuve across the Atlantic. The French plan was to make Nelson think that they were going to attack the West Indian islands, but instead return to Europe immediately. But Nelson guessed their plan and sent word to the Admiralty by means of a fast ship. When Villeneuve reached France, he was unable to force his way up the Channel and sailed south to Cadiz. On 21 October 1805 Nelson tracked him down and destroyed his fleet at the Battle of Trafalgar. The threatened invasion of Britain would never take place.

Nelson on the deck of his flagship HMS Victory *during the Battle of Trafalgar.* ▲

1810 COLONIAL CONQUESTS

WITH FRENCH attention increasingly occupied on events in Europe, British forces took the opportunity to occupy colonies around the world. Many of these were returned at the end of the war, but some key additions were made to the empire. Ceylon and the Cape of Good Hope, which became the basis of South Africa, were taken from the Netherlands, Malta was occupied and retained the islands of Tobago, St Lucia and Mauritius were taken from France and Heligoland was also occupied. On the map these additions to the empire looked unimpressive, but they were to prove very significant. The age of sail was about to give way to the age of steam, and many of these colonies were to prove important refuelling stations throughout the nineteenth century.

1815 WATERLOO

WHEN NAPOLEON returned from Elba in March 1815, he knew that he had to defeat the enemy forces quickly as 200,000 Austrian and Russian troops were advancing from the east. He struck north immediately and met Wellington at Waterloo on 18 June 1815. The French army attacked the British line all day, but the British infantry held out against the French cavalry, just as Marlborough's forces had at Blenheim. At about 5.30 p.m. the Prussian army arrived and fell on the flank of the French. Wellington ordered a general advance and the French army collapsed. Napoleon fled and surrendered to a British warship. This time he was exiled to St Helena where he died in 1821.

1820s THE EASTERN QUESTION

FROM THE 1820s the Eastern Question loomed ever larger in the minds of British foreign secretaries. It concerned the fate of the provinces of the Turkish Empire in the Balkans. As Turkish authority grew weaker, public opinion in Britain usually sided with their Christian subjects, as in the case of Greece in the 1820s, but British

Turkish sultan Abdul Aziz. ▲

governments became increasingly concerned that the decline in Turkish power would lead to an advance by Russia towards the Mediterranean. British policy was normally to support the Sultan against attacks by Russia and attempts by his governors to break away from the authority of Istanbul. So, in spite of public opinion, when the governor of Egypt, Mehemet Ali tried to become independent in the 1830s and '40s, Britain backed the Sultan.

English statesman George Canning. ◀

1822 GEORGE CANNING

AFTER VISCOUNT Castlereagh's suicide in 1822, George Canning became foreign secretary. Although he had fought a duel with Castlereagh in 1809 and the two men had been enemies ever since, their approaches to foreign policy were very similar. Canning believed even more strongly than his predecessor that the great powers should not interfere in events outside their own countries. He supported the Greek rebellion in the 1820s, which led to the creation of the Greek state and he threatened to use the British navy to prevent intervention in the revolts that broke out against Spanish rule in South America. He said, 'I have brought in the New World to redress the balance of the Old'.

1830   LORD PALMERSTON

IN 1830 LORD Palmerston became British foreign secretary. Until his death in 1865 his polices dominated British foreign policy. Palmerston was a strange mixture. On the one hand he was a skilled diplomat, who settled the difficult question of Belgian independence in 1839, on the other hand he was a keen exponent of gunboat diplomacy and did not hesitate to use force to support British interests around the world. In 1850 he compelled the Greek government to pay compensation to an extremely dubious character, Don Pacifico, who claimed that he had lost documents worth more than £20,000 in a fire in Athens. At the same time Palmerston supported liberal revolutions throughout Europe. In 1860 he allowed British warships to protect Giuseppe Garibaldi as he crossed from Sicily to Naples during his campaigns in southern Italy.

1833   THE GREAT TREK

IN 1833 SLAVERY was abolished in the British Empire. The two areas most affected by this decision were the West Indies and South Africa. In the West Indies compensation was paid to slave owners, but in South Africa the slave-owning Boers left the colony and travelled north to set up two new states, the Orange Free State and the Transvaal. Their journey became known as the Great Trek and acquired great significance in the history of South Africa. The two new states retained their independence until the 1870s, when they were threatened by the Zulus. The refusal of the Boers to accept the abolition of slavery was the basis of the apartheid system, which was formalised in South Africa after the Second World War.

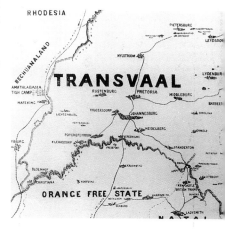

Map showing the Transvaal and the Orange Free State, where the Boers set up new colonies.

1845   QUEST FOR THE NORTH-WEST PASSAGE

IN 1819 Lieutenant John Franklin was part of an expedition sent to map the north coast of Canada. In 1825 he returned to explore the Mackenzie River and in 1845 led a third expedition to try to find the north-west passage in his two ships, the *Erebus* and the *Terror*. Although Franklin was well prepared, his ships became trapped in ice during the winter of 1846–47. He himself died in June 1847 and the rest of the party died the following winter. The bodies of some of the men have been discovered recently and they were found to have died from lead poisoning. Franklin had carried supplies of food in lead cans, unaware at that time of the risk that this entailed.

1854   THE CRIMEAN WAR

IN 1854 BRITAIN and France went to war with Russia to protect Turkey. Russia had occupied the provinces of Moldavia and Wallachia the previous year, in an effort to put pressure on Turkey to allow Orthodox priests the right to control the holy places in Jerusalem. This dispute triggered an

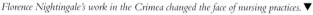

Florence Nightingale's work in the Crimea changed the face of nursing practices. ▼

invasion of the Crimea by a Franco-British force of 125,000 men, because the British government was afraid that Russia was planning to expand into the Balkans and take control of the Straits. The army spent two years besieging Sevastopol in appalling conditions and suffering very heavy losses from disease, relieved somewhat by the arrival of Florence Nightingale, who took over the hospital at Scutari. The British army displayed incredible heroism at the battles of the Alma, Balaclava and Inkermann, although the British commander, Lord Raglan, who had last seen action at the Battle of Waterloo in 1815, frequently referred to the French, Britain's allies, as the enemy.

1857 THE INDIAN MUTINY

BY 1857 the East India Company, still a private company, governed virtually the whole sub-continent of India. The only limit on its authority was the reduction of the monopoly of trade. Since 1800 it had vastly

The Indian Mutiny, which eventually led to British government over India. ▲

improved in its territories. Universities had been set up in Calcutta, Bombay and Madras, roads, railways and canals had been built and elementary-and secondary-school systems had been started. But in 1857 some soldiers of the East India Company's army mutinied. The most serious trouble occurred in northern India around Delhi, caused by the introduction of a new cartridge. Rumours spread that it was smeared with either pig fat, which was unclean to Muslims, or the fat of a cow, which was a sacred animal to Hindus. The revolt was ruthlessly suppressed, but it led to the end of the East India Company. In 1858 the British government took over the government of India.

1861 BRITAIN AND THE AMERICAN CIVIL WAR

IN 1861 CIVIL war broke out between the states of the USA. Thirteen slave-owning states in the south attempted to secede from the union and the president of the USA, Abraham Lincoln, sent the Federal army into action against them. The British government sympathised with the South, from where Britain obtained most of its cotton. When representatives of the Southern states (Confererates) were taken off a British ship, the *Trent*, by Federal officers, there appeared to be a risk that Britain might enter the war on the Confederate side, but the crisis blew over. It soon became clear that public opinion in Britain backed the North. Cotton workers in Lancashire accepted long lay-offs when the blockade of southern ports by the Federal navy prevented supplies reaching Britain.

1871 LIVINGSTONE

ALTHOUGH ONE reason for the Scramble for Africa was the wealth that Africa was believed to hold, some Europeans were in Africa for a very different reason. David Livingstone was a Scottish missionary and explorer who made extensive journeys across Africa in the mid-nineteenth century. In 1849 he crossed the Kalahari Desert and in 1853–56 crossed the entire continent, discovering the Victoria Falls on the way. In 1858 he set off from the Zambezi and discovered Lake Nyasa and in

Scottish missionary David Livingstone, who made explorations across Africa. ▲

1866 discovered Lake Tanganyika. By this time his travels had caught the attention of the world and when he failed to emerge from Tanganyika, H. M. Stanley, an American journalist, set out to find him. The two men met in the famous encounter on the shores of Lake Tanganyika in 1871.

1879 THE ZULU WAR

IN 1879 WAR broke out between the British in South Africa and the Zulus, led by King Ceshwayo. At the Battle of Insandhlwana, in January, a British column was massacred, but the Zulus lost so many men in the attack that Ceshwayo tried to restrain any further attacks. His decision was backed up by the experience of a Zulu army, which attacked a small British force at Rorke's Drift, a mission station. However, the British were not prepared to leave the Zulus alone. Reinforcements arrived from Britain and the Zulus were crushed at the battle of Ulundi in July. Ceshwayo surrendered the following month. During the Zulu War, the Boers had accepted the annexation of the South African Republic, but once the Zulu threat was removed they wanted independence.

British soldiers fighting the Zulu warriors. ▲

1880 THE FIRST BOER WAR

IN 1880 THE Boers in the Transvaal revolted against British rule. At
Laing's Nek and Majuba Hill they defeated British forces and the
government signed the Treaty of Pretoria in 1881, which gave the South
African Republic its independence. Foreign policy was to be handled by
the British government, however. In 1886 the whole situation was
transformed, when gold was discovered in the Transvaal. Miners rushed
from all over the world and the city of Johannesburg appeared almost over
night. By 1890 it had a population of 100,000 and there were 450 mining
companies operating in the area. The Boers treated the miners as
foreigners, *Uitlanders*,
they had no rights,
could not vote and
paid extra taxes.
They began to look
to Britain to
protect them.

1895 RAIDS IN AFRICA

THE JAMESON raid
of 1895 was a futile
attempt to create
trouble in the South
African Republic.
Cecil Rhodes believed
that there was an
impending revolution

*Gold mining in the Transvaal, South Africa; the discovery of gold
brought an influx of foreigners desperate for riches.* ▲

in Johannesburg and organised an armed raid by his friend Starr Jameson,
along with 600 men, into the Republic. Rhodes heard too late that the
revolt was not going to take place and tried to stop the raid. He failed and
it was a disaster. Jameson and his men were either killed or rounded up and
he was handed over for trial in Britain. In disgrace, Rhodes was forced to
resign as prime minister of Cape Colony; it was virtually the end of his
career. He died soon afterwards.

Industry and Invention

1802 FIRST IMAGES

IN 1802 THOMAS Wedgwood, son of the famous potter Josiah Wedgwood, reported his experiments in recording images on paper or leather sensitised with silver nitrate. Although he could record silhouettes of objects placed on the paper, he was not able to make them permanent and, to his disappointment, he failed to record a camera image. The first photograph was taken in 1826 or 1827 by the French physicist J. Niepce, using a pewter plate coated with a form of bitumen that hardened on exposure. His partner Louis Daguerre and the Englishman William Fox Talbot adopted silver compounds to give light-sensitivity, and the technique developed rapidly in the middle decades of the nineteenth century.

1804 THE FIRST RAILWAYS

RAILED TRUCKS had been used for mining as early as 1550 at Leberthal, Alsace and by Ralph Allen from Combe Down to the River Avon in 1731, but the first self-propelled locomotive ever to run on rails was that built by

French photography pioneer Louis Daguerre. ▶

Richard Trevithick, designer of the first self-propelled locomotive. ▲

Richard Trevithick (1771–1833) and was demonstrated over 14 km (9 miles) with a 10.2 tonnes load and 70 passengers in Penydaren, Glamorgan, on 21 February 1804. The earliest established railway to have a steam-powered locomotive was the Middleton Colliery Railway, set up by an Act of 1758 running between Middleton Colliery and Leeds Bridge, Yorkshire built by Matthew Murray in 1812. The Stockton and Darlington colliery line, County Durham, which ran from Shilden through Darlington to Stockton opened on 27 September 1825.

1807   HARNESSING THE WIND

BRITISH WINDMILL construction was improved considerably at this time by sail refinements and by the self-correcting device of the fantail, which kept the sails pointed into the wind. Spring sails replaced the traditional canvas rig with the equivalent of a modern venetian blind, the shutters of which could be opened or closed, to let the wind pass through or to provide a surface upon which its pressure could be exerted. Sail design was further improved with the 'patent' sail in 1807. Here the shutters were controlled on all the sails simultaneously by a single lever inside the mill. With these and other modifications, British windmills adapted to the increasing demands on power technology, until the use of wind power declined sharply in the nineteenth century with the spread of steam.

1829 THE GREAT BUILDER

THE FAMOUS engineer and inventor Isambard Kingdom Brunel was born in 1806. He began his working life by helping his father Sir Marc Brunel in the construction of the first tunnel to be built under the River Thames. In 1829 he won a competition for the Clifton Suspension Bridge and construction began in 1833. By then he had been appointed chief engineer to the Great Western Railway. Then,

The Clifton Suspension Bridge. ▲

at the age of 27, he was responsible for building the new line from London to Bristol with all its bridges, tunnels and viaducts. He built in all about 2,500 km (1,553 miles) of railway track in England and Wales and was a consultant for many overseas lines. He also constructed or improved many docks.

English scientist Michael Faraday, whose experiments with electricity and magnetism paved the way for further communication developments. ▲

1831 INVISIBLE POWER

THE PIONEERING work on the use of electricity was done by an international collection of scientists including Benjamin Franklin of Pennsylvania, Alessandro Volta of the University of Pavia, Italy and Michael Faraday of Britain. It was the latter who demonstrated the nature of the relationship between electricity and magnetism in 1831, and his experiments set off the development of both the mechanical generation of electric current and the utilisation of such current in electric motors. Both the generator and the motor depended on the rotation of a continuous coil of conducting wire between the poles of a strong magnet: turning the coil produces a current in it, while passing a current through the coil causes it to turn. Both generators and motors underwent substantial development in the mid-nineteenth century.

1837 OPENING UP THE WORLD

THE GREAT INNOVATIONS in communications technology derived from the new knowledge of electricity. The first was the electric telegraph, invented for use on the developing railway system by two British inventors, Sir William Cooke and Sir Charles Wheatstone, who collaborated on the work and took out a joint patent in 1837. Two years earlier, in 1835, the American inventor Samuel Morse devised the signalling code that was subsequently adopted all over the world. In 1843 Morse obtained financial support from the US government to build a demonstration telegraph system 60 km (35 miles) long. Wires were attached, by glass insulators, to poles alongside a railway. By 1858 the first transatlantic telegraph cable was laid bringing the main political and commercial centres into instantaneous communication.

1839 BIRTH OF THE BICYCLE

THE FIRST two-wheeled, rider-propelled bicycle was the wooden *draisienne*, invented by Baron Karl de Drais de Sauerbrun and exhibited in Paris on 6 April 1818. The seated rider propelled himself simply by paddling his feet against the ground. It was not until Scot Kirkpatrick

Macmillan's lever-driven bicycle. ▼

Macmillan completed four years of experiments in 1839 that a self-propelled bicycle appeared. Macmillan's machine had wheels rimmed with iron and, though lighter than the *draisienne*, it was still heavy. With a steerable front wheel about 75 cm (30 in) in diameter and a driven rear wheel of about 100 cm (40 in) in diameter, it could move at a brisk pace; in 1842 Macmillan successfully challenged a post carriage.

1840   MUCK AND BRASS

THE GREEKS and the Romans had used farm manure and vegetable waste as fertilisers to replace the chemicals extracted from the soil by growing plants. Eventually intense cultivation led to natural resources running out. South American guano (sea-bird droppings) were imported into England from 1840 to replenish the soil but by then it had been learnt that nitrogen, phosphorus and potassium were the key elements and so it became possible to replace natural fertilisers by synthetic. The widespread use of phosphate fertilisers was due to the work of Sir John Bennet Lawes who used a bedroom in his ancestral home as a laboratory. In 1840 he patented a process for making a phosphate fertiliser and in 1843, with Sir John Gilbert, founded the famous Rothamsted Experimental Station.

1856   FROM A MESS TO SUCCESS

THE FIRST DYES to be used were all naturally occurring substances such as indigo (from woad) and Tyrian purple (from a sea snail). William Henry Perkins did much to change the colour of the world in 1856 when he made the first synthetic dye. The discovery was made by accident when he was an assistant at the Royal College of

The world's first synthetic dye was created in 1856. ▶

Chemistry in London. While trying to make the white solid, quinine, he ended up with a blackish mess from which he extracted a purple substance, which he found would dye silk. He patented the product and began manufacturing the dye. The dye was known as mauve, Queen Victoria wore a dress dyed with it and the penny purple postage stamps issued in 1881 owed their colour to it.

1863   GOING UNDERGROUND

THE FIRST underground line in the world was in London, and opened in 1863. The linking of two terminal stations at the West End and the City was achieved in 1884 with the opening of the Metropolitan Railway. Early development of underground railways in London was helped by the clay on which the city is built, which was easy to excavate, the spoil providing raw material to make bricks for lining the tunnel walls. Improved deep-tunnelling techniques after the First World War allowed a rapid expansion of the underground network, while the Piccadilly, Bakerloo, Central and Northern lines opened up hundreds of square miles of rural Middlesex and Essex for suburbanisation.

Construction work on the London Underground near King's Cross. ▼

The invention of the torpedo changed the nature of battle at sea. ◄

1866 THE BIRTH OF THE TORPEDO

THE CIGAR-SHAPED underwater guided missile known as the torpedo was invented by a British engineer, Robert Whitened, in 1866. His first design was about 4.26 m (14 ft) long and 36 cm (14 in) in diameter. It carried an 8.16-kg (18-lb) warhead of dynamite, was powered by a propeller driven by a compressed air engine and was held at a set depth by a hydrostatic valve that operated horizontal rudders at the rear. Vertical rudders, controlled by a pre-set gyroscope to give lateral steering were added in 1896. The early torpedoes were launched from specially designed torpedo boats. Modern torpedoes are driven by battery-operated electric motors, have full guidance systems and can also be launched from submarines and aircraft.

1892 THE THERMOS

THE THERMOS vacuum flask was invented by the British chemist and physicist Sir James Dewar in 1892. He devised it to preserve liquefied gases by preventing the transfer of heat from the surroundings to the liquid. The evacuated space between the walls is practically a non-conductor of heat; radiation is reduced to a minimum by silvering the glass or steel from which the walls are made. The idea was patented by a German glass-blower Reinhold Burger in 1904 who helped Dewar put it into practice and the proprietary name Thermos, from *therm*, was suggested by a member of the public in a competition.

Culture, Arts and Leisure

1804 'JERUSALEM'

THE ENGRAVER, poet and artist William Blake (1757–1827) was an enigmatic genius, unrecognised in his own lifetime. He claimed to see angels, developed his own complex mythology and at the low-point of his life, found himself arrested on trumped-up charges of sedition. His pictures were of a kind never seen before and his verses were stark and complex, and grow more influential with each century that passes. But it is his poem 'Jerusalem' (1804) – with its reference to 'dark satanic mills' – that is best known, part of a cycle of poems about Milton written and engraved between 1803–08. The now-famous tune was finally added to turn it into a patriotic song during the First World War.

The Brighton Pavilion was built by John Nash for the extravagent Prince Regent. ▼

1815   BRIGHTON PAVILION

WHILE GEORGE III (1738–1820) remained insane, his profligate son
George (1762–1830) acted as Prince Regent, stamping his style on the
architecture of London, Brighton and Bath. His friend, the architect John
Nash (1752–1835), who was working in partnership with the landscape
gardener Humphrey Repton (1752–1818), influenced him greatly. In
1815, Nash began what would be eight years work remodelling the
Prince's notorious Pavilion in Brighton, mixing neo-classical style with
Gothic, Chinese, Egyptian and Indian influences. It was designed, it must
be remembered, for a flamboyant prince who left £10,000 in small change
in his various suits after his death in 1830.

1818   FRANKENSTEIN

APART FROM BEING the wife of the great romantic poet Percy Bysshe
Shelley, Mary Shelley (1797–1851) was the daughter of two radicals – the
pioneer feminist Mary Wollstonecraft and the writer William Godwin. Her
greatest work, the gothic novel *Frankenstein, or The Modern Prometheus* was
begun when she, Byron and Shelley were writing ghost stories to pass the
time during a summer in Switzerland. She wrote several other novels after
her husband's death, and the death of two children and two miscarriages,
but none caught the imagination of the public like the story of the
monster who creates horror in anyone who sees it, but desperately needs
to be loved.

1821   DEATH OF KEATS

THE ROMANTIC POET John Keats (1795–1821) died in Rome of
tuberculosis at the age of only 25. He had only given up his work as an
apprentice to an apothecary-surgeon five years before to concentrate on
poetry, yet his work marked the full flowering of the Romantic movement – in fact most of his great poems, like 'The Eve of St Agnes' and
'Ode to a Nightingale', were written in two years of productivity in
1818 and 1819. Keats struggled with money, as well as with his love for
Fanny Brawne; Percy Bysshe Shelley was drowned in the Bay of Spezia
in 1822; and Lord Byron died of fever, fighting for the Greek nationalists
in 1824.

Madame Tussaud, owner of the famous waxworks in London's Baker Street. ▶

1835   MADAME TUSSAUD'S

THERE HAD BEEN waxworks in London before, notably at Westminster Abbey – where the unkempt representations of royalty were known as the 'ragged regiment' – before Madam Tussaud (Marie Grosholtz, 1760–1850) set herself up in England in 1802. She had been imprisoned for three months in Paris during the French Revolution, and had even modelled some of the revolutionary leaders from their heads after being taken from the scaffold. Her collection of 300 figures was first seen at the Lyceum in the Strand, but moved to a permanent home in London's Baker Street in 1835. The Chamber of Horrors was opened there, and included the knife from the Paris guillotine that had executed 22,000 people in the Revolution.

1836   THOMAS CARLYLE

THE SOCIAL THEORIST, historian and writer Thomas Carlyle (1795–1881) brought himself to the attention of the country with his 1836 study *The French Revolution* – 'itself a kind of revolution', he wrote later. In this, and later works, he attacked unfettered industrial capitalism, affirming moral certainties at a time of revolutionary change, and insisting on the importance of the individual. He was fascinated by heroism, and his lectures *On Heroes, Hero-Worship and the Heroic in History* (1841) marked the beginning of his search for strong leaders, which was so influential on the Victorians who came after him. Those deeply influenced by his work included the novelist Charles Dickens (1812–70) and the critic John Ruskin (1819–1900).

1836   NEW HOUSES OF PARLIAMENT

PARLIAMENT BURNED down in 1834, and as many as 97 architects entered the competition that was held to replace it. The winner was Charles Barry (1795–1860), with his design that incorporated Elizabethan and medieval styles to blend in with Westminster Hall and Westminster Abbey next door. Barry actually preferred designing classical buildings, like the Reform Club in London (1837–41), but was also responsible for one of the first Gothic-revival buildings in Britain, St Peter's Church in Brighton (1823–26). He was helped in the design for Parliament by the great Gothic revivalist Augustus Pugin (1812–52), who was later driven mad by his own eccentricities. Once built, the Victoria Tower, opposite Big Ben, was then the tallest building in the world.

The Houses of Parliament as they look today. ▼

England's greatest novelist and social commentator, Charles Dickens. ▲

1843   *A CHRISTMAS CAROL*

THE REPUTATION of the great novelist and social reformer Charles Dickens had been made by the publication of *The Pickwick Papers* in 1836–37, but it was his novella *A Christmas Carol* (1843) that first made the link between Dickens and Christmas. His Christmas stories were collected together later and published in 1852, most of them ending – like the first – with a glowing sense of *bonhomie*. His voluminous novels, stories and magazines changed the way we live, and the monthly publication of his stories held mass audiences enthralled on both sides of the Atlantic. Large crowds gathered at American ports to read the latest instalments as they arrived – or to hear him read from his own works towards the end of his life. He died exhausted at the young age of 58.

1846   **THE BRONTË SISTERS**

Charlotte Brontë. ▼

WHEN THE BRONTË sisters, Charlotte (1816–55), Emily (1818–48) and Anne (1820–49), published their first poems in 1846, they used the androgynous pseudonyms Currer, Ellis and Acton Bell. They used the same names the following year when all three published novels. Charlotte's *Jane Eyre* and Emily's *Wuthering Heights* were both immediate successes, and Anne's *Agnes Grey* remains in print a century and a half later. Within two years, their identities had been revealed – causing astonishment that a woman could have written a novel as brutal as *Wuthering Heights*. By this time Emily, Anne and their alcoholic brother Branwell (1817–48) were dead. Charlotte survived until 1855, but succumbed to complications in pregnancy.

The Pre-Raphaelite Dante Gabriel Rossetti. ▶

1848 THE PRE-RAPHAELITES

WHAT KEATS and Scott had done for literature, the Pre-Raphaelite Brotherhood was doing for painting. The original members of the brotherhood, John Everett Millais (1829–96), William Holman Hunt (1827–1910) and Dante Gabriel Rossetti (1828–82), were admirers of fifteenth-century Italy and set about illustrating medieval life, or high moral subjects, with their strong colours and detailed illustrations. The brotherhood began in 1848 and dissolved during the 1850s, but its members continued to react against the ugliness of modern life. They were a formative influence on the poet, designer and philosopher William Morris (1834–96) – whose wife Jane was a regular model for Pre-Raphaelite portraits – as well as the Arts and Crafts movement and utopian socialism that he inspired.

1852 MUSIC HALLS

WHEN PUB LANDLORD Charles Morton (1819–1905) took over the Canterbury Arms in Lambeth in 1849, he added popular musical evenings to the food and drink. It was so successful that, in 1852, he opened the first music hall – the Canterbury – offering sing-songs and variety entertainment for the working classes. Morton was given the title 'Father of the Halls', though a rival contender to the Canterbury was the Evans Music-and-Supper Rooms in King Street, Covent Garden, where the entertainment was considered so shocking that women could only watch from behind a screen. Music halls, with names like 'Palladium', 'Alhambra', 'Empire' or 'Hippodrome' were soon more numerous than theatres, but they were overshadowed by cinema and radio after 1914.

1868   *THE MOONSTONE*

THE DETECTIVE story, where one intelligent outsider is able to see through the mists of confusion, was the invention of the American writer Edgar Allan Poe (1809–49) in the 1840s, but it was Wilkie Collins (1824–89) – the son of a landscape painter – who made the idea British. His novel *The Moonstone* in 1868 introduced the character of Sergeant Cuff, and was serialised in Dickens' magazine *All the Year Round*. His other great success was *The Woman in White* (1860). Collins used his own advice to himself: 'Make 'em laugh, make 'em cry, make 'em wait'. His career petered out in ill-health and private confusion: at one point he shared his home with two of his mistresses simultaneously.

1877   WHISTLER VS RUSKIN

WHISTLER WAS an American by birth, but settled in London in the 1860s under the influence of the Pre-Raphaelite group. His almost abstract and atmospheric paintings, often with musical names like his series of *Nocturnes*, changed the direction of British art – but also infuriated the great critic, John Ruskin. In fact the disagreement between them ended up in court after Ruskin visited Whistler's 1877 exhibition at the Grosvenor gallery and accused him of 'throwing a pot of paint in the public's face'. Ruskin was having one of his periodic breakdowns, and was unable to defend the libel action in person, but Whistler was awarded damages of only a halfpenny. Despite this setback, Ruskin's resistance to industrial culture remains a major influence a century later.

1880   W. G. GRACE

WHEN DR WILLIAM Gilbert Grace (1848–1915) began his career in first- class cricket at the age of 16, the game was still rough and ready. By the time he retired at the age of 50, the rules were set and – partly through his influence – cricket was established as England's national summer game. He became the most famous cricketer in history, winning a total of 54,904 runs in his first-class career – including 126 centuries and 877 catches. He captained England 13 times, but the pinnacle of his career came when he scored the first-ever test century, against Australia in 1880. In 1903, he also became the first president of the English Bowling Association.

William Morris was renowned for his textiles, art and writing. ▲

1890 *NEWS FROM NOWHERE*

THE INFLUENCE of William Morris on poetry, furniture, printing, interior decor and politics has been immense. His horrified reaction to overwrought Victorian design led to a fascination with the simplicity of the Middle Ages. He was influenced by the Pre-Raphaelites, and converted their ideas into poetry – including long translations from Icelandic – and political tracts, like *The Dream of John Ball* (1886–87). In his utopian socialist novel *News from Nowhere* (1890), he imagined waking up a century later, and travelling down the Thames from his homes in Hammersmith and Oxfordshire, finding London transformed into a pastoral idyll of his own Arts and Crafts movement. His wallpaper company made a fortune, and he died at the relatively young age of 63 – according to his doctor 'of being William Morris'.

1891 SHERLOCK HOLMES

THE GREAT DETECTIVE Sherlock Holmes is probably among the most imitated and parodied characters in literature. He and Dr Watson appeared for the first time from the pen of the doctor-turned-writer Arthur Conan Doyle (1859–1930) in the novel *A Study in Scarlet*, published in *Beeton's Christmas Annual* for 1887. But it was not until the short stories began for *The Strand Magazine* in 1891 that Holmes acquired a mass audience. Doyle borrowed some of the literary method from Poe, and Holmes's scientific method from one of his teachers at Edinburgh University, but tried to kill him off in *The Memoirs of Sherlock Holmes* (1894). Popular demand brought Holmes back from the dead, and by 1927 there had been four novels and 56 short stories.

Conan Doyle's greatest character, Sherlock Holmes. ▲

1895   THE IMPRISONMENT OF OSCAR WILDE

OSCAR WILDE (1854–1900) was the best-known and one of the most outrageous members of the Aesthetic movement, which espoused art for art's sake. The year 1895 was the most important of his life: not only was his brilliant comedy *The Importance of Being Earnest* an enormous success, but he also ended up in Reading Gaol. Although his homosexuality was an open secret, he made the mistake of suing for libel the Marquis of Queensberry (1844–1900) – the father of his lover – over a note accusing him of being a 'somdomite'. He lost the case and became the first person prosecuted under the new homosexuality laws. He died in Paris five years later, a tragic and broken figure.

Oscar Wilde was the first man to be imprisoned under the new homosexuality laws in Britain. ▲

Religions, Belief and Thought

1833 THE OXFORD MOVEMENT

THIS MOVEMENT was to have a great effect on the Church of England. John Keble (1792-1866) preached a sermon called 'National Apostasy' in July 1833. His sermon raised the question of reform within the Church. From Oxford in 1833 emerged 'Tracts for the Times', a series distributed to the clergy. They advocated a *via media* (or 'middle way') between Protestantism and Catholicism. In the first tract, its author John Newman (1804–90) had said 'choose your side', for it was very difficult to remain neutral. Tract 90 in 1841, was the final straw, Newman's words brought cries of 'Popery' and 'Antichrist at the door'; various clergy objected and extracted a promise that no more tracts would be written. Newman felt the ever-growing attraction of Rome and in 1845 he joined the Catholic Church.

1844 WILLIAM GLADSTONE

WILLIAM EWART Gladstone (1809–98) was strongly Anglican though he acquired Nonconformist aspirations towards the end of his life. During his life, or at least until 1844, he claimed to see himself as an Anglican who happened to be a politician. In truth, regardless of his political creed, he was devoted to Christian charitable concerns but the ambiguity of his Christianity revealed itself in his approach to slavery. (His father had been a slave owner.) He recognised the validity for the disestablishment of the Anglican Church in Wales and presided over the disestablishment of the Church in Ireland (1871). He was a true missionary, in that he sought to live out Christian principles in a political context and in such an overt manner that he was, probably, one of the greatest men of his time.

1848 THE COMMUNIST MANIFESTO

THE WORD 'Socialism' first appeared in France in the 1830s to describe ideas and people opposed to a market economy that benefited the rich and

Prime minister William Gladstone. ▲

Karl Marx, who advocated a communist society and condemned the capitalist regime. ◄

powerful. Some socialists advocated the abolition of property and were called 'communists'. It was in this context that *The Communist Manifesto* appeared in 1848. Marx (1818–83) appeared to believe that revolution would sweep away capitalist society and create a new economic order. In effect, Marx was the founder of what was essentially a new religion. This included its own mythology, its Chosen People (the working class) whose entry into the Promised Land of a just society would be reward for their pilgrimage. The philosopher Bertrand Russell (1872–1970) believed Marx had too many shortcomings, he said Marx was 'too practical, too much wrapped up in the problems of his time'.

1850s SCIENTIFIC AND CULTURAL CHANGE

INDIVIDUAL DETERMINISM, which was growing at this time, was very different from the Christian ideas that lay behind the Enlightenment or the free-thinking individuals envisaged by Renaissance ideals. Science struck its heaviest blows at religious belief in the West by undermining the authority of Scripture. Christianity had grown lazy, being concerned either with its own internal disputes or focused on social welfare and missionary work. The authority of the Catholic Church and the emphasis on Scripture by the Protestants inhibited any possible critique of biblical revelation. The acceptance of the literal truth of Scripture essential to nineteenth century, had ironically not been part of the teaching of the early church. The scientists, believing in individual determinism, slowly replaced the priests as the keyholders to the future and a better life. The power of individualism was to become the root of post-modern thinking in the late-twentieth century.

1859 MAKING OF MAN: CHARLES DARWIN

DARWIN (1809–92) was probably the most popular influential scientist of the century. His book *The Origin of Species* (1859) set out his theory of evolution though he did not use the word in the early editions of his book. In 1871 *The Descent of Man* made explicit his theories of natural selection as they applied to humans. Natural selection acted as a hammer blow against Christians and Jews who accepted the literal truth of the Bible. Darwin made it impossible for any thoughtful person to believe the Bible was literally true from cover to cover (though many did so and some even continue to do so). A turning point was a debate where a colleague of Darwin, Thomas Huxley, verbally tore the Bishop of Oxford, Samuel Wilberforce, to shreds. Darwin became a reverent agnostic, he could 'hardly see how anyone ought to wish Christianity to be true; for if it be so, the plain language of the text seems to show that the men who do not believe… would be everlastingly punished. And this is a damnable doctrine.'

Darwin's studies led him to form his theory of the 'survival of the fittest'. ▶

Slums in London, reflecting what Arnold called 'vast, miserable, unmanageable masses of sunken people'. ◀

1859 THE EVANGELICALS

THE EVANGELICAL experience was closely bound up with conversion and had less interest in ecclesiastical authority or the sacraments. Early evangelicals acquired a sense of responsibility to the weak and exploited and found a cause in the slave trade. By 1850 evangelical teaching had been accepted in the Church of England but it followed a quieter path. Later in the century (*c.* 1859) a second evangelical resurgence arrived from America. The hymn 'Stand up, stand up for Jesus' is one that remains from that era, but the zeal and enthusiasm of the people caused some staid English evangelicals to hold back. Lord Shaftesbury (1801–85) was one of the leading evangelicals of this period. He was, like his co-evangelicals, committed to the poor and unwittingly laid the foundations of the twentieth-century welfare state.

1869 VICTORIAN COUNTRYMEN: MISSIONARIES AT HOME

MATTHEW ARNOLD (1822–88) believed the 'peace of God' was the Christian phrase for civilisation. In *Culture and Anarchy* (1869) he described London's East End as containing 'these vast, miserable, unmanageable masses of sunken people'. In reality he battled with belief and un-belief and gave up orthodox Christianity as a 'fond but beautiful dream'. Charles Dickens (1812–70) was less influenced, if influenced at all, by institutional religion. His 'mission' was to draw attention to the hypocrisy and exploitation in society. Dickens was a prophet, his novels personified social evils and revealed him as an analyst of society. He was religious but attacked the narrowness of Christian interpretations of the New Testament. He was a Christian, intent on revealing the devils at home rather than the devils overseas.

1879　JOHN HENRY NEWMAN

NEWMAN (1801–90) had fascinated many while he was an Anglican and still retained that interest when he became a Catholic. Originally an evangelical, he became vicar of the university church in Oxford and ceased to be a Calvinist. While working with Keble he edited 66 tracts in two years. His Protestant friends and admirers were amazed that so articulate and intelligent a man should affirm dogmas and miracles they believed to be nonsense. Newman, a liberal, had submitted to an authoritarian Church but it was not until Leo XIII became pope that the official attitude to him

Cardinal John Henry Newman. ▲

eased enough for him to be acknowledged a true Catholic. In 1879 he was made a cardinal; for him it was a symbol that he was recognised and accepted by the Church he had joined.

CHAPTER 8

The Twentieth Century

Power and Politics

1901   EDWARD VII

EDWARD VII, the eldest son of Queen Victoria, came to the throne in his sixtieth year – 1901. The beginning of the Edwardian era witnessed the build-up to the First World War. Edward, popular among his subjects, though tiresome to his mother for his playboy lifestyle, nevertheless proved to have an asset for his foreign-policy ventures. In 1903 he visited Paris to promote the Entente Cordiale between the United Kingdom and France successfully. In 1907 the Triple Entente, which now included Russia, was recognised. Although no explicit promise was made by the British to go to war if one of the other two powers was attacked there seemed little reason to believe that would not be the case. The *rapprochement* between the three states certainly raised German suspicions.

Edward VII succeeded Queen Victoria in 1901. ▲

1914   THE START OF WAR

ON 28 JUNE 1914, Archduke Franz Ferdinand, the heir to the Austrian throne, was shot dead by a Serbian protester. It was to trigger a four-year-long savage and cruel bloodbath to be inflicted on the world (mostly Europe) by competing royal houses. The Austro-Hungarian Empire went to war with Serbia; Russia, Britain's ally, went to Serbia's defence. Germany then agreed to aid its Austrian ally. Within months Britain, like the rest of Europe, had been drawn into war. At first the conflict was popular. By the end of war almost 10 million had lost their lives. Britain, and soldiers from its empire, sustained the fifth-largest total loss of life. Never has the fate of an archduke been so momentous.

1915 ASQUITH AND LLOYD GEORGE

OVER £40 BILLION was spent by the major powers to sustain the war effort between 1914–18. Britain spent the second-highest amount, £7.8 billion. Despite the propaganda that Britain was at one during the war, this was evidently not the case. No more was this better demonstrated than in government. When the war began Britain was ruled by the Liberal party headed by Asquith, but internal factions led to this becoming a coalition government by 1915. Asquith differed from other politicians, including Lloyd-George and Winston Churchill, about the need for conscription. Lloyd-George who was at first thought to have opposed the war, publicly and unequivocally supported conscription and by December 1916 had replaced Asquith.

The assassination of Archduke Franz Ferdinand in Sarajevo. ▲

1917 GEORGE V

AN AVID stamp collector, George V was a popular monarch due to his sense of royal duty during the First World War. Also an emperor of India, the first four years of his rule, which began in 1910, witnessed two general elections, the establishment of the Union of South Africa and a Home Rule Bill for Ireland pass through Parliament. His devotion to duty was evidenced when he formed the National government in 1931 in response to the economic crisis of the time. In 1917 George V was responsible for changing the Germanic name of the royal house from Saxe-Coburg to Windsor, a name that remains today.

During the First World War, women began to take on roles traditionally associated with men. ▲

1918   THE RISE OF WOMEN

IF THERE COULD be such a thing as a beneficiary from the First World War, women were one group whose standing in society certainly grew as a result of the war. The emancipation of women, or at least the beginning of the process, can be directly linked to the Great War. It seems to have acted as a catalyst, vastly speeding up the process of female liberation. Women's work at the front and at home in offices, transport, munitions and other factories, led to a breaking down of the sex barriers. Previously engineering work was seen as the preserve of men. After the war this was no longer the case. By 1918, the Representation of the People Act handed the vote to most women aged 30 and over. Women over 21 got the vote in 1928.

1924   THE FIRST LABOUR-PARTY
GOVERNMENT

THE LABOUR party came to replace the Liberals as one of the two major political parties in Britain after the First World War. Renamed in 1906, from the Labour Representation Committee formed in

Ramsay Macdonald, the first Labour PM. ▲

1900, the Labour party pulled together factions from various strands of the working-class movement such as the trade unions and the Fabian Society. The party had served in the wartime coalition government and became popular after the war. The fall of the Liberals left a political vacuum. Labour, in a move that would be repeated in the 1990s, broadened its appeal to the middle classes making it more electable. In 1924, the first Labour government, headed by Ramsay MacDonald, came to power. A second government was formed in 1929, which lasted until 1931.

1936 EDWARD VIII AND CONSTITUTIONAL CRISIS

IN JANUARY 1936, Edward VIII came to the throne. His brief reign came to an end before the year was out. Although the story of his relationship with the American divorcee Mrs Wallis Simpson has often been told as one of history's greatest-ever love stories it also sparked a constitutional crisis among the British Establishment. The

Edward VIII, who abdicated after just a few months on the throne to marry divorcee Mrs Simpson. ▲

power of Parliament over the monarchy was proven when the prime minister Stanley Baldwin, backed by the Church, forbade the king from marrying Mrs Simpson if he wanted to remain king. Edward VIII chose to abdicate. Subsequently, it appears the politicians were fearful of Edward's pro-Nazi leanings though whether they used the marriage crisis as a pretext to remove him from the throne is still unclear.

1939 WAR AGAIN

ON 3 SEPTEMBER 1939 – two days after the Nazis invaded Poland –
Britain was again at war with Germany. By April 1940, the German armies
had successfully invaded Norway, Finland and Denmark and also claimed
their first British political casualty – Neville Chamberlain. In response to
criticism of his handling of the campaign in Scandinavia, Chamberlain
resigned. Chamberlain will always be associated with the discredited policy
of appeasement towards Hitler. Strongly opposed by politicians such as
Churchill, appeasement was actually quite popular among the people at
the time. The guarantee of peace Chamberlain secured from Hitler in 1938
at the time of the Munich crisis
though, proved to be a mirage.
Chamberlain joined the Churchill
government but resigned just
before his death in October 1940.

1940 WINSTON CHURCHILL

A POLITICIAN with a patchy
record before the outbreak of war,
Winston Churchill emerged at the
end of war as a politician whose
status was assured both in Britain
and abroad. Elected as a
Conservative MP in 1901,
Churchill crossed the floor of the
House to join the Liberals in
1904. He was also elected as a
constitutionalist in the 1920s. A
consistent opponent of

*The great political leaders of the 1940s (l to r):
Churchill, Roosevelt and Stalin.* ▲

appeasement during the 1930s, Churchill was appointed First Lord of the
Admiralty in 1939. When Chamberlain resigned as wartime prime
minister he took over the reigns of government in May 1940. During the
war he established himself as a great politician and orator. His reputation
abroad was secured with his central role in the peace negotiations.

1945 THE END OF THE WAR

BY THE END of 1945 the war in both Europe and in Japan was over. In Britain there would be a marked swing to the left with the landslide election of a Labour government later in the same year. Labour's massive victory – they won 394 seats, to the Tories' 210 – represented a new direction being taken in British politics. The politics of an interventionist State had been given credence during the

Celebrations in the street on VE Day in 1945. ▲

war and Churchill's Cabinet included left-wing MPs such as Ernest Bevin. The new breed of Tories emerging also advocated a stronger role for the State after the war, both politically and economically. Seen in this context, Churchill's defeat at the polls, despite leading Britain to victory, seems less of a surprise.

1948 NATIONALISATION

THE LABOUR party, under Clement Atlee, won the 1945 general election and embarked upon one of its major policy initiatives – nationalisation. In basic terms this meant the purchase of private industry and business by the State so that they could provide, their supporters claimed, for the national good. The rail, gas, coal and electricity industries were among those purchased by the State. The National Health Service was established in 1948 and has been state-owned ever since becoming the sacred cow of British politics. A lot of policies of nationalisation were reversed by the Thatcher government in the 1980s, who sold many of the above industries back to the private sector.

1950s   THE POLITICS OF CONSENSUS

THE 1950s and early '60s marked a conciliatory time in British politics with successive Labour and Conservative governments embarking on very similar social and economic policies. This was the period of consensus politics where the tenets of social democracy and a strong welfare state were generally supported across the political spectrum. Keynesian economics were pursued by both parties in an attempt to sustain full employment. A new term, 'Butskellism', entered the dictionary. A hybrid of a Conservative and a Labour ministers' names, Butler and Gaitskell, it was meant to demonstrate the closeness with the which the parties operated. Both parties advocated state intervention to deal with economic downturns. Internally it was a time of peace, including in Northern Ireland.

1952   ELIZABETH II

ELIZABETH II is the fourth monarch from the manufactured dynastic House of Windsor. Her family's name was originally Saxe-Coburg but this was changed in 1917 as its German associations were seen as inappropriate during the First World War, where the main enemy was Germany. She came to the throne in 1952, the year Britain tested its first atomic bomb, and has survived 10 prime ministers, beginning with Winston Churchill. Tony Blair is the eleventh head of government during her reign. Her rule has overseen vast changes in Britain, politically, culturally and socially, as well as many changes to the royal family. Although its fundamental role has not changed for many years, its tone has. Since the mid-1990s there have been increasing calls for Britain to become a republic.

The coronation of Elizabeth II in 1953. ▲

Conflict grew between the British and Egyptian governments over control of the Suez Canal. ◀

1956 SUEZ

FROM THE END of the Second World War, Britain had retreated from its colonies unable or unwilling to maintain an empire. India – the jewel in Britain's colonial crown since 1858 – was granted self-government in 1947. Countries around the world soon followed. But its rapidly diminishing world status was most clearly brought home to Britain during the Suez Canal Crisis of 1956, when Britain, which had controlled the canal since 1875, pulled out its troops in 1956, the Egyptian government nationalised Suez. British prime minister Anthony Eden responded by sending in troops to regain control. What followed was worldwide condemnation. The United States, Britain's main ally, signalled its disgust, sterling was threatened and British troops were ignominiously withdrawn.

1957 HAROLD MACMILLAN

HAROLD MACMILLAN was the Conservative prime minister between 1957 and 1963. His premiership oversaw political trends that marked post-war Britain. Elected in the wake of the Suez disaster he came to power on the back of the slogan 'You've never had it so good' and a national mood

Prime minister Harold Macmillan, one of the great leaders of post-war Britain. ▲

reflecting a desire for domestic prosperity. Consumer-led affluence continued to create a feel-good factor following the years of war and post-war austerity. He advanced Britain's retreat from its colonies with his 'Wind of Change' speech in Africa and set Britain on course to gain entry to the European Economic Community though this was vetoed by the French. Macmillan's rule was undermined by both illness and a spy scandal involving his war minister, John Profumo. He retired in 1963.

1957   TREATY OF ROME

THE THEORY of building new European political institutions began to take formal shape in 1957 with the signing of the Treaty of Rome by six countries. Britain was not one of those six countries. The government, led by Harold Macmillan, refused to join. The signatories – France, Germany, Italy, Netherlands, Belgium and Luxembourg – signed up to a treaty that established a Common Market and began the process of developing pan-

European institutions. From this beginning, the concept of Europe has now grown massively in importance and scale. Areas of policy include the Common Agricultural Policy and a Common Fisheries Policy. The Common Market became the European Community in 1967 and the European Union in 1993.

1960s DE GAULLE

IN 1960 BRITAIN was a founder member of the European Free Trade Association. This comprised seven European nations and was formed after the failure of non-EEC members to extend the area of free trade throughout western Europe. Its remit focused solely on economic matters. By 1961, however, Britain had indicated it wanted to join the Common Market as a solution to economic difficulties but its application was rejected. In 1967, under Labour, Britain applied again, but was again rebuffed. Britain accused the French leader de Gaulle of blocking its attempts to join the

French leader Charles de Gaulle, who was accused of hindering Britain's entry to the Common Market. ▲

Common Market. Some saw this as a blatant anti-British stance by de Gaulle, but it is more likely the French premier feared Britain's relationship would threaten France's more independent foreign policy.

1973 BRITAIN JOINS THE COMMON MARKET

IN 1973 AFTER YEARS of trying, Britain, under Conservative prime minister Ted Heath, finally joined the Common Market. Along with Denmark and Ireland, who joined at the same time, the EEC swelled to a membership of nine. But membership did not stop the debate in Britain about whether or not it should belong to a pan-European political organisation. In 1975 the country went to the polls in a ground-breaking referendum to vote on continued membership. A bitter campaign was fought with the political parties largely split about which way to vote. The result was a resounding 'yes' as two-thirds voted in favour, but the splits on Europe hardly became less rancorous in succeeding decades.

1979   WINTER OF DISCONTENT

IN 1976 BRITAIN'S deteriorating economic position was emphasised when the Labour government went to the International Monetary Fund for financial assistance. By 1979 the Conservatives had been returned to government after a sustained period of industrial unrest, known as the 'winter of discontent', brought down the Labour government. An ailing economy refused to pick up despite the Wilson and the James Callaghan administrations watering down wage demands from the trade unions. But fears over jobs and wages refused to go away and led to a rash of strikes in the public sector in 1979. Even council gravediggers went on strike. As well as ushering in a new government, the winter of discontent marked the end for the use of Keynesian economic policies in Britain.

1979   MRS THATCHER

IN 1979 BRITAIN elected its first woman prime minister – Margaret Thatcher. She became the longest-serving and one of the most controversial prime ministers of the century. Mrs Thatcher advocated right-wing politics, a monetarist policy, sustained privatisation and a more vigorous foreign policy, especially in Europe, which earned her the title of 'Iron Lady' abroad. Her

Marines in training during the Falklands War in 1982. ▲

government's policies were deeply unpopular at first, but she was returned to Number Ten on the back of populist opinion after the Falklands dispute with Argentina in 1982. Although she commanded large Commons' majorities that enabled her to pursue her policies, her vote in the country was less impressive. She was driven from office by her own party in November 1990.

1986 EUROPEAN ACT

'NO! NO! NO!' thundered Margaret Thatcher in 1990 when asked about her government's position on the prospect of more political control passing from national government to Brussels. Opposition to greater political integration in Europe was well documented during her 11-year reign as prime minister and led to many

Margaret Thatcher, Britain's first female prime minister. ▲

conflicts with other European Community countries especially over budgetary contributions. On political integration she demurred; economically she promoted trade between the European partners. She vetoed Britain joining the European Exchange Rate Mechanism until only a month before her resignation in October 1990. However, in 1986 Mrs Thatcher signed Britain up to the Single European Act, which gave fresh impetus to closer economic integration by planning the creation of a single market by 1 January 1993.

The royal family has seen a decline in popularity over the last decade. ▲

1990s   THE CHANCES OF A REPUBLIC?

THE DECLINE in fortunes of the monarchy allied with doubts over the usefulness of its role in the modern age provoked increasing calls among some sectors of the British public for the restoration of a republic. Although support for the retention of the monarchy remains in the majority, there is little doubt that opposition to the institution, at least in its present form, has grown in the last years of the twentieth century. At the beginning of the 1990s, support for the monarchy was between 80 and 90 per cent. According to some polls, by 1997 this had slipped to around two-thirds. The royal family, in attempts to show it could adapt in the after-math of the death of Diana, Princess of Wales, showed signs of some modernisation, albeit largely cosmetic.

1997 THE END OF TORY RULE

THE CONSERVATIVE party, first under Margaret Thatcher and then John Major, had ruled Britain for 18 consecutive years between 1979 and 1997. Four successive elections were won by the Tories. But on 1 May 1997, the party was all but wiped from the political map of Britain. In the fallout from the Labour landslide victory it was clear this was no ordinary defeat for the Tories. They returned just 165 MPs to the Commons, losing 171 seats all in all. No Conservative MPs were returned in either Scotland or Wales. It was the party's worst defeat for 91 years. Symbolic of all their losses was the defeat of Michael Portillo, seen by many as the party's next leader, in his north London constituency by Labour newcomer, Stephen Twigg.

1997 LABOUR'S VICTORY

THE GENERAL ELECTION victory in 1997 for Labour was far and away the best the party had ever recorded. Its final total number of seats, 418, was the most the party had ever won; its 13.5 million votes the highest since 1951 and its share of the vote – 43 per cent – the highest it had recorded since 1966. Under Tony Blair, party leader since 1994, Labour had become more voter-friendly, continuing a process set in place by Blair's predecessors Neil Kinnock and John Smith. Moving to the right, it courted large parts of 'middle England', usually seen as traditional areas of Conservative support. In power, it has continued to appease the middle classes to the dismay of those on the left of the party.

Tony Blair led the Labour Party to victory in 1997. ▲

1997 DEVOLUTION IN SCOTLAND

ONE OF THE MAIN tenets of Labour's election-winning manifesto was the aim, after in-party battles, of creating a Scottish Parliament and devolving more powers away from Westminster. Following a referendum of the Scottish people in September 1997, the government set about passing legislation to establish a Scottish parliament with genuine power in 1999. The Scots will elect their own MPs to the parliament in Edinburgh and the parliament will have tax-raising powers and control a budget of over £17 billion. Critics have suggested the creation of a Scottish parliament could lead to the end of the Union, with Scotland eventually choosing independence. Labour's main political competitor in Scotland is now the separatist Scottish National Party.

The death of Diana caused an unprecedented outpouring of public grief. ▲

1997 THE DEATH OF DIANA

DIANA, PRINCESS of Wales, died a commoner but her effect on the monarchy could hardly have been greater if she had died as the ruling monarch. Letters in the national press compared the reaction to the revolutions in eastern Europe in 1989. Married to the heir to the throne in 1981, Diana soon proved to be a popular choice. The couple provided an heir to the throne, William, in 1982, but the marriage was to end in divorce in 1996. After the divorce she proved more popular and controversial than ever. She criticised the Conservative government, took up the cause of the banning of landmines (Britain was one of the biggest exporters of arms) and started a relationship with a wealthy Muslim, Dodi Al-Fayed.

1997 DEVOLUTION IN WALES

DEVOLUTION IN WALES was not as radical in concept as the planned changes for Scotland. Although Wales would elect its own MPs to the Welsh Assembly, the new body's powers would not equal those in Scotland. The Assembly would take control of the £7-billion budget previously controlled by the Welsh Office, and would decide where the money should be spent, but it would have no tax-raising powers. The plans for Welsh devolution were narrowly accepted by the Welsh electorate in September 1997 in a referendum. Critics of the Welsh plans said the proposed devolution was 'half-baked' as it allowed for only a measure of reform compared to that in Scotland.

1998 NORTHERN IRELAND

THE 1973 NORTHERN Ireland Constitution Act states 'it is hereby affirmed that in no event will Northern Ireland … cease to be part of the United Kingdom'. But a political and constitutional solution to the period of violence known as the 'Troubles' came to the fore in the 1990s. A ceasefire, sporadically broken most notably in the summer of 1998 with the Omagh bombing, has now been secured and the focus now lies on the politicians rather than the military strength of all sides. The Good Friday Agreement of 1998 paved the way for a referendum of the Northern Irish people who now had their own Assembly with limited powers, led by the Unionist First Minister David Trimble.

The 'Troubles' in Northen Ireland have become characterised by terrorism and bitter conflict. ▶

1998 THE MODERN ROLE OF PARLIAMENT

'PARLIAMENTARY SOVEREIGNTY is a busted flush,' said the greatest-ever commentator on British constitutional affairs, Bagehot, in the nineteenth century. Some would say his comments would still hold true today. Although reform has been proposed for the upper house, the House of Commons is coming under increasing pressure to find a new role. The strait-jacket of party politics, say the critics, means Parliament has been subjugated to the whim of the party rather than concentrating on its role as scrutiniser of government policies. In 1998, after the influx of New Labour politicians and the party's strict discipline, Parliament was labelled by one critic as an 'election machine'. The rise of the European Union and its ever-increasing involvement in top-level decisions has also eroded Parliament's powers.

1999 THE EURO

IN FEBRUARY 1992, the leaders of the European Union signed up to the Maastricht Treaty. This set out a timetable for one of the most ambitious projects in post-war Europe – the establishment of a European central bank and single currency by January 1999. The treaty moved the governments into greater political co-operation by agreeing foreign and security responsibilities. A reluctant Britain secured an opt-out clause

freeing it from adopting the currency – the Euro. The New Labour government did not rule out joining the Euro, but not when it began on 1 January 1999. Opposition to the policy was strong. In June 1998, the *Sun* newspaper asked of Tony Blair, 'Is this the most dangerous man in Britain?', accusing Labour of warming to the Euro.

The adoption of a single European currency has caused dispute amongst politicians in Britain. ◀

Ordinary Lives

1909 THE PEOPLE'S BUDGET

THE PEOPLE'S BUDGET, formulated by the Chancellor of the Exchequer David Lloyd George (1863–1945), was the culmination of a series of measures to tackle poverty by the Liberal government. Parliament backed old-age pensions for the over-70s, which reduced the threat of the old workhouse for many. Labour exchanges followed in 1909, and a limited national insurance scheme was introduced in 1911. These measures followed a string of detailed reports revealing detailed inner-city poverty by leading sociologists like former shipping magnate, Charles Booth (1840–1916), and Seebohm Rowntree (1871–1954), the son of a chocolate magnate. 'A West End and an East End', wrote the American journalist Jack London (1876–1916) in 1902, '… one end is riotous and rotten, the other end sickly and underfed.'

1912 CHIVALRIC IDEALS

THE SINKING of the British liner *Titanic*, after striking an iceberg in 1912, happened to coincide with the deaths of the ill-fated British Antarctic expedition, led by Captain Robert Falcon Scott (1868–1912). Both tragedies became mythic events, wrapped in tales of heroic self-sacrifice, a theme which would continue with the enormous casualties of the First World War. This was a period of chivalric ideals, brought to a head in the apotheosis of British imperialism celebrated during Queen Victoria's Diamond Jubilee in 1897, with 50,000

Captain Robert Scott perished on the return journey from the Antarctic. ▲

The 'unsinkable ship' the Titanic, *which sank after hitting an iceberg on its maiden voyage.* ▲

troops marching through London and a gigantic celebration outside St Paul's Cathedral. Responsibility and sacrifice were also the ideals of the Boy Scouts (1908) and Girl Guides (1909), created by the hero of the siege of Mafeking, Sir Robert Baden-Powell (1857–1941).

1916 CONSCRIPTION

THE ISSUE OF compulsory military service divided the ruling Liberals, but before the Military Service Act of 1916 the New Army of Lord Kitchener (1850–1916) relied on volunteers, 2.25 million of whom came forward. At the outbreak of war, so many men came forward at Great Scotland Yard, that the duty officer took 20 minutes just to reach his desk. It was not enough: British volunteers reached a peak of 5.3 million. 16,000 conscientious objectors were screened by local tribunals, and 41 were condemned to death by the military – but imprisoned instead after a political outcry, joining the 6,000 others who spent some time in prison for the same reason.

1916 WOMEN BUS CONDUCTORS

THE SHORTAGE OF men back home meant that women were beginning to fill roles that would have been unthinkable a few years before. Women became bus conductors from 1916, housemaids fled their jobs to go into factories – with as many as 900,000 women in the munitions factories by the end of the war – and the number of women

A woman bus conductor during the First World War. ▶

working in banks increased sevenfold in the same period. Others played prominent roles in the wartime voluntary organisations, distributing 12 million bandages, 16 million books and 232 million cigarettes to the troops. These new roles changed women's fashions for ever, leading to shorter skirts – six inches above the ground – and by 1916 the brassiere was beginning to oust the old-fashioned corset.

1920 THE UNKNOWN SOLDIER

IN A NATIONAL outpouring of grief in 1920, the Unknown Soldier was buried in Westminster Abbey, and the Cenotaph – designed by Sir Edwin Lutyens (1869–1944) – was unveiled in Whitehall. With nearly a million British Empire deaths and over two million wounded, barely a family remained untouched by the war. By 1922, 900,000 war pensions were being paid out; six years later, 65,000 shell-shock victims were still in mental hospitals. A revulsion against jingoism spread through the country as the true horrors became apparent, described in the bleak war paintings of Paul Nash and the writings of Robert Graves, among others, and a determination that peacetime should be better.

1939 THE ENEMY ALIENS

AS A COUNTRY at war, Britain could not afford to let enemy aliens – German or Italian citizens – have complete freedom to move about, and mix with the general population. There was a chance they might be spies, or become spies, even if they were also refugees or had lived in Britain for years, and had British husbands or wives. About 50,000 aliens, including many who had fled from Nazi Germany in the late 1930s, were therefore rounded up and placed in detention camps, most of which were on racecourses on the Isle of Man. Some were sent to America, but not all of them arrived. Ships carrying enemy aliens were torpedoed and sunk in the Atlantic by Nazi submarines, with heavy loss of life.

1940 EVACUATION

TO AVOID the dangers of air attack, the government planned to evacuate urban children – and sometimes their mothers and teachers – to safety in the countryside. In the event, 1.5 million went – more than had been

Thousands of children were evacuated from London during the Second World War. ▼

planned for. Another two million left the cities of their own accord, but by early in 1940, a million had returned home. A second wave followed when the Blitz began later that year. There were problems from the start, for example providing country shoes and warm clothing; many children were from the slums and had lice. The better-off homes the evacuees stayed in were a revelation, and helped increase support for a post-war Welfare State. Some government departments also left London, including part of the Admiralty, which moved to Bath.

1940   THE BLITZ

THE FIRST air-raid sirens went just as prime minister Neville Chamberlain (1869–1940) finished announcing the outbreak of war, but the expected aerial deluge did not happen for almost a year. But a black-out was enforced and car headlights banned – deaths on the road doubled during the first month of the war. When it came in 1940, the Blitz was a military failure for the Germans, but caused enormous damage to cities – especially London, Liverpool, Liverpool, Manchester, Sheffield and Coventry. More raids followed in 1942, and the V-rocket raids in 1944. 60,000 civilians were killed during the war and 200,000 houses destroyed. People broke into underground stations for shelter at first, and this became institutionalised, though even at the height of the Blitz, six out of 10 people slept at home.

The Blitz on London caused extensive damage, particularly in the East End. ▶

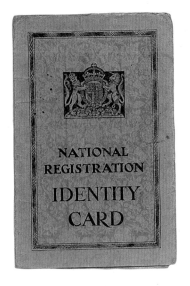
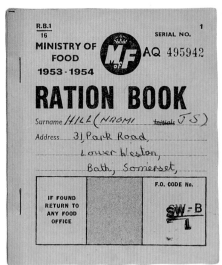

Rationing was introduced in Britain in 1940. ▲

1940 THE START OF RATIONING

GERMAN U-BOATS were already threatening food supplies, and food rationing began in 1940. This was based on a formula related to people's nutritional requirements, and covered butter, bacon and sugar. Its first effect was to raise food consumption, because people liked to buy their whole ration. Meat was soon rationed, too, followed by most other foods except for bread and potatoes, under direction of the food minister Lord Woolton (1883–1964), the former chairman of John Lewis. Clothes rationing began in 1941, leading to the government campaign 'Make do and Mend' and to the simple 'utility' look, designed by Norman Hartnell (1901–78). Schools offering meals doubled early in the war and these meals became a social service, canteen eating was encouraged, as was the campaign to 'Dig for Victory'.

1946 THE NATIONAL HEALTH SERVICE

FREE MEDICAL care was passed by the Labour government in 1946, after difficult negotiations with the medical profession conducted by health minister Aneurin Bevan (1897–1960), fulfilling some of the objectives of the Beveridge Report. It was believed that demands on the National Health Service would reduce as people became healthier, but the opposite was the case – and by the 1970s it was the biggest employer in Europe. Under financial pressure during the Korean War in 1951, Bevan resigned in protest at the introduction of charges for dentures and spectacles. The NHS was part of the new Welfare State, which included comprehensive National Insurance and a National Assistance Act, which meant that neighbours were no longer responsible for the poor.

1947 THE NEW LOOK

THE NEW LOOK dresses emerged after the coldest winter in Europe for 40 years, launched in Paris by the French designer Christian Dior (1905–57). Designers turned their back on the utility looks of the war, by introducing their padded shoulders, low waist and billowing skirts. Their luxury and expensive designs flew in the face of British government austerity recommendations about conserving cloth, and were condemned by government officials, afraid that it would undermine policies of exporting clothes to earn badly needed foreign currency. But it thrilled women in the year when 1-km (1,000-yard) queues were regularly forming just to buy nylon stockings. The New Look dominated fashion until 1954.

1953 THE CORONATION OF ELIZABETH II

THE CORONATION of Elizabeth II (b. 1926) in 1953 was a sumptuous affair marking the end of the austerity years and the beginning of the television age,

The coronation of Elizabeth II. ▶

Edmund Hillary, reaching the top of Mount Everest. ▶

building on the popular success of the Festival of Britain two years before. Although it rained throughout, TV pictures of the 25-year-old queen excited a sense that the country was on the verge of a second Elizabethan age – enhanced when the news was released the same day that a British team had become the first to conquer Mount Everest. It also marked the beginning of a period when the monarchy would have to respond increasingly to media coverage, often intrusive, with a greater openness about the workings of the royal household.

1960s AIMING FOR INDEPENDENCE

IN THE 1960s, determined moves were made in Wales and Scotland for a measure of independence from England. The Irish, too, resolved to detach Northern Ireland from English dominance and in 1969 there was a renewal of terrorism aimed at forcing English agreement. The Welsh and the Scots proceeded differently. Their main methods were political, though some Welsh nationalists destroyed English holiday homes in Wales to make their point. The first MP to sit for Plaid Cymru, the Welsh nationalist party, was elected in 1966 and the first Scottish National Party MP in 1967. Another 30 years passed, however, before the Welsh and Scots were given the chance to vote for devolution and their own assemblies separate from Parliament in London.

1963 CONTROLLING IMMIGRATION

THOUGH THE Notting Hill Riots had been an isolated incident at the time, it became clear before long that the resentment against Blacks, which started them, was widespread. By 1963, popular concern was such that the government had to take action. New rules imposing work permits on immigrants came into action at midnight on 1 July 1963. During that day, there was a rush of people trying to beat the deadline. Jamaicans on board an aircraft delayed by bad weather nearly lost their chance, after they landed at Belfast almost an hour too late. An exception was made for them and they stayed. For others, though, the new rules were strictly enforced: several Indians and Pakistanis without work permits were repatriated.

1967 THE MINISKIRT

THE FASHION designer Mary Quant (b. 1934) had been running her Bazaar shop in London's King's Road since 1955, but it was a decade later that she developed the item of clothing that came to symbolise the decade – the miniskirt, which reached its shortest in 1967–68. The miniskirt stood for a new generation of women, and was modelled by a new generation of achingly thin models. It helped make the King's Road the centre for fashion in the Beatles' and hippy eras, although it was briefly overtaken by London's Carnaby Street. With the emergence of people like Quant and the Beatles, fashion, music and youth culture rapidly became one of Britain's main exports.

The miniskirt was designed by Mary Quant and became the fashion item of the 1960s. ▶

Beatle John Lennon, one of the icons of the 1960s. ◀

1969 THE DIVORCE ACT

COMMENTATORS DIFFER about the beginning of the so-called 'permissive society'. Did it begin with legalising suicide in 1959, ending conscription in 1960, or legalising abortion and homosexuality in 1967 under the regime of Labour home secretary Roy Jenkins (b. 1920)? The Sexual Offences Act only legalised homosexuality between consenting adults over 21 in private, and only for England and Wales, but it was part of a string of legal changes that altered the moral atmosphere of Britain. Others included the introduction of the pill, the abolition of the death penalty, and reduction of the voting age to 18, but the most influential of all was probably the 1969 Divorce Act, which allowed fault-free divorce after the 'irretrievable breakdown' of the marriage. The divorce rate has risen steadily ever since.

1971 OPEN UNIVERSITY

A MODERN economy needed more higher education, said the Robbins Report of 1963, recommending a target of 60 universities in Britain by 1980. They never reached it, but universities like East Anglia, Essex, Lancaster, Sussex, Warwick and York all received charters in the 1960s, and by 1972 there were 45 – plus a growing sector of polytechnics, which themselves

Sussex University, which received its charter in the 1960s. ▲

became universities in 1993. The number of students had doubled in a decade, ready to play a leading role in the ferment of 1960s youth politics. The Open University, started in 1971, was a scheme of prime minister Harold Wilson's (1916–95), using radio, television and correspondence courses to take university education to adults at home. Its innovative techniques have been copied all over the world.

Refugees fleeing from war-torn Vietnam. ▲

1975   VIETNAMESE REFUGEES

AS THE VIETNAM War drew towards its bloodstained close in 1975, Britain was among several countries that admitted refugees. On 6 April, for example, 105 Vietnamese orphans were flown in from South Vietnam. Their need for shelter and succour was so great that, to save time, immigration arrangements were finalised on the way. Adults were also allowed in and the public mood of sympathy was such that the man who protested that the new immigrants were 'ethnic Chinese' was very much a lone voice. This act of mercy was repeated during the civil war in Yugoslavia that began in 1991, when Bosnians were rescued from the widespread destruction and again when persecuted Kurds, who were treated with especial brutality in Iraq, took shelter in Britain.

1979   THE WINTER OF DISCONTENT

THE ATTEMPT by Labour minister Barbara Castle (b. 1910) to control growing trade-union power, outlined in the white paper *In Place of Strife*, was defeated by the Cabinet and TUC in 1969. By 1975, a Gallup poll voted the general-secretary of the Transport and General Workers Union, Jack Jones (b. 1913), as the most powerful person in the country. By 1978, relations between the government and unions had broken down completely over a five-per-cent pay limit announced by the government of James Callaghan (b. 1912), and a number of key trade unions went on strike. The impact was made worse by the severe winter, and the experience paved the way for the anti-trade union legislation of the Thatcher government that took office in 1979.

1981   BRIXTON RIOTS

A MISUNDERSTANDING in Brixton in April 1981 was all that was needed to unleash the most destructive riot in Britain since the war, followed later in the summer by a series of copycat disturbances around the country, notably Southall and Toxteth. There was only one death – a disabled man run down by a police van in Toxteth on the day of the royal wedding – but a combination of tension between police and the black community, plus youth unemployment, exploded to shift government attention on to the inner cities. A report by the Church of England in 1986, after a second Brixton riot in 1985, urged action to tackle social disintegration. Even the Prince of Wales (b. 1948) spoke publicly about his fears of inheriting a 'divided kingdom'.

1986   AIDS AWARENESS

MARGARET THATCHER came to power in 1979 promising that the NHS was 'safe with us', but the strains were beginning to show.

A campaign to increase awareness of the AIDS virus was launched in 1986. ▶

REACH OUT AND TOU

U.K. HIV/AIDS PROCESSION WITH FLOW

Although smoking was on the decline and inoculation was defeating many old diseases, the stresses of modern life and the progress of medical science were taking their toll on NHS funding at a time when successive governments were trying to squeeze public spending. The arrival of Aids in 1981 highlighted the problem: fearing an epidemic, the government launched an unprecedented public-information campaign in 1986. The epidemic never happened, and the impact of AIDS was blunted by an expensive cocktail of drugs.

1990   RIOTS AT STRANGEWAYS

THE PRISON RIOT at Strangeways in Manchester in 1990, when inmates took control of the building for 25 days, was a symbolic moment in the increase of crime – a continuing story since the 1960s. Recorded crimes mushroomed from 2.7 million a year in 1980 to a peak of 5.6 million in 1992 in England and Wales; the peak of 590,000 a year came earlier in Scotland in 1991. Most crimes are traditionally committed by young men – 80 per cent by men under 35 – so the shrinking population of teenagers was beginning to feed through into better figures. But because of an enthusiasm for prison as a solution among successive home secretaries, the prison over-crowding crisis continued.

A prisoner at Strangeways during the riot there in 1990. ▲

The case against five young white men accused of murdering black teenager Stephen Lawrence collapsed, causing widespread outrage. ▲

1993 STEPHEN LAWRENCE MURDERED

AFTER THE 1981 race riots, which were duplicated in Hull, Reading and elsewhere, black leaders named as the root causes black poverty, unemployment and the negative attitude of the police towards people of colour. Despite the Race Relation Acts of 1965, 1968 and 1976, designed to reduce racial conflict, the problem remained unsolved. Police leaders had made many efforts to build bridges of understanding with the black community, but their quest for better relations was dogged by incidents such as the murder of black teenager Stephen Lawrence, who was killed in 1993. The case against five young whites seemed strong, but it collapsed for legal reasons. The Lawrence family pursued the case, without success, though the police publicly admitted their failure to handle the crime properly.

1995 TECHNOLOGY TAKES OVER

THE LAUNCH IN Swindon of Mondex – the computerised money system developed by NatWest, Midland and BT – was a sign of the growth of information technology in every area of British life. The first cashpoint in Britain was opened by Barclays in Enfield in 1967, but the wide distribution of credit cards in the 1980s also changed the way people used money, as well as contributing to a total of over £500 billion in personal debt. Computer technology filtered into UK homes and offices, taking off in the mid-1990s with the arrival of the Internet. By 1998, as much as seven per cent of the UK population had access to it – rising at a rate of 75 per cent every year, with 250,000 on-line shopping transactions every month.

Cash dispensing machines began to appear around Britain in the late 1960s. ▲

1996 THE ROYAL DIVORCE

THE DIVORCE of the Prince and Princess of Wales in 1996 was one of the most public of all time, after their wedding had been watched on television by record numbers around the world in 1981. The divorce fuelled the growing debate about the future of the British monarchy, but it also provided a mirror to the British people – who were divorcing faster than any other European country apart from Denmark. More than one in three marriages were breaking up, with widespread implications for planning and welfare. As many as 10 per cent of households were headed by a single parent, and a quarter contained just one person – twice as many as 1961. The result was growing isolation and a prediction of 4.4 million new homes needed for southern England.

Britain in the World

1900 THE SECOND BOER WAR

IN 1897 SIR ALFRED Milner became British High Commissioner in South Africa. He became convinced that the only way to settle matters with the Boers was through war. He demanded that the *Uitlanders* be given the vote and refused to compromise. Kruger declared war on 12 October 1899, realising the weakness of British forces in South Africa. Until the end of the year, the British suffered defeat after defeat, but the arrival of General Roberts with reinforcements in January 1900 turned the tide. By

September 1900, both Boer republics had been occupied and their capitals captured, but the war was to drag on for another 18 months as the Boers resorted to guerrilla tactics. General Kitchener, who took over command in November 1900, built blockhouses to defend railway lines and herded Boer civilians into concentration camps before he could force their leaders to surrender.

Lord Kitchener, who led the British to victory over the Boers in South Africa. ◄

1904   ENTENTE CORDIALE

A MUCH MORE important step in British foreign policy was the
Entente Cordiale signed between Britain and France in 1904. It was not a
treaty as such, but a settling of long-standing sources of friction. Britain
recognised French influence in Morocco and the French recognised
British influence in Egypt. Territorial disputes in Canada, Africa and Indo-
China were also settled. More significant, however, was the fact that the
Entente led subsequently to discussions on naval issues. The two navies
agreed to divide responsibility for European waters. In 1912 the British
navy withdrew its forces from the Mediterranean and the French navy
withdrew its forces from the Channel.

1907   THE TRIPLE ENTENTE

IN 1907 BRITAIN signed an entente with Russia. As in the case of the
Entente Cordiale, its most immediate effects were the settlement of
outstanding disputes between the two countries in Persia, Afghanistan and
Tibet, but the agreement also drew Britain into the system of alliances,
which had dominated European politics since 1870. Britain was now
clearly aligned with France and Russia against the powers of the Triple
Alliance, Germany, Austria and Italy. The Triple Entente, as it came to be
known, did not commit Britain to defend
or support the other two powers, but it did
make British support for them much more
likely in the event of war.

1912   SCOTT OF THE ANTARCTIC

CAPTAIN ROBERT Scott led an
expedition to Antarctica in 1902. In 1903
he landed on the continent and marched
south to 82 degrees, a new record. Scott
returned in 1910. Although he was mainly
interested in scientific research, he became

*Captain Robert Scott, leader of the ill-fated
expedition to the Antarctic.* ▶

involved in a race to the true South Pole and set out, with four others, in November 1911. He reached the pole on 16 January 1912, only to find that the Norwegian Amundsen had beaten him by exactly one month. Scott's refusal to use dog sledges was one reason for his failure. On the return journey, Scott and his party all died from exhaustion in a blizzard on about 29 March 1912.

1915   GALLIPOLI

THE IMPOSSIBILITY of breaking through the front lines on the Western Front in France led to an attempt to strike at the enemy from the south. In April 1915, Allied forces landed at Gallipoli in Turkey. The aim was to force Turkey, Germany's ally, out of the war and then link up with the Russian army. The landings succeeded, but little further progress was made. The Allied troops had to attack up-hill against well-trained and well-dug-in Turkish troops. A second landing was made at Suvla Bay in August, but this failed to break the deadlock. In December 1915 the Allied forces were evacuated by night. This, rather ignominiously, was the most successful part of the operation.

1915   YPRES

BY THE END of October 1914 the remnants of the BEF (British Expeditionary Force) found itself in the pleasant Belgian market town of Ypres. The town was very low-lying and was surrounded by shallow hills occupied by the Germans. It had an enormous cloth hall and a cathedral, both with tall spires. They

Scene from the Battle of Ypres. ▲

made excellent targets for the German gunners. Every day, shells rained down on the town, nowhere was safe. The British held Ypres (they called it 'Wipers') for four years and by 1918 there were virtually no buildings left standing. In 1915 the Germans attacked from the north at Langemarck and used poison gas for the first time; 8,000 soldiers were killed. In 1917 the British tried to break out and planted 18 enormous mines under the German lines and exploded them at the same time, some German soldiers were killed by shock rather than by the explosion.

1916   THE SOMME

IN DECEMBER 1915 Douglas Haig became the commander-in-chief of the British forces on the Western Front. He believed that the deadlock could be broken by weight of numbers and prepared for a major battle in 1916. Originally he planned to attack near Ypres, but the German attacks on Verdun, which began in February, made him change his plans. Instead the attack would take place near the River Somme and would, it was hoped, take pressure off the French forces further east. Haig believed that a heavy bombardment would destroy the German defences. The infantry would

Sir Douglas Haig, whose tactic of sending men 'over the top' led to many thousands of casualties in the Somme offensives. ▲

then walk across and clear the way for a massive cavalry advance. The result was very different. On the first day the British army suffered 70,000 casualties and when the attacks were called off in November, less than five miles of land had been gained.

British prime minister David Lloyd George with his wife and daughter. ▲

1919 THE TREATY OF VERSAILLES

THE LEADERS of the Allies met at Versailles in March to discuss the peace terms to be imposed on Germany. David Lloyd George, the British prime minister, had fought a general election in December 1918 with the slogan 'Make Germany Pay', but when he arrived at Versailles he wanted to avoid really harsh conditions, for fear that these might provoke a backlash in Germany. Lloyd George did manage to tone down the demands of the French to some extent, but overall the Germans came to see the treaty as humiliating. Britain gained most of the German colonies, under League of Nations mandates, and was handed the German fleet. When the crews heard the terms of the treaty they scuttled all the German ships in the Scapa Flow.

1920 THE LEAGUE OF NATIONS

THE LEAGUE OF NATIONS came into being on 1 January 1920. It was the idea of Woodrow Wilson, the President of the USA. It was intended to have a Council of nine members, five of them permanent, an Assembly, which met once a year and a secretariat headed by a Secretary-General. Although it was not appreciated at the time, there were fundamental weaknesses in its organisation and make-up. Despite Wilson's leadership, the USA did not join, as Congress refused to ratify Wilson's actions. Although the League could apply military sanctions against members, it did not have any military forces and had to persuade members to declare war on countries, that broke the Covenant. But in the long run, its most fundamental weakness was that when three of the permanent members of the League, Japan, Italy and Germany, left in the 1930s, the remaining two, Britain and France, bore the whole burden of enforcing the League's decisions.

1939 POLAND

HITLER INVADED Poland on 1 September 1939. On 2 September the British government sent a note to Berlin demanding that the German forces withdraw, or agree to withdraw, by 11 a.m. on 3 September. Hitler ignored the note and the invasion continued. He believed that Chamberlain was bluffing as he had not taken any action in the past. Chamberlain now had no option as the British government had promised to defend Poland; on the other hand, in the past Britain had had no such treaty obligations to Czechoslovakia or Austria. At 11 a.m. on 3 September, Britain went to war with Germany. Chamberlain announced the declaration on the BBC Home Service in a special broadcast at 11.45 a.m. Everything he had worked for had collapsed.

1940 THE BATTLE OF BRITAIN

IN AUGUST 1940 the *Luftwaffe*, the German airforce, began to attack the Royal Air Force. It was assumed in Britain that this was a prelude to an invasion. First, radar stations on the coast were attacked and then airfields were bombed. Finally the *Luftwaffe* attempted to destroy Fighter Command. The British fighter planes, the Hurricane and the Spitfire, were more than a match for the opposition, but Britain had only a limited

A Hawker Hurricane plane used against the Luftwaffe duing the Second World War. ▼

number of trained pilots, and it was this that began to tip the balance at the beginning of September. Once again Hitler intervened and on 7 September ordered the *Luftwaffe* to stop attacking Fighter Command and attack London instead by night. This gave the RAF a chance to recover. When the next daytime attack took place on 15 September, the RAF defeated the *Luftwaffe*. The Battle of Britain was over.

1942 NORTH AFRICA

AT THE BEGINNING of the Second World War, Egypt and Palestine were held by Britain. Italy was occupying Libya and invaded Egypt in September 1940. The invasion failed completely and the British were able to force the Italians back and take more than 100,000 prisoners. In April 1941 General Rommel was sent by Germany to support the Italians and he advanced into Egypt once again. He captured Tobruk and then reached El Alamein, about 110 km (70 miles) from Alexandria. In October 1942 the British Eighth Army, under General Montgomery attacked Rommel at El Alamein and drove the Germans out of Egypt. In December, US forces landed in Morocco and by May 1943 all of North Africa was in the hands of the Allies.

General Montgomery, leader of the war in North Africa. ▶

The D-Day landings in Normandy proved the turning point for the Allies in the war. ▲

1944   THE TIDE TURNS

ON 6 JUNE 1944 Allied forces landed on five beaches in Normandy to begin what was hoped to be the liberation of Europe. It was the biggest operation of its type ever. British and Commonwealth forces landed on three beaches and US forces on the other two. Breaking out of the beachhead took more than a month, but after that Paris was liberated in early August and the Rhine was reached in September. The British army tried to seize the bridges across the Rhine at Arnhem, but failed. Germany was not invaded until the following spring. On 30 April 1945, Hitler committed suicide in Berlin, and eight days later Germany surrendered to the Allies, bringing the war in Europe to an end.

The symbol of the United Nations, set up in 1945. ▲

1945 THE UNITED NATIONS

THE UNITED NATIONS was set up in April 1945. The name had been invented by Franklin Roosevelt to describe the countries that had fought against the Axis powers during the Second World War and all three Allies had agreed to take part in the UN at the conferences of Yalta and Potsdam. Britain, along with the USA, the USSR, France and China, became a Permanent Member of the Security Council. This gave her special importance, prestige and power. It meant that Britain was right at the heart of the UN and could also veto any Security Council Resolution. Britain has retained her place on the Security Council ever since.

1948 THE MURDER OF GANDHI

MOHANDAS GANDHI returned to India in 1915, having already led campaigns against racist laws in South Africa. He had supported Britain during the First World War and, like many Indians, expected that the British would introduce substantial changes to India by way of a reward. He became the leader of the Congress and began a series of campaigns of civil disobedience. He preached 'Satyagraha' or non-violent protest. Gandhi wanted a united India, in which people of all faiths could live

Mahatma Gandhi, who became known as the father of the Indian nation. ▶

together. He opposed the efforts by Hindus, Muslims and Sikhs to create their own states, but in the end he failed. The violence that erupted in India after the Second World War convinced him that unity was impossible. He was murdered in January 1948 by a Hindu extremist, who believed that Gandhi had favoured Muslims.

1948 THE BERLIN AIRLIFT

IN 1947, BRITAIN and the USA united their zones in Germany in what was called 'Bizonia' and set about helping the country to recover from the effects of the war. In 1948 the French were also included. When the Allies attempted to introduce a new currency in the western zones, Stalin closed the borders with the west, preventing contact by land, canal or rail between the Allied sectors in Berlin and in West Germany. For ten and a half months the Allies supplied West Berlin by air; approximately one third of the flights were undertaken by Britain. When the blockade was lifted in May 1949, Britain, the USA and France established the Federal Republic of Germany, with its capital in Bonn.

1949 APARTHEID

THE BEGINNINGS of apartheid can be traced back to the Great Trek of 1836, when the Boers left Cape Colony rather than free their slaves. However, many whites in South Africa regarded the native Africans as inferior, as Gandhi found when he lived in South Africa at the beginning of the twentieth century. But institutionalised apartheid really began in 1949 with the founding of the National Party. In theory, apartheid meant 'separate development', the idea that blacks, whites and coloureds should live apart. What made the system so objectionable was that 'apart' came to mean completely different standards, which were controlled by the whites. A black African had to carry a pass, was not allowed in certain areas and could not use the same facilities or schools as a white. In the 1960s and '70s these laws were rigorously enforced, by violence if necessary.

Institutionalised apartheid began in 1949, and ended with Nelson Mandela's campaigns in the 1990s. ▼

1949 NATO

THE NORTH Atlantic Treaty Organisation was set up in 1949 in response to the Berlin Blockade. Thirteen countries signed the treaty including Britain and the USA. The most important aspect of the treaty was the clause that stated that an attack on one member would be taken to be an attack on all of the members. This was intended to deter any

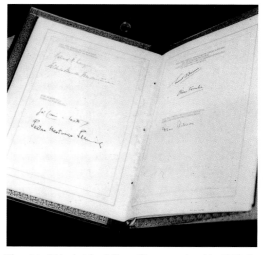

The original North Atlantic Treaty Document, signed in 1949. ▲

attacks from eastern Europe. By signing the treaty Britain was linking her security to that of western Europe. US bases were set up in Britain and eventually nuclear weapons were located there. This was the first time that Britain had undertaken a long-term treaty commitment to continental Europe. To this day, none of the members of NATO has been attacked.

1950s DECOLONISATION

DECOLONISATION IS the withdrawal of Britain from her colonies in the period after the Second World War. The first example was the independence of India and Pakistan in August 1947; this was followed by independence for most of Britain's colonies in Africa in the 1950s and '60s. Ghana was the first in 1957 and then Nigeria in 1960. In most cases British withdrawal was achieved without violence, but in Kenya the Mau Mau, a terrorist organisation, began to attack white settlers. It took four years of fighting (1952–56) to defeat the Mau Mau. Kenya finally became independent in 1963.

In 1956, Britain and Egypt fought for control of the Suez Canal. ▲

1956 THE SUEZ CRISIS

BRITAIN HELD responsibility for Egypt from the 1880s until 1922, but continued to station troops in the Suez Canal Zone. In 1952 there was a revolution in Egypt, which forced the king to abdicate and then set up a republic. In 1954 the British troops were forced to leave, British and French banks were nationalised and in 1956 the Suez Canal Company, which was owned by Britain and France, was taken over. In October 1956, Britain and France landed troops and seized control of the canal. The Israeli army invaded Egypt at the same time. It was the type of action that Britain had carried out many times in the nineteenth century, but in 1956 it was condemned by the United Nations and by the US government. The British forces were withdrawn and Britain had to accept the actions of the Egyptian government, led by President Nasser.

1965 UDI

RHODESIA, WHICH had been founded by Cecil Rhodes in the 1890s, was dominated by about 200,000 white settlers. When the neighbouring colonies gained independence as Zambia and Malawi in 1964, the white Rhodesians decided to prevent a similar occurrence by declaring UDI, a Unilateral Declaration of Independence. This was announced by the prime minister, Ian Smith on 11 November 1965. For 10 years Rhodesia survived, but in the late 1970s there were increasing attacks from guerrillas led by Robert Mugabe. Eventually sanctions forced Ian Smith to allow free elections in 1980 and Mugabe's party won 57 seats out of 80. He became the first prime minister of the new country of Zimbabwe.

1973   BRITAIN JOINS THE EEC

IN THE LATE 1940s there was a series of discussions about plans to unify Europe. These led to the setting up of the European Coal and Steel Community in 1951, which was the basis of the European Economic Community when it was formed in 1957. Britain took little part in these proceedings, believing that her links with the Commonwealth and the USA made them irrelevant, but it soon became clear that the Common Market, as it came to be known, was a success. In 1961 and 1967 Britain applied to join, but was prevented by the French president Charles de Gaulle. He believed that Britain's links with the USA were too strong and that she was not committed to Europe. After de Gaulle's death in 1970, Britain applied for a third time and became a member in 1973.

1982   THE FALKLANDS WAR

BRITAIN TOOK possession of the Falkland Islands in 1771. In 1838 Argentina tried to force Britain to hand them back and Britain blockaded the Argentine coast in reply. Further demands were made in the twentieth century but all were refused. In March 1982, 10,000 Argentine troops landed on the Falkland Islands and South Georgia was occupied at the same time. The handful of British troops on the islands surrendered. A task force of 3,500 men was assembled in Britain to retake the islands. The first landings were made at San Carlos and then forces moved south to Goose Green and east to Tumbledown. The Argentine forces surrendered in June. Altogether more than 330 British servicemen were killed retaking the islands.

Britain retaliated in 1982, when Argentina landed forces to reclaim control of the Falkland Islands. ▶

The election of Nelson Mandela as president marked the end of apartheid in South Africa. ▲

1994 ELECTION IN SOUTH AFRICA

ON 11 FEBRUARY 1990, Nelson Mandela, the vice-president of the African National Congress was released from prison in South Africa. He had been in prison since 1963. Since then there had been increasing pressure on South Africa by Britain, the Commonwealth and the United Nations to end its policy of apartheid. By releasing Mandela the South African government hoped that it would be possible to reach a compromise with the ANC. This did not happen. Talks dragged on for four years before a general election, the first the whole population was allowed to vote in, was held in April 1994. The ANC won with 62.5 per cent of the votes and Nelson Mandela became the president of South Africa. One of his first actions was to apply for readmission to the Commonwealth, which the old apartheid regime had left in 1961.

Industry and Invention

1900 LIGHTING-UP TIME

THE PRINCIPLE of the filament lamp was that a thin conductor could be made to glow by an electric current, provided that it was sealed in a vacuum to keep it from burning out. Around 1878, Thomas Edison and British chemist Joseph Swan experimented with various materials for the filament and both chose carbon. The resulting lamp did not immediately supersede gas lighting, which remained popular for some forms of street lighting until the middle of the twentieth century. Electric lighting became an accepted part of urban life by 1900. The tungsten-filament lamp was introduced during the early 1900s and became the principal form of electric lamp, though more efficient fluorescent gas discharge lamps have now found widespread use as well.

An early vacuum cleaner. ▲

1901 CLEANING UP

THE FIRST electrical vacuum cleaner was invented in 1901 by the Scot Hubert Booth. He had the idea when he saw how much dust was blown out of a carpet by a jet of compressed air. His system used an electric pump to remove the dust from a carpet by sucking air along a tube and through a cloth filter. The equipment was bulky and noisy and was improved on by US janitor J. Spangler. He used an electric motor to rotate a brush at the front of his portable machine and a fan behind it to suck the dirt into a collecting bag. Patented in 1907. Spangler did not have the money to promote it and sold the rights to a relative, William Hoover, whose name is now synonymous with the invention.

1901   WIRES AND WIRELESS

THE ELECTRIC telegraph was followed by the telephone, invented by
Alexander Graham Bell in 1876 as a result of Faraday's discoveries in
electromagnetism, and adopted quickly for short-range oral
communication in the cities of America and Europe. About the same time,
theoretical work on the electromagnetic properties of light and other
radiation was beginning to produce astonishing experimental results, and
the possibilities of wireless telegraphy began to be explored. By the end of
the nineteenth century, Guglielmo Marconi had transmitted messages over
many miles in Britain and was preparing the apparatus with which he
made the first transatlantic radio communication on 12 December 1901.
The world was thus being drawn inexorably into a closer community by
the spread of instantaneous communication.

1903   FIRST FLIGHT

THROUGHOUT THE nineteenth century, investigations into
aerodynamic effects were carried out by inventors such as Sir George
Cayley in England, who, by 1799 had established the basic configuration of
the modern aeroplane with fixed wings, fuselage and tail unit. Several
designers perceived that the internal-combustion engine promised to
provide the light, compact power unit that was a prerequisite of powered

The Wright brothers made the first flight at Kittyhawk in North Carolina in 1903. ▼

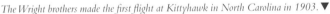

flight, and on 17 December 1903, Wilbur and Orville Wright in their *Flyer I* at the Kill Devil Hills in North Carolina achieved sustained, controlled, powered flight. The *Flyer I* was a propeller-driven adaptation of the biplane gliders that the Wright brothers had built and learned to fly in the previous years. By 1908, the brothers were flying across the Atlantic to Europe to give demonstrations.

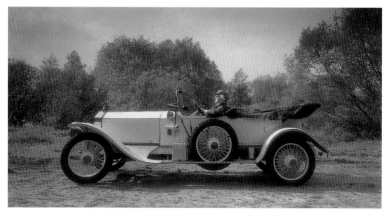

The famous Rolls Royce Silver Ghost. ▲

1903 TOYS FOR THE RICH

IN THE DEVELOPED world the automobile entered the transportation market as a toy for the rich at the beginning of the twentieth century. In 1885, Germans Gottleib Daimler and Karl Benz built and ran the first petrol-driven motor car. The pattern for the modern car was set by Mercedes in 1901, with mass-production on an assembly line introduced at the Ransome Olds factory in America in the same year. From 1904–08, 241 automobile-manufacturing firms went into business in America. One of these was the Ford Motor Company, which was organised as a corporation in June 1903 and sold its first car on 23 July. The company produced 1,700 cars during its first full year of business. In 1906 the British Rolls Royce company produced the legendary Silver Ghost.

1915 ARMOURED VEHICLES

TANKS WERE invented in the First World War for use as armour-shielded assault vehicles that could cross the muddy, uneven terrain of the trenches. Several European nations worked on ways to adapt internal-combustion gas engines to tracked vehicles, and in 1915 the British Admiralty's 'Landship Committee' became the first to adapt several tractors for military use. The first of these 'tanks' were dispatched to France the following year and on 15 August 1916 were assigned to combat at the first Battle of the Somme. These early tanks were lightly armed with machine guns and small-calibre guns. Tanks first played a decisive role in the First World War in the Battle of Cambrai (1917), when 474 British tanks broke through the German lines. After this they were increasingly used by the Allies.

1915 THE NAVY INVENT THE DEPTH CHARGE

A DEPTH CHARGE is a canister of explosives, which was first used as an anti-submarine weapon by the British navy in 1915. The canisters were originally dropped or thrown from the stern of a ship in a pattern of five. The explosive, detonated by a hydrostatic fuse set at a particular depth, caused serious damage even if it exploded at some distance from the submarine because the pressures built up by underwater explosions are much greater than those in the air. Today, computerised launching systems are used; the canisters are propelled over greater distances and can carry nuclear charges that can destroy a submarine up to 1.61 km (1 mile) away from the explosion.

1922 ADVANCE WARNING SYSTEM

THE DEVELOPMENT of radar can be traced to the work of German physicist Heinrich Hertz. Hertz proved the existence of radio waves and demonstrated that they can be reflected like light waves. The possibility of using the radio-reflection phenomenon for detection purposes was further explored after the engineer Guglielmo Marconi elaborated its principles in 1922. During the 1930s several countries, including Great Britain, France, the US, Germany and Japan, initiated research on radar systems capable of detecting aircraft and surface vessels at long range and under poor visibility.

Before the outset of the Second World War, Britain had constructed a network of radar stations designed to provide early warning against approaching enemy aircraft. By late 1939, Germany had begun production of similar ground-based aircraft-warning units called *Freya*.

1926 SOUND AND VISION

IN 1926, JOHN Logie Baird demonstrated a mechanical scanner able to convert an image into a series of electronic impulses that could then be reassembled on a viewing screen as a pattern of light and shade. However, it was the ideas of fellow Brit A. Cambell-Swinton that helped to advance television further. In 1908, Cambell-Swinton had pointed out that cathode-ray tubes would best effect transmission and reception and cathode-ray tubes were used experimentally in the UK from 1934. In 1932 the Radio Corporation of America demonstrated all-electronic television using a camera tube called the iconoscope (patented by Vladimir Zworykin in 1923) and a cathode-ray tube in the receiver. In 1929 the British Broadcasting Company began broadcasting experimental TV programmes using Baird's system and in 1936 they began regular broadcasting from Alexandra Palace, London.

Television became more widespread throughout the 1950s. ◀

The Empire State Building in New York was the tallest construction for over 40 years. ▲

1931   REACHING FOR THE SKY

IN THE SOUTH of England at this time construction industries and new service industries such as hotels and the shops of London flourished. London grew enormously. Here, as in the rest of the world, conventional methods of building in brick and masonry had reached the limits of feasibility in buildings up to 16-storeys high, and the future lay with the skeleton frame or cage construction pioneered in the 1880s in Chicago. The Americans were using abundant cheap steel, for columns, beams and trusses, and to make efficient passenger elevators. The Empire State Building was built in 1931, with its total height of 381 m (1,250 ft) and 102 storeys, and achieved a limit not exceeded for 40 years, but set a world-wide trend for building taller structures.

1933 FORD AND FERGUSON

THE VERY FIRST tractors had appeared at the end of the nineteenth century. Early models invented by Hart and Parr in the USA and D. Albone in England were soon superseded when Henry Ford began mass production of Fordson tractors in 1916. However, competition and much patent legislation came with the invention of the Ferguson tractor in 1933. Harry Ferguson was born in Northern Ireland and worked on his father's farm from the age of 14. His tractor was designed for use on smaller farms and was much lighter and less cumbersome than the Fordson and utilised pneumatic rubber tyres. It was launched in England in 1936 and, in collaboration with Ford, in the USA in 1939.

1940 CODES AND COMPUTERS

ALAN TURING was a brilliant English mathematician and logician. In 1936 he described a 'universal computing machine' that could theoretically be programmed to solve any problem capable of solution. This concept, now called the 'Turing Machine' foreshadowed the computer. During the Second World War he worked with the Government Code and

Henry Ford began by producing tractors, founding one of the greatest automobile empires in history. ▲

The first computer, known as Colossus, developed in part by Alan Turing. ▲

Cypher School at Bletchley Park where he helped build a computer with vacuum tubes. It was known as the Colossus and was designed to decipher the German 'Enigma' codes, which it did in 1940. After the war, Turing worked in the construction of early computers and the development of programming techniques. He also championed the idea that computers would eventually be capable of human thought (Artificial Intelligence), and he devised the Turing test to assess this capability.

1941 THE MANHATTAN PROJECT

ON 25 JULY 1941 a British committee chaired by G. P. Thomson and code-named Maud, issued a report that concluded that building an atom bomb was a proposition, and that it would 'lead to decisive results in the war'. Its recommendations were accepted by the British Prime Minister, Winston Churchill, in August. American scientists supported the findings of the Maud committee and US President Franklin Roosevelt established the Manhattan Project to harness all the various activities. General L.R. Groves was put in charge and he chose Robert Oppenheimer, a professor of Science at the University of California, to direct a new central laboratory where the new bomb would be built. The laboratory opened at Los Alamos in April 1943.

1947   THE SPEED OF SOUND

THE GAS TURBINE underwent substantial development since its first successful operational use at the end of the Second World War. The high power-to-weight ratio of this type of engine made it ideal for aircraft propulsion, so that in either the pure jet or turboprop form it was generally adopted for all large aircraft, both military and civil, by the 1960s. The immediate effect of the adoption of jet propulsion was a huge increase in aircraft speeds. The very first piloted aeroplane to exceed the speed of sound in level flight was the American aeroplane *Bell X-1* in 1947. By the end of the 1960s supersonic flight was becoming a practicable proposition for civil-airline users.

1948   OBJECTS IN LIGHT

HOLOGRAPHY IS a method of producing three-dimensional images by means of laser light. The photographic recording of the image is called a hologram,

The post-war years saw the development of lasers and holography. ▶

which appears to be an unrecognisable pattern of stripes and whorls but which, when illuminated by coherent light, organises the light into a three-dimensional representation of the original object. Dennis Gabor, a Hungarian-born British scientist, invented holography in 1948, for which he received the Nobel Prize in physics more than 20 years later (1971). Gabor considered the possibility of improving the resolving power of the electron microscope, first by utilising the electron beam to make a hologram of the object and then by examining this hologram with a beam of coherent light.

1956   NEW ENERGY

SOON AFTER THE discovery of nuclear fission was announced in 1939, it was also determined that the fissile isotope involved in the reaction was uranium-238 and that neutrons were emitted in the process. Newspaper articles reporting the discovery mentioned the possibility that a fission chain reaction could be exploited as a source of power. After the Second World War, reactor development was placed under the supervision of the leading experimental nuclear physicist of the era, Enrico Fermi, at Columbia University. On 2 December 1942 Fermi reported having produced the first self-sustaining chain reaction. His reactor was later called Chicago Pile No. 1 (CP-1). In 1956 the opening of Calder Hall in Britain seemed to herald a new age of cheap nuclear electricity.

1957   THE LARGEST RADIO TELESCOPE

AFTER THE SECOND World War the British Astronomer Alfred Lovell began working at the University of Manchester's botanical site at Jodrell Bank with war-surplus radar equipment. Researching radio and radar astronomy, he began to construct the Lovell telescope, a fully steerable radio telescope with a reflector that measures 76 m (250 ft) in diameter. Operation of this, the largest radio telescope, began in 1957 shortly before the launch of *Sputnik I*, and the satellite's carrier rocket was tracked at Jodrell Bank. Most operational time there is devoted to astronomy rather than tracking and communication, but the telescope has been part of the tracking network for the US programme of space exploration and monitored most of the Soviet accomplishments.

Modern telescopes provide extensive information about other planets and the ways of the universe. ▼

Satellites were developed throughout the 1960s, increasing communication possibilities on Earth. ▲

1958   SOUNDS THROUGH SPACE

IN 1945 THE BRITISH author-scientist Arthur C. Clarke proposed the use of an Earth satellite for radio communication between, and radio broadcast to, points widely removed on the surface of the Earth. The station would be positioned at an altitude of about 35,900 km (22,300 miles) so that its period of revolution about the Earth would be the same as the period of the Earth's rotation. The first satellite-communication experiment was the US government's Project SCORE, which launched a satellite on 18 December 1958. *Prospero* was the first of four X-3 satellites orbited by the UK. Launched with a British missile in 1971 from Australia, it was designed to test the efficiency of a new system of telemetry and solar-cell assemblies.

1959   CROSSING ON AIR

PERHAPS THE FIRST man to research the air–cushion vehicle concept was Sir John Thornycroft, a British engineer who, in the 1870s, began to build test models to check his theory that drag on a ship's hull could be reduced if the vessel was given a concave bottom in which air could be contained between hull and water. The proper development of the hovercraft was due to the Englishman Sir Christopher Cockerell. His early experiments on air cushions were carried out on tin cans but, by 1955, he had built a working model from balsa wood and taken out his first patent. The *SRN1*, capable of carrying four men at 45 kph (28 mph) was launched in 1959 and crossed the English Channel on 25 July.

The latest in hovercraft design, an idea originally conceived in 1959. ▼

1966   LIGHT SIGNALS

OPTICAL FIBRES are glass or plastic waveguides for transmitting visible or infrared signals. Their use was first suggested by Dr Charles Kao, born in China and trained and working in Britain, in 1966. Once it became possible to make the fibres of sufficiently pure glass, new optical-fibres began to replace the old metal ones in the UK and the US in the late 1970s. The first transatlantic optical-fibre cable was laid in 1988 and an integrated services digital network's (ISDN) were installed all over Europe. This network can transmit at speeds up to 64,000 bits per second. ISDN links have wonderful potential for the future of telecommunication and computer technology.

1966   VERTICAL TAKE-OFF

THE HARRIER JET is a single-engine, 'jump-jet' fighter-bomber designed to fly from combat areas and aircraft carriers, to support

A British Harrier Jump Jet, designed for aerial combat. ▼

ground forces. It was made by Hawker Siddeley Aviation and first flew on 31 August 1966, after a long period of development. The several versions of the Harrier could take off straight up or with a short roll, and thus did not need conventional runways. Powered by a vectored-thrust turbofan engine, the plane diverted its engine thrust downward for vertical take-off using rotatable engine exhaust ports. It could carry a combination of armaments, including air-to-air missiles, air-to-surface anti-ship missiles, rockets and bombs. The Sea Harrier saw combat in the Falkland Islands War of 1982.

1972   THE NEW CERAMICS

A WHOLE NEW range of ceramic-like materials have been made in recent years from oxides of aluminium and zirconium, silicon carbide and nitride, as well as synthetic materials known as sialons, first made at the University of Newcastle upon Tyne in 1972. Sialons are made by baking powders (sintering) in high-temperature kilns, under pressure if necessary, and are shaped by abrasives. The materials are extremely hard, resistant to corrosion and highly refractory. Many of them have excellent electrical, magnetic and optical properties and they have been used in making cutting tools, bearings, hip-replacement joints and heat shields for spacecraft. Cermets are composite materials containing a hard ceramic with a metal such as cobalt. These are easier to manufacture yet similar to ceramics and are used in making cutting tools.

1973   SEEING THROUGH THE BODY

GODFREY HOUNSFIELD, the British electrical engineer, headed the team that pioneered the development of computerised axial tomography (CAT) in 1973. Unknowingly, his team was working on the project at the same time as the American physicist Allan Cormack. They both shared the Nobel Prize for Medicine for the CAT scan device in 1979. The CAT scan enables detailed X-ray pictures of 'slices' of the human body to be produced and displayed as cross-sections on a viewing screen. Using views taken from varying angles, a three-dimensional picture of any organ or tissue irregularities in the body can be analysed and used as an aid in diagnosis, without the need for surgery.

Nuclear power has been a fast-growing industry since the Second World War. ◄

1987 LINKING TWO NATIONS

THE OFTEN-CONSIDERED idea of constructing a tunnel under the English Channel was revived in 1986 by the UK and France. A rail tunnel was chosen over proposals for a suspension bridge, a bridge and road-tunnel link, and a combined rail and road link, and the project was privately financed by British and French corporations and banks. Digging began on both sides of the Strait of Dover in 1987–88 and was completed in 1991. The tunnel was officially opened in May 1994. The tunnel runs between beneath the English Channel for 50 km (31 miles), and actually consists of three tunnels, two for rail traffic and a central tunnel for services and security. Trains can travel through it at speeds of 160 kph (100 mph).

1995 NUCLEAR FUTURE

THE MOST WIDELY used nuclear reactor is the pressurised-water reactor, which contains a sealed system of pressurised water that is heated to form steam in heat exchangers in an external circuit. It was designed in the USA and was fitted on the submarine USS *Nautilus* in 1954. The first nuclear reactor of this type built in England was Sizewell B on the Suffolk coast. It cost nearly £3 billion and has an output of 1200 MW. It first fed electricity into the national grid in February 1995. Worldwide data for 1993, released by the International Atomic Energy Agency (IAEA), showed there were 430 nuclear-power units in operation in 29 countries, with a total capacity of 330,651 MW.

Culture, Arts and Leisure

1904 *FRY'S MAGAZINE*

C. B. FRY (1872–1956) was the pre-eminent amateur sportsman of his generation. He played soccer for Southampton and England, captained the England cricket side – scoring six centuries in succession in 1901 – and played first-class rugby too. All of that was in addition to finding time to be an Oxford scholar and a successful athlete, equalling the world long-jump record. His popularity was such that his own publication, *Fry's Magazine*, had a wide circulation from its launch in 1904 until the First World War. Fry was so famous that as well as representing India at the League of Nations after the First World War, he was even offered – and refused – the throne of Albania. He devoted his retirement to sail-training for boy's clubs.

Cricket, always popular, has now become the typical English summer sport. ▼

Charlie Chaplin was the first true British film star. ◀

1913 CHARLIE CHAPLIN

LONDON'S FIRST purpose-built cinema opened in 1912, but the world's first international movie star did not make his first appearance until the following year – and he was British. Charlie Chaplin (1889–1977) was on a tour of the USA when his talent was recognised by the Keystone Studios, and he made his first film in 1913, soon gaining his trade-mark bowler hat, moustache and walking stick. By 1918, Chaplin was internationally famous and instantly recognisable, and he was able to command a fee of $1 million for his performance in *Shoulder Arms*. He went on to be co-founder of United Artists. 'Chaplin means more to me than the idea of God,' said the French director Francois Truffaut (1932–84).

1915 WAR POETS

THE OUTBREAK of the First World War had a great impact on writers, none more so than on the romantic socialist poet Rupert Brooke (1887–1915), who described going to fight as 'swimmers into cleanness leaping'. His poem 'The Soldier' ('If I should die …') had an enormous impact when it was published in 1915, just before Brooke died of blood poisoning on his way to the Dardanelles. But the war will be remembered more for the poets who described its horrors, like Wilfred Owen (1893–1918), Siegfried Sassoon (1886–1967) and Isaac Rosenberg (1890–1918), whose work had a profound effect on the years afterwards: 'My subject is War, and the pity of War,' wrote Owen just before his death – a week before the armistice.

Wilfred Owen, one of the best-loved poets of the First World War, who was killed just a week before the Armistice. ▲

1926   WINNIE-THE-POOH

THE PLAYWRIGHT A.A. Milne (1882–1956) was a former assistant editor of *Punch* magazine who became known for his successful light comedies – and then he published the verses written for his young son Christopher Robin, starting with *When We were Very Young* (1924). But it was the stories about Christopher Robin's toys that, to his frustration, made him internationally famous. *Winnie-the-Pooh* (1926) and *The House at Pooh Corner* (1928) were enhanced by the illustrations by E. H. Shepard (1879–1976) – who did the same service for *The Wind in the Willows* – and concerned Pooh and Piglet's minor adventures involving birthdays and the weather. Milne's verses about nannies were set to music and have been lampooned ever since.

1930   *PRIVATE LIVES*

THE ACTOR and playwright Noel Coward (1899–1973) began by shocking his audiences with a play about drug addiction, *The Vortex* (1924), but made his reputation with patriotic set pieces, comic songs and stylish comedies. His song 'Mad Dogs and Englishmen' caught the public mood, though his wartime 'Don't Let's be Beastly to the Germans' caused a

Ralph Vaughan Williams, who used much traditional folk music as the basis for his compositions. ◄

public furore and forced him to leave the country to perform to troops instead. But it was his comedy *Private Lives*, first performed in London in 1930, which was the pinnacle of his career. The play concerns a divorced couple who meet by accident on their respective honeymoons, and the cast of four included Coward himself, Gertrude Lawrence (1898–1952) and Laurence Olivier (1907–89).

1934   VAUGHAN WILLIAMS

'WHAT WE WANT in England is real music,' said the composer Ralph Vaughan Williams (1872–1958), which 'possesses real feeling and real'. When he first overheard the folk song 'Bushes and Briars' in an Essex village in 1903, he felt he had known it all his life, and went on to weave traditional songs into his music. His 'Fantasia on Greensleeves' in 1934 knits together the traditional song 'Greensleeves', said to be by Henry VIII, and 'Lovely Joan' – a folk song he discovered in Norfolk in 1908. His songs, like 'Linden Lea' (1903) and 'On Wenlock Edge' (1908) – using the poems of A. E. Housman (1859–1936) – have come to represent our sense of what it means to be English.

1940   LUNCHTIME RECITALS

'THERE IS NO SUCH THING as culture in wartime,' said the *Daily Express* in 1940, complaining about a government grant to CEMA, the forerunner of the Arts Council. In fact, the upsurge of creativity, theatre, film, music and dance was already proving them wrong, even in a blacked-out and half-empty London. Within weeks of the outbreak of war, the pianist Myra Hess (1890–1965) began her famous lunchtime recitals, which became a symbol of cultural resistance. They took place in the National Gallery, with its bare walls because its pictures had been hidden in a Welsh quarry, and continued throughout the war. The audience moved to basement shelters during air raids and performers often played through the noise of falling bombs.

1943 *THE FOUR QUARTETS*

THE POET AND playwright T. S. Eliot (1888–1965) was born in America but came to London in 1915 and worked as a clerk in Lloyds Bank. His poem cycle *The Waste Land* (1922) was one of the most influential examples of modernist writing, edited into shape by the poet Ezra Pound (1885–1972) – who was later discredited for broadcasting from fascist Italy during the war. Eliot became increasingly religious during the 1920s, a change that culminated in *The Four Quartets*, which were first published together in 1943. Eliot demonstrated a whole new way of writing poetry, obscure and spiritual, but it was his *Old Possum's Book of Practical Cats* (1939) that became his greatest success after his death. It was turned into the musical *Cats* by Andrew Lloyd Webber (b. 1948).

T. S. Eliot's epic poem The Waste Land *was one of the most influential works of its era.* ▲

The image of Big Brother from the film of George Orwell's Nineteen-Eighty-Four. ▲

1949 *NINETEEN EIGHTY-FOUR*

GEORGE ORWELL was once a policeman called Eric Blair (1903–50) in imperial Burma, but he became well known as a powerful social prophet – lambasting unemployment in his book *The Road to Wigan Pier* (1937). But he became increasingly disillusioned with Soviet-style totalitarianism, which he ridiculed in his novel *Animal Farm* (1945). *Nineteen Eighty-Four* (published in 1949) is an ironic commentary on the world in 1948 when he was writing it, where Britain has been transformed into Airstrip One in a superstate called Oceania, ruled by the image of Big Brother. The hero commits thought crimes by keeping a diary and falling in love. It became one of the most important texts of the Cold War.

1954 THE FOUR-MINUTE MILE

RUNNING A MILE in under four minutes was a symbolic, but apparently unreachable goal for athletes, and the world record – set by Gunther Hargg (b. 1918) – had been unchallenged for eight years before 1953 when Christopher Chataway (b. 1931) ran two miles in a world-

Roger Bannister breaking the four-minute mile. ▶

record time of 8 minutes 49.6 seconds, just a week before the Coronation. Middle-distance runner Roger Bannister (b. 1929) finally passed the magic four-minute mark in 1954 on the Iffley Road running track in Oxford, with a time of 3 minutes 59.4 seconds. His achievement was crucial to the development of British athletics, inspiring the next generation of Olympic athletes such as David Hemery (b. 1944) and Sebastian Coe (b. 1956).

1954 *THE LORD OF THE RINGS*

A SELECT GROUP of academics met every Tuesday in the Eagle and Child pub in Oxford throughout the war. The results, among other writings, were the children's classics by C. S. Lewis (1898–1963), starting with *The Lion, the Witch and the Wardrobe* (1950), and the fantasy epic *The Lord of the Rings* by the Anglo-Saxon scholar J. R. R. Tolkien (1892–1973). Tolkien invented a whole new mythology for his imaginary land 'Middle Earth', and the whole conception of Shire hobbits fighting the evil enemy in the East owes a great deal to the experience of the war. But *The Lord of the Rings* also began a whole new style, and gave birth to a new genre of fantasy and science fantasy, culminating in the Hollywood epic *Star Wars* in 1978.

1958   CLIFF RICHARD

ACROSS THE ATLANTIC, the record companies and the emerging teenage market had discovered rock 'n' roll as created by Bill Haley (1927–81) and Elvis Presley (1935–77). It took longer in the UK, where the number one album throughout 1959 was the soundtrack of the film *South Pacific*, but before long Britain had its answer – an 18-year-old called Cliff Richard (b. 1940). He had been born in India as Harry Webb, and produced his first chart success – 'Move It' – in 1958, on his way to being Britain's most

Cliff Richard became the UK's contribution to the new wave of rock 'n' roll music. ▲

successful recording artist. He and his group, the Drifters, met in a London coffee bar called 21s. Their first number one single and gold disk came the following year with 'Livin' Doll', and by 1960 they had changed their name to the Shadows.

1962   NATIONAL THEATRE

THE FOUNDATION stone for a national theatre had been laid three times, twice by the Queen Mother, until the institution finally became a reality. 'Why don't they put it on castors?' she asked on the last occasion. Actors and critics since David Garrick had been calling for one, but not until 1962 – when the National Theatre opened at the Old Vic theatre in London under Laurence Olivier – did the idea become a reality. Its first production, of *Hamlet*, was a success, and the director Peter Hall (b. 1930) took over in 1973, moving it to its present site on

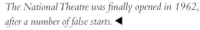

The National Theatre was finally opened in 1962, after a number of false starts. ◀

the South Bank in 1976. Together with the Royal Shakespeare Company, the Royal National Theatre is one of the best-known and most successful subsidised theatre companies in the world.

1962   'PLEASE PLEASE ME'

THE BEATLES achieved their first number one hit with 'Please Please Me' in 1962, but it had been a long slog since John Lennon (1940–80) first met Paul McCartney (b. 1942) in a Liverpool band called The Quarrymen in 1957. They confirmed Liverpool as the capital city of the so-called beat generation, stamped their mark on the 1960s and became the ultimate international pop success. The Beatles' story culminated in the universal popularity of *Sergeant Pepper's Lonely Hearts' Club Band* in 1967, just in time for the explosion of hippy culture the following year. Legal wrangles over their company, Apple, meant that by 1970 they could no longer bear to be in the same room together. Hopes that they might reunite ended when Lennon was shot in New York a decade later.

1966   THE WORLD CUP

THE WORLD CUP final took place at Wembley Stadium in 1966 in front of the Queen and the world's television cameras, and brought football to the forefront of British culture when it was won by the home team. The architect of this success for the England team was Alf Ramsey (b. 1920), who had made his reputation by taking Ipswich from

The Beatles, who remain one of the most successful bands in the history of pop music. ▶

the third division to the league championship between 1955 and 1962. His achievement as England manager was to reconnect the game in the UK with the new techniques in the rest of the world, and he stayed in the job until 1974. The final itself was won by West Ham's Geoff Hurst (b. 1941), who scored three goals against West Germany. The final score was 4–2, and Hurst finally received a knighthood for his efforts in 1998.

1967   THE DEATH OF ORTON

THE ACTOR Joe Orton (1933–67) was briefly the *enfant terrible* of British theatre, specialising in exuberant black farces, starting with *Entertaining Mr Sloane* (1964). He was influenced by the playwright Harold Pinter (b. 1930) and the French writer Jean Genet (1910–86), but he increasingly developed his own style, which took the plays into forbidden areas of sex, incest and violence, culminating in *Loot* in 1966. His plays thrived in the permissive period after the end of theatrical censorship, part of a cultural revolution that affected most areas of British life. His last play, *What the Butler Saw*, was produced in 1969, two years after Orton had been murdered by his lover, who then committed suicide.

The original members of Monty Python's Flying Circus, *demonstrating one of their 'Silly Walks'.* ▼

1969   MONTY PYTHON

THE ANARCHIC comedy of the type represented by the BBC series
Monty Python's Flying Circus had never been seen before when it hit Britain's
TV screens in 1969. Its bizarre characters sometimes spilled out between
scenes, or even between episodes, but the series became famous all over the
world – and so did its catchphrases, such as 'Now for something completely
different'. So did its most memorable sketches, like the Dead Parrot or the
Ministry of Silly Walks. It made the careers of its leading members, like John
Cleese (b. 1939) as a film actor, Michael Palin (b. 1943) as a documentary-
maker and transport campaigner and Terry Gilliam (b. 1940) as an
international film director. Python films followed, including *Monty Python's
Life of Brian* (1979).

1976   'ANARCHY IN THE UK'

THE SEX PISTOLS, the creation of
Kings Road clothes-shop owner
Malcolm McLaren (b. 1946), shot to
notoriety after swearing during a TV
interview at the end of 1976. The
Damned achieved the first punk single,
but it was the Sex Pistols' 'Anarchy in the
UK' that really launched the
phenomenon in Britain, with its
characteristic spiky hair and anarchic
bondage-style fashion created by
designer Vivienne Westwood (b. 1941) –
turning the conventional rock industry
upside down in the process. Their first
album, *Never Mind the Bollocks, Here's the
Sex Pistols* was banned from TV and shop
windows because of the word 'bollocks'.
They disbanded in 1978 after the suicide
of band member Sid Vicious (1957–79).

Johnny Rotten, the icon of the punk era. ▶

1981 *CATS*

THE 'COMPOSER' Andrew Lloyd Webber (b. 1948) achieved his first successful West End musical in partnership with lyricist Tim Rice (b. 1944) with *Jesus Christ Superstar* in 1973. For *Cats*, he used the children's poems from *Old Possum's Book of Practical Cats* by the poet T. S. Eliot, and the result was the most successful stage musical of all time, and led to the domination by British musicals of both the West End and Broadway throughout the 1980s. Its success was also due in part to director Trevor Nunn (b. 1940) from the Royal Shakespeare Company. The main song 'Memory' was first sung by Lloyd Webber's future wife Sarah Brightman (b. 1961): within 10 years, it had been recorded as many as 150 times around the world.

1984 TORVILL AND DEAN

BRITISH ICE-SKATERS had performed well in the late 1970s and early '80s, but it was the partnership of Jayne Torvill (b. 1957) and Christopher Dean (b. 1958) that took the world by storm. They were British champions from 1978 to 1983, with a surprise comeback after a period as professionals, in 1994 – the same year they repeated their Olympic success to win a bronze medal; but it was in 1984 that they thrilled Olympic viewers with their performance to win the gold medal, at the same time popularising their chosen accompanying music, Ravel's *Bolero*. As a result, ice-skating enjoyed a burst of popularity in Britain, with new rinks opening in Oxford and open air in the new Broadgate development in London.

Ice dancers Torvill and Dean, who took the gold medal at the 1984 Olympics. ▶

1986 LLOYD'S BUILDING

THE MID-1980s property boom, and the development of dock areas in London, Merseyside and Glasgow, brought the future of architecture into the forefront of debate. Prince Charles (b. 1948) led the assault on modernist architects with his attack on a design for the National Gallery extension as 'a monstrous carbuncle on the face of a much-loved friend'. Together with James Stirling (1926–92) and Norman Foster (b. 1935), architect Richard Rogers (b. 1933) was the most high profile, and was particularly celebrated for his design of the Pompidou Centre in Paris. His Lloyd's Building in 1986, with its big atrium of light in the centre, and its mixture of glass and colourful tubes, became the most famous new building in London.

The Lloyd's Building in the City of London, created by architect Richard Rogers. ▲

1988 THE SATANIC VERSES

THE WRITER Salman Rushdie (b. 1947) arrived in Britain in 1965, from India where he was born. His novel *Midnight's Children* was based in his native Bombay and won the Booker Prize in 1981, reflecting the increasingly diverse culture that now made up the UK. But the diverse culture began to pose a serious threat to him after the publication of his 1988 novel *The Satanic Verses*. What some of the Muslim community around the world saw as an attack on Islam led to the book being banned in India. It also led to book-burnings around the world and a death sentence – or *fatwa* – against him announced by the Ayatollah Khomeini (1900–89) of Iran. Rushdie was forced into hiding, from which he only partially emerged, until the fatwa was lifted in 1998.

The Spice Girls, who became the pop phenomenon of the 1990s. ▲

1996   THE SPICE GIRLS

THE POPULARITY gap left by the all-boy pop group Take That was filled in 1996 with the all-girl group the Spice Girls. The five girls had been sharing a house together in Maidenhead, Berkshire in 1993 before they shot to international fame with their first hit single 'Wannabe'. The marketing mix was an enormous success, partly because of the concept of 'girl power' – which meant that, although the five could be attractive to men, their heady female aggression made them enormously popular among teenage girls and young women. They hit the political headlines in 1997 in an interview for the *Spectator* magazine when they claimed they supported the Conservatives and that former prime minister Margaret Thatcher (b. 1925) was the first spice girl.

1997   TELETUBBIES

THE BBC's attempt to tailor a regular television series directly at children aged two to five years old gave birth to the *Teletubbies*. The series involved four brightly coloured characters of indeterminate sex, Tinky Winky, Dipsy, Laa Laa and Po, who were created after months of research to find out the way very young children respond to TV, and how best to prepare them for pre-school education. The programme often repeats whole sections, which young children like. Adults even found they enjoyed it and the series gained a worldwide cult status, with the Teletubby dolls selling out in the shops before Christmas 1997.

The Teletubbies, *the latest success in children's programming.* ▼

Religions, Belief and Thought

1900s   AFRICA

'WE WERE LIKE you, going about naked … with our war paint on, but when we learned Christianity from the Romans we changed and became great. We want you to learn Christianity and follow our steps and you too will be great.' So said Sir Harry Johnston to the Basagra people in Africa, 1900. Although a black bishop, Samuel Growther, was consecrated in 1864, he

Gold miners in the Transvaal in South Africa; Africa was one of the main targets for Christian missionaries in the 1900s. ▲

was forced to resign and much of the missionary activity in Africa was in concert with white domination. David Livingstone (1815–73) travelled throughout Africa for many years converting no one to Christianity and died penniless and defeated in 1873. The missionaries failed to recognise the hugeness of Africa and its immense diversity. Christianity took hold in parts of central and southern Africa on the back of imperial power.

1900s   FEMINISM AND THE ROLE OF WOMEN

THE ENLIGHTENMENT tradition was probably more prominent than evangelicalism in the formation of feminism, though evangelicalism introduced women to various forms of political activity. The theology of the Virgin Mary emphasising her obedience and making her a symbol of motherhood, rather than woman, was irreconcilable with radical feminism. Three issues undermined the traditional role of women in the twentieth century. The first was the growth of the industrial economy i.e. teachers,

The traditional role of women was subsumed by radical feminism in the twentieth century. ▶

telephone operators etc. The second was better contraception and the third, technology. Congregationalists had had female ministers since 1919; the Church of Scotland from the late 1960s and in 1994 the Church of England ordained its first women priests.

1909   ARCHBISHOP WILLIAM TEMPLE

THE MOST influential clergyman of the inter-war years was William Temple (1881–1944), (Archbishop of York 1929–42 and of Canterbury 1942–44), for he tried to reverse the decline in organised religion and to make England an Anglican nation again. He failed and the Church became a voice of social criticism that led it to be seen in a much more secular light. Temple was 'The People's Archbishop'. He had presided over meetings, written books, formulated statements, yet he was still immensely popular with people who never read his books or heard him preach. It may have been his commitment to education and his presidency of the Workers Educational Association from 1909 that endeared him to so many people.

1912   INDIA

BY THE TWENTY-FIRST century the Christian population of India would be around two per cent. The missionaries failed to understand the Indians and the depth of the Hindu religion. Various Christian denominations agreed to 'carve up' India between them to avoid acting against each other and they did found schools in India that continue to influence the articulate, intellectual elite. The Catholics were more successful because they did not use English priests; the Anglicans' first bishop, by contrast, was appointed in 1912. As elsewhere, the activities of Christian missionaries were littered with good intentions; they combated infanticide and the execution of widows, provided education, hospitals and raised the dignity of women, but it was still perceived as 'British religion', the religion of power and might.

The war not only saw the physical destruction of many churches, but it also led to a spiritual crisis. ◀

1914 CHURCH IN CRISIS

THERE WAS a crisis of authority in the Churches after the First World War, with the possible exception of the Catholics. Non-conformism was in decline, even in Wales and Scotland. The Church of England spoke of cohesion and discipline but appeared ineffective and increasingly irrelevant. Britain was still a Christian country, the Monarch was the Supreme Governor of the Church of England, shops closed on Sundays; the 1928 Anglican Prayer Book caused furious debate among those who were interested, and the Anglo-Catholic and evangelical wings of the Church resumed their vigorous battles. The Churches were still present, in the Scouts and the Church Brigade but the war had created a form of secular religiosity whereby the formal trappings reminded people of their inheritance and their past.

The role of women changed inexorably during and after the First World War. ◄

1914–45   WAR: PRESSURES AND STRAINS

THE ROLE OF women would be radically changed by the two wars, the Churches would continue to lose influence and there would be a rise of interest in humanism and secularism. Religion continued to be largely irrelevant, most people were neither committed nor anti-religious, they had a strong neighbourhood sense, with the family being the sacred institution. As the century developed there would be a continuing tension between science and religion; the wars raised issues of pacifism. The success of Hitler and the Nazi movement from 1933 had a parallel voice in Britain through the activities of Oswald Mosley; and the development of eugenics would cast a long shadow across the medical ethics of the century.

1916   PACIFISM

THE CONSCRIPTION ACT of 1916 created the term 'conscientious objector' and most of these were Nonconformists. Some were not willing to play a part in war at all while others would take non-combatant roles. The 16,500 recorded as conscientious objectors were treated very badly and when the government did grudgingly recognise they existed it was largely because of the work of the Free Churches and humanists. The distinction between 'pacificism', which is the attempt to prevent war by political means, and 'pacifism', which is the refusal to take part in any war whatever the reasons and whatever the consequences was never coherently resolved. The pacifist came to sound like an appeaser and even sound like a sympathiser and by 1939 the Peace Pledge Union had dissolved. However, many individuals remained true to their pacifist beliefs.

1920s   LUDWIG WITTGENSTEIN

WITTGENSTEIN (1889–1951) was the leading analytical philosopher of the twentieth century, and his influence has moulded philosophy since the 1920s. He spent many years teaching in Cambridge, though born in Vienna and having fought in the Austrian army during the First World War. Two of his most influential works were *Tractatus Logico Philosophius* (1921) and *Philosophical Investigations* (1953). He was a dissolver of orthodoxies. 'I am not a religious man but I cannot help seeing every problem from a religious point of view', he is reported to have said. He revealed that philosophical theories were as open to challenge as religious ones. His agnosticism left the door open to religious faith, which influenced the balance of the debate between religion, science and philosophy.

The Austrian philosopher Ludwig Wittgenstein, who taught at Cambridge. ▼

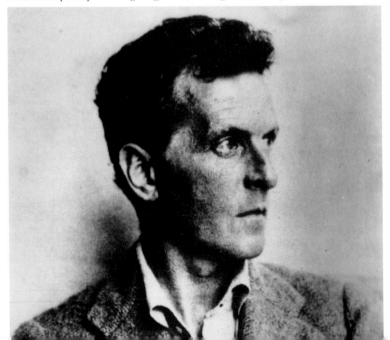

Sigmund Freud, the inventor of psychoanalysis. ▲

1923 UNCONSCIOUS PROBLEMS: SIGMUND FREUD

IF DARWIN HAD destroyed a naive Christian view of human development, Freud (1856–1939) was to challenge the Church even more. Freud founded psychoanalysis and his importance is now related to popular culture. *The Ego and the Id* was published in 1923. His views on religion were encapsulated in *The Future of an Illusion* (1927). His theory stated: children both love and hate their parents, each wishes to kill the parent of the same sex. Society will not allow this so these illicit desires are repressed. Religion is therefore a projection of the father figure, which is identified with a totem that can not be killed save on ceremonial occasions when the identification of the totem with the father figure is renewed. Religion is therefore, crudely, an illusion.

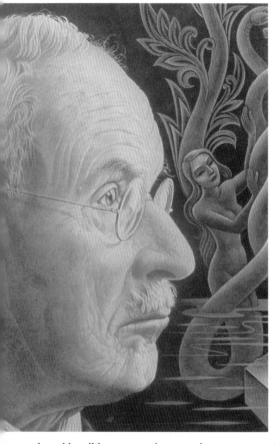

Carl Gustav Jung incorporated religion into his theories on the human mind. ◄

1930s ARCHETYPES AND IMAGES: CARL JUNG

THE WORK OF Darwin, Newton, Freud and others had created a post-Christian world in which people still attended churches but the physical removal of the institutions and symbols of religion would have made little difference to many living in the cities. This may account for the popularity in Christian circles of Carl Gustav Jung (1875–1961). For him, religion was not an illusion. He came to the conclusion that humans have a natural religious function. In the 'collective unconscious' are 'archetypes' that are shared by all humans and may make appearance in our dreams. These archetypes are the equivalent of religious dogmas and parallel all known (to him) religious ideas. He believed religion had practical value and attributed the lack of balance in the mental state of Europeans in the 1930s to the decline of religious life.

1944 THE EDUCATION ACT

Lord Butler, who initiated the Education Act of 1944. ▲

THE EDUCATION ACT of 1902 greatly antagonised the Non-conformists; the Established Church would be strengthened, the Non-conformists undermined. The 1944 Act, in which William Temple played a large part, was a seminal piece of legislation for the religious life of the country. The Anglicans could not afford to keep all their schools and the Nonconformists wanted to get rid of denominational teaching. The eventual agreement whereby each local education authority would have its own Religious Education syllabus determined by an ecumenical conference was successful. The view taken was that the Anglicans had lost control of education. In 1971 R. A. Butler, the architect of the Act, wrote in his memoirs 'the perfunctory and uninspired nature of religious instruction provided in all too many local authority and controlled schools had begun … to imperil the Christian basis of our society'.

1950 BERTRAND RUSSELL

AS WITH MANY philosophers and mathematicians Russell (1875–1970) is considered to have produced his best work when he was young. *Principia Mathematica* (1910–13), written jointly with Alfred North Whitehead (1861–1947), was a magisterial work but his best-known publication is probably *History of Western Philosophy* (1946). In the public's imagination, however, he is best known for being a pacifist. He was imprisoned during the First World War and in his later years worked tirelessly for the Campaign for Nuclear Disarmament. He won the Nobel Prize for Literature in 1950. In *Why I am Not a Christian* (1957) he stated 'all the great religions of the world are both untrue and harmful' (and he included Communism among the great religions).

1950s BUDDHIST APPEAL IN THE WEST

BUDDHISM HAS A lack of dogmatism and an emphasis on free enquiry, personal experiences and development. This in itself is an attraction to those who believe institutional religion has lost its moral authority. In many ways the Buddhist ideal is a natural progression from the humanism of the Enlightenment and it has an appeal to intellectuals in the West.

There are certainly many forms of Buddhism in Britain today and there are probably 50,000 active Buddhists in the country. Buddhism does not disassociate itself from other thought-systems rather it associates with them in order to bring about the realisation of a Buddhist system.

1960s BLACKHAM AND THE HUMANIST ASSOCIATION

'A HUMANIST MOVEMENT … is pledged to work for a particular view of human advancement. Therefore it is universal in politics… Humanism is a concern to understand and to change

The popularity of Buddhist philosophies spread throughout the western world from the 1950s. ◀

The liberal humanist philospher John Stuart Mill. ▶

the world so that human life is more valuable to more people.' So said H. J. Blackham (b. 1903), who belongs to – the tradition of liberal ethical humanism associated with J. S. Mill (1806–73). Blackham believes in an 'open mind' and 'open society', which Christians and communists both deny. An open society must be a plural society in which no one set of values prevails, except those of tolerance, respect for the liberty of others and humanity. Humanism is, therefore, an attitude of mind with emphasis on intellectual humility and tolerance. It is clear how this view is derived from the humanism of the Enlightenment, in fact, it is the natural corollary of Enlightenment thinking.

1980s CHURCH AND STATE: COMPLEX RELATIONS

MUCH LIBERAL Protestantism in the West is a blend of biblically oriented Christianity and democratic liberalism. In Europe the principle of *Cuius Regio Eius Religio* has been applied, 'Of whom the government, of them the ideology'. Patriotism has become the new martyrdom and millions have died for it. But is Britain, in the twentieth century, a 'Christian Country'? The answer, technically, is 'Yes', for the monarch is the Supreme Governor of the Church of England, with Church and State intertwined, but does this mean Jews, Muslims, atheists etc. are not fully British? The statement of the Prince of Wales that he wished to be the

St Paul's Cathedral, one of the finest examples of religious building in England. ▲

'Defender of Faith' rather than 'the Faith' caused controversy yet it is clear the future monarch was trying to be inclusive. If the monarch were to preside over a Council of Religions then religious pluralism would be linked to the potent symbol of the monarchy, not just the Church of England.

1990s HUMANISM: A STANCE FOR LIVING

HUMANISM IS explicitly naturalistic, it denies any supernatural reality and seeks to pursue a bettering of the human condition. Human beings must decide for themselves to achieve a good life, decide what they mean by 'good', and contribute to a just society fulfilling their own potential. Values are the means to resolving particular issues and are, therefore, relative to particular situations. There are different emphases within humanism, for example, secular and ethical humanism, but both are firmly based on the Enlightenment's 'rule of reason'. Comte's (1798–1857) words sum up the humanist position succinctly. 'Man has his highest being, his 'God', in himself' whereas for Sartre (1905–80) human life just happens and is absurd. What is important is that humanism is not just secularism or humanitarianism. It is a positive commitment and the British Humanist Association has (in the 1990s) a membership of 3,500.

The existentialist John-Paul Sartre. ▶

Glossary

AESTHETIC MOVEMENT
During the 1880s artists such as Oscar Wilde believed idealised beauty and art to be the pinnacle of human existence.

AGNOSTICISM
A belief that the existence of God is indeterminable, but one that does not exclude belief in other spiritual existence.

ANABAPTISTS
Members of Protestant movements, generally sixteenth century ones, who rejected child baptism in favour of adult baptism.

ANGLICANISM
Belief in the Christian teachings and doctrine of the Church of England as opposed to that of the Roman Catholic Church.

ANGLO-SAXON
Germanic Angle and Saxon tribes settled England from the fifth century taking advantage of Roman withdrawal to set up kingdoms.

ANTI-SEMITISM
Semitic is another word for Jewish and anti-Semites may discriminate against Jews and or deny their right to a homeland.

APARTHEID
An Afrikaans word to describe the segregation of races in South Africa based on a belief in white superiority.

ATHEISM
Unlike agnostics, who are sceptical about God, atheists tend to preclude the existence of a Christian God.

BENEDICTINE RULE
A sixth-century document composed by St Benedict of Nursia that serves to rule and organise life in monasteries.

BRONZE AGE
Describes the period after 2000 BC when people began using metal-making technology based on copper and its alloys.

BUDDHISM
Buddha's sixth-century teachings were that following virtuous paths could attain the destruction of mortal desires and anguishes.

BYZANTIUM
An ancient Greek city at the centre of a Mediterranean empire with a distinctive architecture and orthodox religious art.

CALVINISM
Strict sixteenth-century Protestant theology of John Calvin, which placed biblical authority above the Church's traditions and influenced the Puritans.

CAPITALISM
An economic system of private rather than state ownership as a means to employ people and produce food and goods.

CAROLINGIAN ERA
A Frankish royal dynasty that ruled France from the eighth to tenth centuries and became Europe's most powerful Christian Kingdom.

CELTIC
Ancient European people, their art and languages marginalised to Wales, Scotland, Ireland and Brittany by the Romans and successive invaders.

CHARTISM
An 1840s British movement campaigning for better industrial-labour conditions and democratic representation for the working classes.

CIVIL WAR, THE
Charles I, who had ruled without Parliament until 1640, prompted civil war in 1642 by attempting to arrest dissenting Parliamentarians.

COLD WAR
A phoney war marked by military tension and nuclear threats between Western alliances and the Soviet Union after 1945.

COMMONWEALTH, THE
Oliver Cromwell's post-civil war seventeenth-century republican Parliamentary protectorate, and Britain's post-1945 association of independent ex-colonies.

COMMUNISM
A classless economic system of public ownership where producing goods and food is a communal activity for the general good.

CONSTITUTION
Fundamental principles on which a State is governed may be written or based on precedent, but should embody individual rights.

CRO-MAGNON
An early type of Stone Age *Homo sapiens*, or modern man, who lived in Europe during Palaeolithic times.

CRUSADES
Eleventh to thirteenth century religious wars fought by European Christian armies to recapture the Holy Land from the Muslims.

DARK AGES
A period in Europe from the fifth to the eleventh centuries noted for its lack of enlightenment in thought or government, law and order.

DEVOLUTION
A process whereby certain powers are passed, or devolved, from central government to regional governments such as Scotland or Wales.

DISESTABLISHMENT
Whereby the Church of England would be denied constitutional involvement in Parliament and no longer be the national institution.

DISSENTERS
Christian believers who refused to conform to the established Church of England. Dissenters could be Catholic or Nonconformist Protestants.

DRUIDISM
A pre-Christian pagan religion of the Celtic people where priests were learned, artistic and important members of the social order.

EAST ANGLES
Eastern English kingdom of the Angles, Germanic invaders who settled in the fifth and sixth centuries. Now known as East Anglia.

EASTER RISING
Continued British denial of Home Rule for the Irish people eventually led to a battle in Dublin's streets in 1916.

ECUMENISM
Thinking that argues for the unity of Christian churches of all denominations from around the world.

ENLIGHTENMENT, THE
A seventeenth-century intellectual movement where rational thought and science came to bear over the irrationality and superstition marking earlier periods.

EPISCOPALIAN
Churches that are governed by the rule of bishops and are in full communion with the Church of England.

EUROPEAN UNION
Originally termed the Common Market this organisation's aim is to maximise Europe's economic power and potential through financial collaboration.

FASCISM
Authoritarian political movements, particularly powerful in the 1930s and '40s, where democracy and liberalism are opposed and nationalistic ideology followed.

FEMINISM

Intellectual and political thinking that argues women's rights to equality in education, the law and the workplace.

FESTIVAL OF BRITAIN

A 1950s celebration of British and Commonwealth post-war optimism marked by building the South Bank arts centre in London.

FEUDALISM

Social and legal system whereby peasant farmers worked a lord's land and in return would serve them in battle.

FIN DE SIECLE

Relates to the prevailing artistic mood at the close of the nineteenth century, one both of optimism and decadence.

FRENCH REVOLUTION

An eighteenth-century popular uprising that saw a decadent, incompetent monarchy overthrown and its aristocracy stripped of land and power.

GAUL

An area of Europe during Roman times covering what is now France and stretching to Northern Italy and the Netherlands.

GLORIOUS REVOLUTION

William of Orange's replacement of James II in 1688 led to the Bill of Rights and constitutional power for Parliament.

GUILDS

Trade associations where members share the same skill, such as silvermaking, in order to maintain craft standards and protect business.

HERETICS

Heretics held beliefs contrary to the teachings of the established Church and were burnt if they would not recant.

HINDUISM

The dominant religion of India, Hinduism's complex system of customs and beliefs include numerous gods, reincarnation and a caste system.

HUGUENOT

Calvinist Huguenots fought the French Wars of Religion (1562-98) against Catholics, coexisted, then fled from persecution in 1685.

IMPERIALISM

The policy and practice of a State to influence or conquer others so to widen its wealth, power and influence.

INDUSTRIAL REVOLUTION

The process by which Britain and other countries were transformed during the eighteenth and nineteenth centuries into industrial powers.

IRON AGE

After 1000 BC barbarian tribes used iron rather than bronze and were contemporaries of classical Mediterranean and African civilisations.

ISLAM
Founded in the seventh century by the prophet Mohammed, messenger of Allah, Islam emphasises God's omnipotence and inscrutability.

JACOBITE
A follower of James II or his descendants wishing to restore the Stuarts to the throne after the Glorious Revolution.

JUDAISM
The religion and cultural tradition of the Jewish people, Judaism follows one God and is based on the Pentateuch.

LIBERALISM
Thinking that attaches importance to civil and political rights of individuals and their freedoms of speech and expression.

LOLLARDS
Under John Wyclif, Lollards challenged Church corruption and emphasised personal not clerical interpretations of the Bible in the fourteenth century.

MATERIALISM
Philosophical idea that the world comprises of tangible matter and what we see or feel is created by our minds.

MAYPOLES
Poles painted with spiral stripes and decked with flowers and danced around on May Day to celebrate the coming spring.

MEDIEVAL
The cultures and beliefs of the Middle Ages; after the Roman Empire's fifth century decline to the fifteenth century Renaissance.

MERCIA
Most powerful Anglo-Saxon kingdom encroached upon by Viking settlers and the Danelaw before disappearing after the Norman Conquest.

MESOLITHIC
Middle part of the Stone Age when the final Ice Age disappeared to produce present-day climates 10,000 years ago.

MESOPOTAMIA
The land between the Tigris and Euphrates rivers, now Iraq, where Sumer and Babylon flourished from around 3500 BC.

MODERNISM
An early twentieth-century approach to the arts that explored Freud's ideas on human consciousness through abstract-artistic techniques.

MUSLIM
Followers of Islam, whose sacred book is the Koran, are members of sects, the main two are Sunni or Shiite.

NAPOLEONIC WARS
Fought between 1803–15, these wars brought much of Europe under Napoleon's dictatorship until France's final defeat by the British.

NAZISM

German fascism of the National Socialist Party led by Adolf Hitler who desired an empire for his 'Aryan' race.

NEANDERTHAL

A type of primitive Stone Age man who hunted and gathered by wandering Europe in late Palaeolithic times.

NEOLITHIC

Final part of the Stone Age period marked by the development of agriculture and forest clearance around 8000–3000 BC.

NOBEL PRIZE

Prizes established by Alfred Nobel, which are awarded for outstanding contributions to fields such as chemistry, physics, literature, medicine and peace.

NORMANS

Viking 'Northmen' who settled France, expanded and took control of what is now Normandy, then conquered England under King William.

OLD ENGLISH

The earliest English spoken by Anglo-Saxons, from their first settlements in the fifth century to twelfth century Middle English.

PAGANISM

From the fourteenth century, worshippers following any religion other than Christianity were not soldiers of Christ and therefore pagans.

PALEOLITHIC

From two million years ago up to the Mesolithic Stone Age period, Palaeolithic times saw modern man develop from earlier types.

PATERNALISM

When a male ruling class or politicians believe that they act parentally in the interests of women and the lower classes.

PATRIOTISM

Historically a devotion to and desire to defend one's nation and way of life, patriotism can now have nationalistic connotations.

PELAGIANISM

A fifth-century version of Christianity, received as heretical, formulated by Pelagius who rejected the idea of mankind's original sin.

PERSIA

Now called Iran, Persia headed an Asian and Mediterranean empire from 550 BC until defeated by Alexander the Great.

PHOENICIAN
A Mediterranean civilisation of explorers and traders that flourished from 1200 BC until conquered by Alexander the Great in 332 BC

PICTS
The Roman name given to Scottish tribes inhabiting Britain before the Celts, the Picts united with Scotland's Celts in AD 844.

PREHISTORIC
From the beginning of life on earth 3.5 billion years ago to 3500 BC when humans began to keep records.

PRE-RAPHAELITES
Mid-nineteenth-century naturalistic movement that shunned artistic conventions used since Raphael and focused on biblical and literary subjects.

PRESBYTERIAN
Sixteenth-century Protestant puritans, following Calvinism, set up Non-conformist churches eliminating Catholic rituals and organ music.

PROTESTANTISM
Takes its name from Martin Luther's 1529 protest for Roman Catholic church reform that precipitated major splits in European Christianity.

PURITANISM
Puritan austerity, opposition to sexual freedom and the divine right of kings brought persecution by Charles I, civil war and exile.

RACISM
A belief in the superiority of one race over another often manifesting itself in social and civil discrimination or violence.

REFORMATION
Sixteenth-century European movement to reform the Catholic Church used by Henry VIII to separate the Church of England from Rome.

RENAISSANCE
Fourteenth-to-seventeenth century European intellectual and artistic movement ending the Middle Ages with its emphasis on science and exploration.

REPUBLICANISM
Support for a system where heads of state are not monarchs was only once realised in England under Oliver Cromwell.

RESTORATION
The period when the English monarchy, in Charles II, was restored after the seventeenth-century civil war and Cromwell's republic.

ROMANTICISM
Late eighteenth,-to early nineteenth-century classical artistic movement in Europe emphasising individual imagination, inspired by revolution and social changes.

SAXONS
German tribes that responded to fifth-century Roman decline by expanding west until absorbed into the Frankish Empire.

SECULARISM
A belief that rejects religion, particularly in political or civil matters, and embraces worldly and material, not sacred, things.

SIKHISM
Belief in the religion founded in the sixteenth century by Nanak as a Hindu sect teaching the belief in one god.

SOLSTICE
Mark the longest and shortest days in the year and were celebrated in pagan ceremonies by Druids at Stonehenge.

STONE AGE
The earliest period of human culture marked by the use of stone implements and covering Palaeolithic, Mesolithic and Neolithic times.

STUART PERIOD
The reigns of James I, Charles I and II ended Tudor rule, brought unity with Scotland and Ireland, autocratic governance and civil war.

SUFFRAGETTES
Fought for female representation and voting rights using direct and violent action from the late nineteenth century until the First World War.

TEUTONIC
Named after fifth-century invaders of Bavaria, Teutonic knights were medieval aristocratic German crusaders taking Roman Catholicism to eastern Europe.

TORYISM
Political ideology of conservative values, from 1680 to modern-day Conservatives, traditionally supported by landed classes and latterly the middle classes.

UTILITARIANISM
Ethical thinking outlined by Jeremy Bentham and John Stuart Mill maintaining that actions are morally right if leading to happiness.

UTOPIANISM
Idea that an ideal society is possible where systems are set in place for humans to live in co-operative communities.

WARS OF THE ROSES
English civil wars fought from 1455-85 between the houses of Lancaster and York over Henry VII's claims to the throne.

WHIGS
Predecessor of the Liberals and opposing the Tories, Whigs enjoyed much power in the eighteenth century advocating commercialism and tolerance.

Author Biographies

Eric Evans: General Editor

Eric Evans is Professor of Social History at Lancaster University. He has contributed to numerous historical studies as well as writing many of his own titles.

David Boyle:
Ordinary Lives; Culture, Arts and Leisure

David Boyle is an experienced journalist and editor of *Liberal Democrat News*. He has written on a range of subjects, from money to the arts.

Alan Brown:
Religions, Belief and Thought

Alan Brown is an educationalist at The National Society. He has contributed to a number of works on all aspects of religion and belief.

Malcolm Chandler:
Britain in the World

Malcolm Chandler is a historian and author, who has written widely on all manner of historical subjects, particularly for schools.

David Harding:
Power and Politics

David Harding is an experienced journalist, who writes on a wide range of subjects. He has contributed to numerous books and magazines and his specialist subject are as diverse as sport and political history.

Brenda Ralph Lewis:
Ordinary Lives

Brenda Ralph Lewis has been writing on historical subjects for 35 years. She has published 85 history books, and has contributed to many others, as well as to numerous magazines and BBC programmes.

Jon Sutherland:
Industry and Invention

Jon Sutherland is an experienced writer and a lecturer is business studies. His specialist interests include economics and science, and he has written over 50 books.

Picture Credits

Christie's Images: 14, 27, 29, 35, 40, 114, 116, 121, 158, 332.

Image Select: 15, 42, 52, 93, 140, 160 (t), 178, 211 (b), 222, 250, 267, 268, 300, 314. Image Select/CFCL: 13, 39, 41, 56, 287. Image Select/Ann Ronan: 16, 65, 73, 76, 89, 95, 99, 100, 106, 119, 124, 149, 165, 173, 205, 214, 216, 239, 263, 279. Image Select/Giraudon: 23, 24, 38, 75, 80 (b), 101, 110, 112, 117, 130, 135, 139, 142 (t), 166, 174, 189, 192. Image Select/FPG: 53, 79, 125, 154, 257, 271, 303.

Mary Evans Picture Library: 12, 17, 18, 20, 22, 25, 26, 28, 43, 47, 51, 54, 57, 59, 60, 63, 64, 66, 67, 68, 69, 70, 80 (t), 81, 83, 84, 88, 92, 96 (b), 97, 107, 118, 122, 123, 126, 128, 129, 134, 136, 138, 141, 143, 145, 146, 148, 150, 151, 153, 156, 159, 160 (b), 164, 167, 168, 169, 171, 172, 175, 180, 182, 183, 184, 185 (t), 186, 188, 193, 195, 196 (t), 197, 200, 201, 202, 203, 204, 206, 207, 208, 209, 210, 211 (t), 213, 217, 219, 220, 221, 223 (b), 224, 226, 227, 230, 233, 236 (b), 237, 240, 241, 242, 243, 247, 249, 254, 264, 265, 266, 270, 278, 280, 281, 282, 283, 294, 297, 299, 309, 310, 312, 324, 325, 333, 335.

Foundry Arts: 179.

Topham Picturepoint: 19, 21, 30, 31, 32, 33, 34, 36, 37, 44, 46, 50, 55, 61, 62, 71, 72, 74, 77, 78, 82, 85, 86, 94, 96 (t), 102, 103, 105, 111, 113, 115, 120, 127, 131, 142 (b), 144, 147, 153, 155, 161, 177, 181, 190, 191, 196 (b), 212, 215, 218, 223 (t), 225, 228, 231, 232, 234, 236 (t), 246, 248, 251, 252, 253, 255, Associated Press 256, Press Association 258, Press Association 259, 260, Press Association 261, 262, 269, 272, Associated Press 273, Press Association 274, 275, Press Association 276, 277, 284, 285, 286, Associated Press 288, 289, 290, Associated Press 291, Associated Press 292, 293, 295, 298, 301, 304, 305, 306, 308, 311, 313, 315, 316, 317, Press Association 318, 319, Press Association 320, 321, 322, Press Association 323, 326, 327, 328, 330, Press Association 331, 334.

Visual Arts Library: 58.

Index